Mine In China

Your comprehensive guide to adopting from China

D0591930

Kelly Mayfield

©Kelly Mayfield 2016

All rights reserved. No part of this publication may be reproduced or transmitted, in any form without the prior permission of the copyright owner.

Cover photo by Linda P. Meineke
Cover design by Matthew and Mary Meineke
Author photo by Bryan Lau Photography

Contents

iv

Introduction

When my husband and I began our first adoption in 2012, the Internet was the first place I turned for information. I did try my local library, but the only book that was about adopting from China was an older one dealing with adopting infant girls with no known medical issues—completely different from the adoption program running in 2012. It was in social media gathering places such as web forums or Facebook groups where I could get my questions answered. Parents exchanged tips for moving the paperwork along faster or the best places to stay in China. If you wanted to know whether it was better to take the van or train to Hong Kong, you could get over a dozen personal experiences to help you decide which was best for your family.

As I became the experienced adoptive parent, I found myself answering the same questions over and over again. Usually the same ones which I had been asking a year previously! I had kept a blog as a travel journal for our trip to China and I began using it as a way to write longer answers to common questions. When someone asked a question, I could simply refer them to the blog post. However, some of my answers made for dauntingly long blog posts. I mean, "How do I choose an agency?" is a question which it isn't easy to answer succinctly—there are simply too many variables! That question spawned a full blog series which was more than twenty pages printed out. It also led to many "You should write a book!" comments.

I decided to write the book that I was looking for in the library in 2012. The one which had the answers to all of my questions. All of everyone's questions, actually. This ridiculously lengthy book is the result. There are so many wonderful books out there which answer the question of "Should we (or I) adopt?" This book assumes that you have made the decision to adopt but are now trying to decide if you should adopt from China. If you have already made that decision, it will hold your hand all the way through the process. I hope when you wake up in a cold sweat at 3 am with a sudden fear and no one is online to answer your question, you can turn to this book and find reassurance. Adopting from China is not any different from adopting in general—it's hard work, but so worth the effort.

1

Choosing to Adopt from China

When a married couple or a single woman decides to adopt, they may consider adopting domestically--either a private adoption or through the foster care system--or internationally. There are many factors for the prospective adoptive parents to weigh when deciding which option is best for them. These include the cost of the program, the age of the child at placement, whether or not they can choose the gender of the child, whether travel is required and if so, how much time the travel will require. Once the decision to adopt internationally is made a similar set of options remains: which countries are they eligible to adopt from and, of those, which is the best match for their family?

International adoption statistics show a boom and bust cycle, with the majority of adoptions taking place from one country for a period of years until the program closes. Another favored program then rises to take its place. Korea was effectively the only international adoption program for four decades. Right around 1990, when Korea began to try and decrease the amount of international adoptions, China and Russia began programs. Both would hold strong over the next twenty years, but Guatemala was a popular option in the early 2000's, followed by Ethiopia after Guatemala closed. Of those programs, Russia and Guatemala are now both closed, while South Korea and Ethiopia's programs place relatively few children compared to the powerhouses they used to be. Through it all, China has plugged along, business as usual from the time their program began in 1991, until they are now the largest placing program for children adopted into the United States from a foreign country. Although the program has undergone many changes and international adoption numbers have plummeted overall, parents continue to choose China as the best option for their family.

Program overview

- Children can be as young as nine months at placement but generally the younger age range of referrals are two to three years old at placement.

- Children are available for adoption until age fourteen, by Chinese law. If the adoption process is not completed by the child's fourteenth birthday they are no longer eligible to be adopted. There are no exceptions to this law.

- Both boys and girls are available, and parents may specify gender. There are more boys than girls waiting to be matched, in part because most adoptive parents prefer to adopt girls.

- Almost all children available for adoption have medical needs. Those who have no medical needs are older children.

- Children may be cared for in social welfare institutions (orphanages), group foster homes, or in foster care with private families.

- You may adopt two unrelated children concurrently.

- You must travel to China to complete the adoption. The adoption is completed in a single trip, usually about two weeks in length.

- It is possible to complete the adoption with only one parent traveling to China.

- Single women may adopt.

- In 2016, a single man was approved by China to adopt for the first time. Single men may now be eligible to adopt under certain circumstances.

- The adoption process can be completed in a little under a year, although it might take longer depending on your child criteria.

- You are able to choose the child you are matched with; you are not assigned a child.

- China will provide updates on the children who are available for adoption, often answering questions you might have about their medical conditions and development. Video of the child is now frequently available.

- The adoption process with China is well regulated with each step taking place in predictable intervals.

If all of this sounds great to you, it's time to consider whether you qualify to adopt from China.

Parent criteria

- You must be thirty years old to adopt from China. There are no exceptions to this law, and both spouses must be thirty years old. It is possible to begin the process a few months before the younger spouse turns thirty.

- If you are married, you must have been married at least two years.

- If either of the parents has previously been married, the couple must be married at least five years. There is a limit of two divorces per spouse.

- There must be no more than fifty years age difference between the younger applicant and the child. This means that a married person could be sixty-three years old and adopt a child who is thirteen years old.

- Large families rejoice--there is no limit on the number of children in the home.

- There is a maximum BMI (body mass index) of forty for applicants.

- China requires a net worth of $80,000 and an income of $10,000 per member of the family. The cost of living of the area will be taken under consideration for this requirement.

- Certain health issues or prior arrests can be problematic with China. It is best to consult with an agency on the specifics of your situation before concluding that you are not eligible.

- For single applications, the age difference is limited to forty-five years between the applicant and child. The net worth requirement is $100,000, with an annual income of $10,000 per family member, plus an additional $10,000. Single applicants may have no more than two children under the age of eighteen at home, and the youngest cannot be under age five.

- China does not currently allow homosexual couples to adopt. Unmarried couples in a long term cohabiting relationship may be allowed to adopt, but you will need to find a placing agency supportive of this arrangement.

China grants considerable latitude for these requirements other than the first one, which is written into China's adoption law and therefore cannot be changed. China is generous in granting waivers for these requirements so do not immediately rule out adoption from China if you do not meet one or more of them.

What is included in the dossier

- A letter requesting China to allow you to adopt

- Birth certificates for both spouses

- Marriage certificate for married couples, divorce decree or death certificate (of spouse) for single applicants who have previously been married

- Family financial information form

- Employment verification

- Police clearances

- Medical exam results

- Letter from a doctor, if necessary, explaining certain medical conditions

- Reference letters

- Copies of passport

- Photos of the couple and their home

- Home study

- Immigration approval letter

- For single applications, a statement of heterosexuality and guardianship letter are also required

Overview of the China adoption process

1. Home study - 2 to 6 months
The requirements for a completed home study from a Hague accredited agency will vary by state. The length of time it takes to complete will depend on how long it takes you to accumulate all of the necessary documents and complete the education hours, as well as how quickly your social worker can get the actual document written.

2. Initial Immigration Approval I800a - 40 to 90 days
After you have a completed home study, you will then request permission from immigration to adopt. This preliminary approval will grant you permission to adopt a non-specified child or children of a certain age range from a particular country. You will include a copy of this document in your dossier so that China is assured that the child will be granted citizenship upon adoption.

3. Dossier Mailed to China (DTC)
After you have compiled all of the documents necessary for your dossier, it will be mailed to China and logged into their computer system. Because a copy of the immigration approval must be notarized, certified, and authenticated, the dossier is usually mailed a few weeks after that approval letter is received.

Those who are matched prior to their dossier being mailed to China will now proceed directly to the next step. Others will wait a few weeks or months to be matched by their agency.

4. Letter Seeking Confirmation (LSC/LOA) - 7 to 100 days
Once you are matched with a specific child or children, you must wait for China to approve the match. They will send you a Letter Seeking Confirmation (LSC) that you want to adopt this child. This is also known as the Letter of Approval (LOA) and is your official permission to adopt the child. Historically, approval times were unpredictable. In recent months, however, China has revised the procedure so that approval times average 40-60 days if you are matched around the time your dossier is sent to China. If you had a long wait to be matched and your dossier has already been translated, the approval can be received in under a week.

5. Final Immigration Approval (I800) - 2 weeks

Earlier, you were granted a general immigration approval. Now you will be approved to adopt a specific child or children. These approvals are given a higher priority than the I800a so approval times are almost always 2 weeks from the time the form is received by USCIS.

6. Receive GUZ Number - 2 or 3 days
The next few steps insure that your child will be granted a visa after the adoption. The visa will be placed in their Chinese passport, and they will become a US citizen when you return to the United States. The GUZ number will be used as a part of the visa process.

7. NVC Letter - 1 to 3 days after GUZ number
This letter confirms that the National Visa Center has forwarded your case to the US Consulate in Guangzhou.

8. Article 5 Drop-off - 10 business days until pick-up
The Article 5 paperwork packet will be dropped off at the US Consulate in Guangzhou where they will prepare paperwork stating that a visa will be granted. This paperwork will then be picked up and submitted to China by your agency so you will be granted travel approval for the child.

9. Travel Approval - 1 to 3 weeks
China now extends an invitation to your family to travel to China and complete the adoption. A travel approval is good for 90 days.

10. Consulate Appointment - 1 to 2 days
After you receive travel approval, your agency will need to schedule an appointment for you at the US Consulate in Guangzhou to complete the final paperwork necessary for the visa to be granted. Once you have this appointment, you can begin to make travel arrangements.

Additional Resources

English language translation of China's law governing adoption
http://guizhou.chinadaily.com.cn/2013-07/11/content_16988069.htm

U.S. Citizenship and Immigration Services website
https://www.uscis.gov/adoption

For a look at the current China program process, I recommend the following documentaries:

Find Me, Global Story2 Films (2015)

The Making of a Family: Our China Adoption, Verge Videos (2015)
https://youtu.be/B-dNBk2mZZQ

2

The New Face of Adoption in China

If there's one thing everyone knows about adopting from China, it's that China has thousands of healthy baby girls abandoned every year because of the One Child Law. I know this because I adopted a boy from China and people constantly ask me "How did you get a boy?! I thought they only had girls to adopt from China!" There were times after our first adoption when I was at a store with my three youngest children--two biological sons and one adopted from China—and I could see people staring at the three, clearly thinking "Okay, so she had two boys and then went to China to adopt . . . a boy??" But I digress.

In the 1990's through the early 2000's, most of the babies abandoned were healthy girls in rural farming areas. The National Geographic documentary *China's Lost Girls,* which aired in 2004 highlighted this for the American population. Most Chinese parents had practical reasons for this stemming from the ancient Chinese land laws, unchanged for centuries. First, farmers were given additional farm land at the birth of a boy but not the birth of a girl. Second, the birth of a boy was needed to secure the ownership of the land. Third, in the absence of a social security system, parents depend on their sons to support them in their retirement. Often, this is taken directly from a son's paycheck. In Chinese culture daughters become part of their husband's family and any income they accrued from a job would contribute to the support of their in-laws. Religious and folk beliefs further contributed to the preference for a boy.

Even so, there were always boys abandoned in China. Statistics kept by the US State Department show that even in the early 2000's, some of the adoptions from China were boys. The circumstances which lead to the abandonment of a son have remained unchanged. A woman might successfully hide a pregnancy but be unable to keep the child and choose to abandon the baby in secret. Parents may already have had a son, so his birth was illegal. There is a stigma against single mothers, so young women who find themselves unexpectedly pregnant, especially in college, face pressure to make the pregnancy disappear in order to continue their education and not bring shame to their family. All births which lack family planning compliance certificates are ineligible to receive a hukou, or birth registration. Without the hukou, a child is shut out of vital government services such as an education and health care, does not have the ability to travel, and because of this censure the prospect of meaningful employment as an adult is bleak. In addition, births without family planning compliance certificates could incur fines equivalent to more than a year's income called "social support" fees. Facing fines of thousands of dollars while having the child be denied basic education and health care caused many families and single mothers to abandon children. These factors are still as relevant in China today as they were in the early 2000's, but now most of the healthy children are adopted domestically.

The Chinese government was aware of the growing problem of child abandonment in rural areas and took serious measures to deal with the contributing factors. The land laws were changed so that additional farm land was received for the birth of a girl or a boy. An exception was made so that in rural areas, if the first child was a girl, the parents could have a second child as long as they waited a certain interval between births. Minority groups were always exempt from the birth regulation laws, which were never the universal One Child Law of popular imagination in America. These changes did have an impact, but the biggest decrease in the abandonment of healthy children was due to the industrialization of China.

The China of today is vastly different from the China of 1980. In 1980, China was still primarily an agricultural society. Since that time, the government has succeeded in pushing through a large program of industrialization. Cities are filled with skyscraper apartment buildings to accommodate the migration of the young to urban cities. The global relocation of factory production to China has raised the standard of living across the nation, but especially for those in the cities. Farming in China was never really more than subsistence level, the average plot of land for a family farm being under two acres, so the opportunities offered by industrialization were welcomed. In what is being called the world's largest human migration, young people from rural areas across China are migrating to the east coast where the factories are located, leaving behind only the very young and the very elderly to hold down the family farm plot.

Because of China's industrial growth, paired with a lack of environmental regulation, it is the most polluted country in the world. This has led to a corresponding increase in birth defects and a rising infertility rate. These factors are behind an increasing interest in domestic adoption in China at a time when the number of healthy infants abandoned has decreased. It has also caused a decrease in the number of children available in China's international adoption program. In 2013, there were about 21,000 official domestic adoptions in China and only around 3,300 Chinese children adopted out to other nations. The era of healthy infant girls available for adoption from China lasted from the early 1990's through 2005, during which time Americans adopted around 60,000 children from China. The "slowdown" began around 2005, when the wait for a referral reached a year. The referral time increased rapidly from that point. People who sent their dossier to China in January of 2006 waited about two years for a referral. Those who sent their dossier at the end of December that same year received their referrals between July and August of 2015, a full seven and a half years after their dossiers were mailed!

Why am I even writing a book about adopting from China if you have to wait at least eight years to adopt a child? China began a second adoption program for children with special (medical) needs around the time of the slowdown in 2005. As waiting times increased, more parents began to consider the special needs program. With only a few referrals being made each year in the standard (healthy child) program, the majority of children who are adopted from China today are through the special needs program. The children who were initially available through the special needs program had relatively minor needs such as heart murmurs, cleft lip, or large birthmarks. As China found that Americans were open to adopting these children, children with moderate special needs were made available as well. Agencies with an established relationship with the CCCWA encouraged orphanages to prepare files for children who were older or with more serious special needs. Until around 2011, children with Down syndrome were not considered adoptable by China. Now they make up 20% of the files available on the shared list.

By far, most children abandoned in China today have birth defects or medical conditions. Does this mean that Chinese parents are casually tossing aside the children with birth defects because they aren't perfect? Not necessarily. China does not have the social services that we have here in America. Imagine if your baby were born needing surgery immediately or he or she would die. Now imagine the hospital demanded you pay for the surgery up front in cash. What would you do? Do you have tens of thousands of dollars available in cash? Neither do the majority of parents in China.

Many of these parents have made the incredibly brave decision to abandon their child to give them the chance to receive the medical care they need. There is no ability to 'make an adoption plan' in China or any other legal method of relinquishment. Sometimes the children are left with notes begging for the child to receive care as soon as possible. Older children might be abandoned because their parents couldn't afford their medical treatment any longer, or because they hoped their child would be able to receive treatment for cancer or a necessary surgery. It can also be the case that a child born with a medical condition such as albinism or Down syndrome is abandoned because of superstition or prejudice, but this makes the Chinese no less enlightened than Americans, who abort 50% of pregnancies with major birth defects and 90% of pregnancies with Down syndrome.

With the recent announcement that the family planning laws have been amended allowing all Chinese married couples to have a second child, many families have wondered what impact it will have on China's international adoption program. The answer is, probably not much. As you have learned, most children in China are abandoned because of their medical needs. If anything, an increasing birth rate in China will lead to a corresponding increase in children being born with medical needs. It is possible that this will lead to even more children being abandoned and eventually being made available for adoption. For the vast number of cases, it is the lack of access to affordable medical care that is at the root of child abandonment in China today, not the family planning laws.

Because the infertility rate has increased in China, and because the government has made it easier for the Chinese adopt, there are a rising number of domestic adoptions. What sort of children do Chinese couples want to adopt? They want healthy young girls, the same as Americans. Raising a boy has become extremely expensive. If you want him to be able to attract a bride, he needs an excellent education, which is expensive. You will also need to buy him an apartment. "Girls are better. They are not so expensive" we were told by our guides and multiple people in China. We were assumed to be extremely wealthy to be able to afford five sons! "Everyone" knows they hate girls and want boys in China. I hope you know now that isn't true. People in China love their daughters as much as we do. Sometimes they even prefer them when the economic situation makes a girl seem beneficial in the way that a boy was beneficial under the agricultural economy. A few decades ago parents were constrained by ancient land laws to choose a boy for their one child. Now, parents in poverty are forced to make difficult choices between keeping a child they love and giving the child the medical care they need. The situation in China is much more complex than "hate girls, love boys."

Additional Resources

National Geographic special China's Lost Girls, 2005.

Xinran. Message From An Unknown Chinese Mother: Stories of loss and love. New York: Scribner, 2012.

The Changing Face of China's Orphans, Love Without Boundaries
   http://www.lovewithoutboundaries.com/adoption/changing-face/

International and Domestic Adoption in China, CRIEnglish.com

http://english.cri.cn/8706/2013/02/27/1942s750864.htm?bsh_bid=414749214

"Birth defects soar due to pollution", China Daily

http://www.chinadaily.com.cn/china/2009-01/31/content_7433211.htm

"Family Planning Law and China's Birth Control Situation", china.org

http://www.china.org.cn/english/2002/Oct/46138.htm

3

When You're Asking the Internet About Adoption

This book is a compilation of all the things I wish I'd known when I was starting out. Much of it is the collected wisdom I've learned from other adoptive parents on the internet. The internet is absolutely one of the best and most educational tools you have as you start your adoption journey. Anything I include in this book will quickly become dated, as China is constantly tinkering with their process. Processing times slow down or speed up. Social network sites and online groups are probably the number one way people get their information. While you can adopt without being involved in these online groups, choosing to participate will guarantee that you are getting the most up-to-date information and even access to tips for speeding up the adoption process. If you aren't on Facebook, I suggest you consider starting an anonymous account specifically for participating in adoption groups. If you are on Facebook but hesitate to join adoption groups for privacy reasons, be aware that any group you join which is "closed" or "secret" will not show on your profile, nor will friends see posts that you make in the groups. Because I will refer you to these online resources throughout the book, I wanted to give you some guidelines to keep in mind when you sit down to ask the internet a question.

Are you in the same time zone?

International adoption has been around for decades. In a Facebook group for people who have adopted through my adoption agency we have people who adopted thirty years ago. You can ask a question about meeting your child for the first time and one of them might pipe up with "Well, when we got to the airport to meet the flight . . ." Interesting, and maybe you feel a tiny bit jealous, but not really relevant to your situation. For some of the questions you want to ask, you need to try to figure out which responses are currently accurate. Include qualifiers with your question. You want to specifically ask "Has anyone recently gotten a waiver for this situation?" or "How much did you pay for your home study within the past year?"

This is especially important to keep in mind when you are looking at resources on the China adoption program. Many people watch National Geographic's *China's Lost Girls* or read *Silent Tears* by Kay Bratt or *The Lost Daughters of China* by Karin Evans. These are excellent resources as long as you keep in mind that they do not reflect the current state of adoption in China. The gender and special needs of the orphan population have changed, as has the care the children receive in institutions.

Sometimes it's better to suck it up and ask

I have a theory that the internet is populated by introverts. It is SO MUCH easier to ask a question anonymously or at least without making eye contact, from the comfort of your computer chair. But sometimes you need to ask yourself if the internet is the best source to be asking. This is particularly true for those who are choosing an agency and have a question about agency policies. For example, you might ask which agencies will allow you to adopt out of birth order. Someone will say "Not agency X! I really wanted to use them but they told me they don't allow it." But I happen to know that agency X has changed their policy on adopting out of birth order, so I ask when this situation occurred.

"Oh, it was three or four years ago" is the response. Agencies change policies all the time--sometimes for the better and sometimes for the worse. If you want to know what an agency's current policy is for adopting out of birth order, two at once, pregnancy while adopting, refunds, or anything else, the best thing to do is call or e-mail the agency directly. You wouldn't want to miss out on working with a great agency because you got outdated information.

You should keep this in mind during the adoption process, too. On my agency group, people constantly ask questions such as "How do I fill out this form?" or "What hotel will we stay at?" during business hours all the time. This is what you are paying these people money for, don't be afraid to ask them questions! Even if someone has adopted from your agency within the past year, they might be unaware of policy changes. It is best to contact your agency directly regarding wait times for a match, how to complete necessary forms, travel arrangements, and many other important aspects of your adoption.

Don't compare apples to oranges

When you are asking questions, make sure you aren't being too broad. A common question to ask is "How long did it take to get your referral?" Answers will be all over the board from "We were matched before we started" to "We've been logged in for over a year and still waiting." Do you mean how long did it take to get your referral for a boy or for girl? Are you open only to minor needs or to a variety of needs? Even the agency you use will make a difference because the wait time for a match can be months longer at some agencies.

Similarly, another common broad question is "How much did your adoption cost?" It is normal to try to compare prices to see how expensive other agencies are. People will name off numbers, but some include travel costs while others don't. Even if you're just comparing travel costs, how many people went on the trip and what time of year? Before you make major decisions based on general responses, you'll want to make sure your comparisons are valid.

Remember that your data pool is skewed

If you have concerns about big topics such as the challenges of attachment or special adoption situations like adopting an older child, it is great to learn from the wisdom of the adoptive parents in these groups. However, keep in mind that most of the people in these groups are there because they love their adoption experience and they want to help you to decide that you should adopt, too! One common question many people ask is "Should I adopt out of birth order?" and usually there are ten to twenty responses, all glowingly positive. In a recent discussion, I brought up the issue of adoption dissolution in conjunction with adopting out of birth order. I was very surprised that multiple people chimed in saying that they had adopted a child from a dissolution and it was because the child had disrupted birth order in the original adoptive family. Those parents who had adopted from an adoption dissolution shared that they thought disrupting birth order was a major factor in failed adoptions. Where were these people in every discussion on adopting out of birth order I'd seen before?

The fact is, it can be hard to bring up the negative aspects of adoption. It can be hard to be the one to speak up and say "That didn't work out for our family" when you see that it seems to have worked out beautifully for everyone else who is participating in the discussion. While it is possible to have difficult and honest discussions about the hard parts of adopting, it doesn't come easily. Many people will gloss over the hard parts so they don't scare others away from adopting. While you shouldn't discount the positive responses, keep in mind that the negative responses will be underrepresented. Particularly for discussing some of those special adoption situations, remember that your social worker and/or agency can also be a great resource on the pros and cons, and will likely be a more impartial resource than the adoptive parents in online support groups.

Be wary of the cheerleader & the naysayer

This one mostly relates to choosing an agency. People can get very personally invested in the agencies they use. You give this organization thousands of dollars and trust them to bring a child into your life during a very stressful and emotional time. When someone doesn't like your agency, it's easy to feel personally insulted. When you ask people opinions on agencies you will get TONS. And usually the longer the comments go on the more pressure people start to apply. "I've adopted through Awesome Agency five times and I would NEVER use anyone else! They have never had a dossier declined from China and I wouldn't trust anyone but their guides!"

It is wonderful that the cheerleader has had such a great experience that she has nothing but good things to say about her agency, but remember that most agencies will get you through this in one piece and with a new son or daughter (or two) at the end. I've seen a cheerleader tell a story about a rough trip in-country where the agency saved the day by moving heaven and earth to get last minute medical tests/providing middle of the night translation/talking China out of canceling an adoption. Actually, I've seen this story told multiple times and about different agencies. You know what? It turns out there are MANY different agencies who will go the extra mile for your family and that is WONDERFUL! So count the cheerleader's vote as a positive but be a little skeptical that you will be in trouble if you don't use Awesome Agency.

A little less common but still surfacing at times is the naysayer, who had a bad experience and wants to let you know it. There are some lousy agencies out there, and it's good to be forewarned. There are also times that agencies have changed policies or personnel that caused negative feedback, but they are still stuck with the negative perception. This can work in reverse when an agency might be skating along on an outdated good reputation while they really aren't that great anymore due to policy or staffing changes. I've found that sometimes the loudest naysayer doesn't even have personal experience with the agency they really dislike. They only know that "everybody knows" the agency is in it for the money or whatever. It can be really tricky to sort out inaccurate information versus an agency that consistently provides lousy service. Good luck on that, but remember not to make your decision based on one person's bad experience.

Don't believe everything you read

I know this should be self-evident, but it bears including in the list. People can sound so authoritative when they share information on the internet that it is easy to believe them. It is very important to try and verify information or use someone's comment as a jumping off point for additional research. For example, I have seen countless posts advising that you do not have to declare the cash you carry out of the country as long as you and your spouse are not carrying more than $5000 each. However, when I researched this I found it was not true. I included a link to the form you must complete if you will jointly be carrying more than $10,000 out of the country in the travel chapter. It is especially important to consult with a medical professional in addition to anecdotal information given by adoptive parents when you are considering special needs. Adoptive parents have the tendency to emphasize how easy a need is because they love their child and want other children with the same need to have families too. However, people being unprepared for the care that a special need will require is sometimes a risk factor for adoption disruption.

Watch out for the wishful thinking fairy

Humans don't deal well with uncertainty. We want desperately for someone to tell us that everything will work out exactly the way we want it to in the end. Hearing the experiences of others can be really helpful in gaining understanding of the range of possibilities. However, it can never give us guarantees. You can ask how long everyone else's adoption took from start to finish, but that doesn't mean yours won't take twice as long. You can ask how long it took for everyone else's school-aged child to gain English fluency, but that doesn't mean it won't take your child longer.

This is especially important to keep in mind when you are in love with a child's photo and are asking other parents for medical information. Other parents can only tell you about their child's situation. They can't tell you how often your child will need a transfusion, or how many surgeries he will need, or if she will need a transplant. They can tell you how quickly their child overcame orphanage delays, but that doesn't rule out the possibility that your child's delays are truly developmental rather than orphanage related. Try to be honest with yourself—are you asking a question because you're looking for reassurance that everything will be fine and you're going to end up with the best case scenario?

As long as you keep that in mind, the adoptive parent community can be a wonderful resource. Many of the medical needs you will encounter in the China program are relatively rare. There might not be anyone else in your community with dwarfism or thalassemia but your child. You can learn which doctors or hospitals are most knowledgeable about your child's medical condition. You can get honest opinions on whether or not you should disclose your child's Hep B or HIV status to their school. Being able to connect with other parents will give you support and help you to ensure that your child is getting the best medical care possible. It can be an especially wonderful place for the opposite of wishful thinking–gaining support. If you ask "Is anyone else struggling with this?", you will find that you aren't alone. When things aren't going as expected, you can ask others who have dealt with the same struggles how they got through the difficult times.

You can find a DTC group composed of other families adopting within the same timeframe as yourself by typing "DTC" into the Facebook search bar. I suggest many other online adoption groups for specific situations in the Additional Resources section found at the end of a chapter.

Acronyms and terminology list

If you wade into the online adoption community you will encounter a specialized vocabulary. Here is your guide to the acronyms most commonly used in China adoption groups.

A5- Article 5, a document issued by the US Consulate in Guangzhou which verifies to China that your paperwork is in order. It takes 10 business days for the document to be prepared by the US consulate. Once this document has been sent to the CCCWA your travel approval will be issued.

CA- Consulate Appointment, your appointment at the US Consulate in Guangzhou where your child's visa will be processed.

CCCWA- Chinese Center for Children's Welfare and Adoption, the agency which oversees China's adoption program.

CWI- Children's Welfare Institute, the name China gives an orphanage which houses only children.

DS260- This is the online application for your child's immigrant visa.

DTC- Dossier to China, when your dossier is mailed to China.

GUZ number- Applications for immigration visas are assigned a number which replaces the SIM number you had with USCIS. Those visas, which will be issued from the US Consulate in Guangzhou, are issued a number which begin GUZ. This is a small step in the immigration process which requires no action on your part.

Hague- An international treaty governing international adoption which was signed on April 1, 2008. Because adoptions from China operate in accordance with this treaty, your home study agency must be Hague accredited.

HS- Home study, the first step in any adoption.

I800A- The first immigration document you must file asking permission to adopt from China. Your I800A approval grants you general permission to adopt a child or children from China.

I800- The second immigration document you must file. Your I800 approval grants you permission to adopt a specific child or children.

LID- Log in Date, the date when your dossier is logged into China's system.

LID only file- A file which is reserved for families who have a dossier already logged into China's system.

Lockbox- Both I800 forms are sent to a USCIS lockbox facility in Texas. The lockbox facility will open the forms, make sure your payment is included, and mail the forms to the USCIS branch in Kansas which handles adoption.

LOI- Letter of Intent, a letter you send to China petitioning to adopt a particular child.

LOA- Commonly referred to as the Letter of Approval, this is a Letter of Action sent by China to confirm that you are approved to adopt the child you are matched with and seeking confirmation that you wish to proceed with the adoption.

LSC- Letter Seeking Confirmation, alternate acronym for the LOA. See above definition.

MCC- Medical Conditions Checklist. A form which tells your agency which special needs you are open to adopting.

NBC- National Benefits Center, the branch office of USCIS in Overland Park, Kansas which deals with adoption immigration benefits.

NVC- National Visa Center, processes the visa your child will be issued to enter the US after the adoption is completed in China. Your child will fly home on a Chinese passport; the visa will verify that they will become a US citizen once their paperwork is processed by immigration at your port of entry.

PA- Provisional Approval or pre-approval, an initial approval granted by China after you have sent a Letter of Intent to adopt a particular child.

Partnership- When a specific agency is paired with a specific orphanage. The agency will provide material aid and training to the orphanage in exchange for being the first agency to receive all the files prepared by the orphanage. They will advocate for the children at the institution and sometimes bear the cost of preparing the files.

Partnership files- The files an agency receives from a partner orphanage. The agency agrees to place at least 80% of the files or they might not be able to keep the partnership. LID files will be designated to the agency for only three weeks, but special focus files are designated for three months to give the agency a longer amount of time to advocate and find a family.

Referral- Your agency will refer a child's file for you to review. When someone says "We have a referral!" it means that they have been matched with a child.

RTF- This is an acronym for rich text format. You will request an e-mail version of your NVC approval letter and they will send it to you in RTF.

SIM number- The number assigned to your immigration application by USCIS.

SF file- Special Focus file, a file which does not require a dossier to be in China for a match. Special focus files are those which China considers to be more difficult to place or they were LID files who remained unmatched after a certain number of weeks.

You do not need to have started the adoption process in order to send a Letter of Intent.

<u>SWI</u>- Social Welfare Institute, the name China gives an orphanage which might also be home to elderly or adults who are unable to live independently.

<u>TA</u>- Travel Approval, a letter issued by China inviting you to enter the country to finalize the adoption. You have 90 days after the TA is issued to complete the adoption.

<u>USCIS</u>- U.S. Citizenship and Immigration Services, the American government agency which approves the Chinese adoption and grants citizenship status to your child.

4

Affording Adoption

Find any internet article or discussion that is in any way related to adoption and you will find a common refrain in the comments: "I'd love to adopt but it costs too much!" International adoption is not cheap. Nor is private domestic adoption for that matter, but that is less related to the purpose of this book. If you are reading this because you're interested in adopting but you are also concerned about the cost involved, please be assured that most of the people who adopt from China are far from rich. The cost of adopting from China is not that much different from buying a new minivan or SUV, a routine purchase for many middle class families. One that you have to plan for yes, but most families make it work in the end.

Before I get into the affording part, I know many people wonder why international adoption costs so much. Earlier generations of adoptive parents were not required to pay nearly as much, even taking inflation into account. Most of the rising cost is due to increased regulation. The Hague convention set many requirements for both governments and adoptive parents to meet. Because home study agencies must be Hague certified, they must pay to earn this accreditation. Your placing agency has the same Hague certification plus paying operating costs in at least two countries. They are usually required to provide financial support within China. Those costs get passed along to you. The US government pays employees to grant parents permission to adopt and process immigrant visas for the adoptees. You pay fees which help the government to pay their paycheck. Yes, I know you already paid taxes. But since when has the government let an opportunity pass to get a little more money out of you?

The costs are higher on the China side as well. China is required to search for birth parents and prepare paperwork. The costs of orphanage care are rising. It turns out, adoptive parents prefer not to adopt from orphanages where babies are kept in cribs or tied to chairs all day while one nanny tries to feed 30 babies at a time. Care has greatly improved in orphanages across China. The nanny-to-child ratios are much lower. Orphanages now have toys for the children to play with, and often provide some form of education for the children. They provide physical therapy as well. Better care costs more. Now that almost all of the children have medical needs, China is paying for surgeries and medications, not merely formula and diapers. Some people are very resentful of the orphanage "donation" required by China. Yes, corruption happens. However, when you consider how much it costs to provide for all of the children in the care of the orphanage, few of which will ever be adopted, the cost of the donation seems entirely reasonable. Certainly, the process could be cheaper and more streamlined, but for now there is no way to change the cost. You can only accept it as a given and come up with a plan for tackling it.

One important point is that you do not have to have all of the money up front. If you do not have all of the funds starting off, be sure to ask potential agencies for a payment schedule. Agencies are very aware of how daunting the cost is for potential adoptive families and will be glad to help you find the resources you need. A few agencies require that you have at least half of the funds upfront. Most agencies will have points where you cannot progress further if you are not paid up, often at either dossier submission (DTC) or travel. At minimum, you will need to pay for the home study before it is released to you. Be sure to budget carefully, knowing what you need to pay and when. My agency had us pay the orphanage donation at LOA, although you could make payments on it until travel. Most other agencies don't have you pay the donation until you travel, but many people were scrambling to come up with the orphanage donation funds plus travel costs all at the same time. If you throw in an agency that requires you to pay several thousand for post placement visits at the same time, that is a big chunk of money to come up with all at once.

If you are beginning an adoption without the full amount of funds available you should give serious consideration to how you expect to come up with those funds. Ideally you would have a large portion of it when you start and a plan for how you are going to bring in the rest. The first place to start is to see if you will qualify for the adoption tax credit. Also, ask if your employer provides an adoption benefit. An increasing number of employers offer between $1000-$5000 and if you are fortunate enough to work for Intel, they recently announced they will offer a $15,000 adoption benefit! Neither the tax credit nor an employer benefit would be received until after the adoption is finalized, but if you know that these funds will be coming, you could arrange for a loan until they are available. Many people utilize home equity loans or borrow from their retirement funds, but there are programs which offer loans specifically for adoption.

The next place to look for funds is to go over your budget to look for ways to save and cut expenses. If you get a tax refund, use it to start your adoption fund. If you take an annual vacation, make it a "staycation" this year. Many families spend a large amount of money every year on dining out and activities for their children. If your children are in multiple activities, maybe you could ask them to choose their favorite and skip the rest for one year. If you aren't at a different activity every night, you'll probably dine out less. Many people are hesitant to withdraw their children from activities because they feel it is unfair to ask their children to make that sacrifice. Consider that is also a way for them to learn to prioritize their time and money. You might find that your children are happy to help contribute to the adoption effort. You could also find that you enjoy the extra unstructured time together. Cooking a meal as a family in the kitchen is not only frugal, but is a wonderful way to spend time together. It promotes conversation in a way that soccer practice with a drive through meal eaten in the van does not.

Perhaps you are looking at these suggestions and laughing at how privileged I must think you are. I remember feeling the same way when I read an article about saving for adoption where the author wrote that she thought they couldn't afford to adopt because they "only" had a six bedroom house. They couldn't afford to buy a larger one so the new child could have her own room. She had the epiphany that children could share rooms and passed along this bit of information, which seemed glaringly obvious to me, as a suggestion to readers to consider doing the same. We all come from different places, and what cutting costs looks like for one family will be very different from another.

You can also look at ways to reduce the cost of your adoption. In a future chapter, I will discuss questions to ask potential agencies to see if they offer grants and to uncover hidden costs. Adopting two children at once is possible through the China program, but this does significantly increase the cost of an adoption because many of the fees are doubled. If you are struggling with the funds to adopt one child you might want to "boomerang" or begin the adoption process again as soon as you return home, using the adoption tax credit and/or employee benefit to from the first adoption to fund the next rather than adopt two children in a single trip. Choosing not to take siblings on the adoption trip will make travel much less expensive, and if you're really short on funds only one parent is required to travel in order to finalize the adoption.

From there you can look at ways to bring in extra money. Some people have the opportunity to work additional hours at their primary job. Many people take a second job delivering newspapers or a seasonal holiday position. Almost everyone seems to find something to sell--have a yard sale, start selling items on eBay, begin an Etsy shop, or set up a table at local craft fairs. People sell their second car, downsize their house, and even sell their wedding rings! Some of you are reading this and thinking it is radical and crazy. But others of you are nodding your head and thinking, "Yes. It is absolutely worth it."

There are many grants available to help you adopt. You can begin applying as soon as you have a finalized home study. Most, though not all, will be based on your financial information and require a Christian church affiliation. Some people will qualify for several while others will receive none despite spending hours and hours of their life filling out applications. Each grant organization might look for different factors when they make their decision, but many people find that demonstrating financial need and having a compelling story are often common themes for families who have a lot of success in receiving grants. In some ways, it might seem unfair that you aren't chosen for a grant because you chose to sell your second car (creating a savings reflected on your grant applications) and wait to be matched for a child after your home study feeling it would irresponsible to you to commit to a child before you have the funds necessary for the adoption. However, someone who writes that the child they want to adopt will be aging out in two months and they only need $2000 more to be able to travel probably seems to have a more urgent need to the grant committee.

Fundraising versus raising funds

Now we arrive at the topic you might have been expecting to pop up sooner in this chapter: fundraising. Until now we have been discussing what might more accurately be described as "raising funds" rather than fundraising. Fundraising is when you ask other people to contribute financially to your adoption through direct donation or participation in a sale, raffle, or similar event. Fundraising used to be relatively rare for adoption but now it is so commonplace that those who do not fundraise seem to be the exception rather than the rule.

Fundraising is hard work. It is often frustrating, too. If you are asking for money, people will feel justified in making critical comments and scrutinizing your finances. Be especially prepared to hear, "If you can't afford to adopt, how do you expect to afford to parent the child once they're home?!" Of course, you understand that day-to-day expenses, particularly medical expenses which are covered by insurance, are in no way comparable to having $30,000+ on hand for a one-time expense. I think the impetus for this comment is that adoption falls under the heading of family planning, which many regard as personal decision and therefore not an appropriate cause to fundraise for. For many people it would be on the same list as asking someone to pay for the hospital bills from the birth of a baby or infertility treatments such as in vitro fertilization.

While you will never be able to please everyone, here are some tips which will make fundraising more acceptable to a greater number of people:

- Be upfront about your costs and goals.

- Don't be shy about what you are contributing. People want to know that you are working hard to fund this adoption, not sitting back and expecting other people to pay for it.

- Fundraisers which involve a product being sold or some sort of raffle will often get more participation than putting up a "donate to me" website. People like to get something out of their donation. If you do need a central website to receive donations, adoptive families find that the YouCaring, Adopt Together, or Pure Charity sites take a smaller amount of the donations out for fees than gofundme.

- Have zero expectations of people. Don't assume that because you have a few friends or relatives who are well off that you can count on a big donation from them. In fact, it is often those who are strapped for money who will be your biggest supporters, because they understand how much a little bit of help can mean. It can be painful for people to hear that a good friend can't contribute but then see them buying luxury items for themselves. Try to remember that they do not owe you a contribution.

- That scrutiny works both ways. Avoid letting people know you have spent money on anything non-adoption related. People assume that if you are fundraising that you have zero extra money to spend. If you are posting on social media every time you dine out or take a vacation, people may wonder why they need to donate. Regardless of whether you change your spending habits, it is best to buck the social media bragging trend and keep purchases quiet for the duration of the adoption.

- Similarly, people will expect you to cut costs in-country as much as possible. If you tell everyone that you are having trouble coming up with the money you need to finalize the adoption, then take your four children to China with you and stop in at Hong Kong Disney for a day on your way home, they will feel angry. It will seem to them that you asked them to pay for the adoption so you could save your money to take your family on a nice vacation.

- If you are taking your children for reasons you feel are necessary, don't be shy about sharing those reasons. If your children are raising the cost of their own airfare, a fairly common occurrence, let people know that as well. They will be less likely to see taking the children along as being frivolous if you are open about these factors.

Looking at fundraising from the aspect of faith

As some denominations within the Christian church have taken up the adoption movement, it has become mixed with a ministry cause. For many families, the decision to adopt now originates not from infertility, but from their church's decision to embrace the biblical call to provide for widows and orphans. We are a little short on needy widows these days, but there is no shortage of children in need of families. Often the decision to adopt internationally rather than through foster care is seen as fitting in with the mandate to spread the gospel, as children from countries where they may not have been exposed to Christianity will be adopted into Christian families.

If you are a part of a church which embraces adoption ministry, you may not feel that fundraising is about asking for money at all. It is giving the others the opportunity to share in "orphan care." Some people are called to adopt and others are called to support adoption through donating funds or prayer support. If you are in this situation, it can be tempting to overemphasize the "rescue an orphan" narrative to encourage more people to participate. It is important to consider the fact that the child you adopt is a real individual who will be in your family for their entire life. Often adult adoptees are very critical of fundraising as a part of church ministry. Here are some of the points they make which you should consider before you begin:

- Adoptees say that hearing that their parents decided to adopt to save an orphan made them feel that they were a charity project rather than a cherished member of the family.

- Some were uncomfortable with comments made by church members about how they helped contribute financially to the cost of the adoption, encouraging them to be grateful for what the church and their parents did for them. It gave them the feeling of constantly being indebted.

- People in the church and greater community being overly familiar with personal information which should have been kept private, such as their medical information or details about their family of origin.

- Adoptees say they grew up feeling ashamed that they were from China because of constant references to China as a pagan, backwards nation with an evil government.

- It is best to avoid referring to adoption expenses and especially the orphanage donation as the "ransom" you have to pay for your child. It really paints the picture of the Chinese government as the bad guy and yourself as the rescuer.

- While fundraisers selling tee-shirts that use the word "orphan" on them are common, many adult adoptees are very negative about the use of this term. First, few of the children adopted from China are true orphans. Almost all have living birth parents. You might feel that you are celebrating adoption when you have your child wear a shirt which says "Orphan No More!" or "One Less Orphan", but many adult adoptees feel that your child might one day wish that you had not placed such a big label on them.

You might be feeling hurt right now by these comments, thinking that whoever has these ideas is completely misunderstanding your intentions. I will discuss the importance listening to adult adoptees later in the book. For now, I will only say that adoptees are not a unified front. They are individuals who all have different feelings about their own adoption, so no, your child might not feel this way at all. But it is important to consider how your child might feel about these things as an adult when you are making these decisions. Try this--when you are thinking of how to market your fundraiser, so to speak, imagine your child as a teenager standing beside you. If you have a sign featuring a picture of your daughter (who is not legally your child yet) and information on where she was found and what her medical condition is, plus general information on how China is a pagan nation which doesn't value girls, how do you think this might make your teenage daughter feel? Would she be happy to invite her friends along to this event, as she might a fundraiser for a school team? Choosing to use positive language and making the focus your desire to welcome a child into your family is a choice which is more respectful of your child's personal history and emotional development.

Moving on to an even more sensitive topic, many Christian families feel that they are called by God to adopt. An aspect of this for them is "stepping out in faith", even though they do not have all, or sometimes any, of the funds required. In online adoption communities, faithful families will encourage each other with testimonies of how God provided all the funds necessary for their adoption even though it seemed impossible when they began. There are many truly amazing stories of God's provision; however, I want people who are considering this route to know that not all families are able to come up with the funds in time and these families are less likely to stay in the adoptive community to share their experience. There is a constant flow of children on advocacy sites who were matched with a family for a time and then released, weeks or months later, because the potential family could not find the funds to complete the adoption. This hurts both the children, who will now be that much older and therefore more difficult to place, as well as the families who feel the heartache of the child they lost, as well as a potential struggle with their faith, because they felt they had a call but it didn't work out the way they had expected. People who are well-connected in the community, have churches with active adoption ministries, or even with popular blogs have highly successful fundraisers. But what if no one wants to buy your tee-shirts and your yard sale is rained out? Carefully consider how and when you think the money will be coming in, and remember that you can choose to delay several months or a year before starting the process if you need to be more financially secure.

I know the best way to close out this chapter would be to give you a big list of grants and fundraiser ideas, but other people have already done that far better than I could. Please see the resources listed below to get you started.

Additional Resources

22 ways to raise funds for adoption
http://www.nohandsbutours.com/2014/03/14/22-ways-to-raise-funds-for-your-adoption/

4 more ways to raise funds for your adoption
http://www.nohandsbutours.com/2014/03/22/four-more-ways-to-raise-funds-for-your-adoption/

Agency provided list of grants and other financial resources
http://www.holtinternational.org/adoption/assistance.php

Applying For Grants - Tips on the grant application process
http://www.nohandsbutours.com/2016/02/11/applying-for-grants/

Growing Family, Growing Faith – a look at 3 different families and resources they used
http://holtinternational.org/blog/2013/11/affording-adoption-feature/

The Resources 4 Adoption website
http://www.resources4adoption.com/

Adoption Fundraiser Planning Facebook group
https://www.facebook.com/groups/769065473129077/

Casper, Lauren. How to Fund Your Adoption: Dispelling the Myth That You Can't Afford to Adopt. Kindle ebook, 2014.

Gumm, Julie. You Can Adopt Without Debt: Creative ways to cover the cost of adoption. Nashville: Abingdom Press, 2015.

Resmer, Jeremy. Fund Your Adoption: A step-by-step guide to adopt debt-free. Kindle ebook, 2014

5

Understanding China's File Designations

Isn't it rough that the most important decision you will make in the entire adoption process happens right up front when you don't really even know how the adoption process works or what questions you should be asking? Should you start by choosing a waiting child or by choosing an agency? If you start by choosing an agency, how can you find the one that will be the best fit for your family? The next two chapters are intended to help you become familiar with the different factors to consider when making these choices. It includes the wisdom of many experienced adoptive parents and will give you the tools you need to make your decision with confidence.

If you ask any sort of "How do I start?" question in a China adoption group, many will respond "We found our child first and just used the agency he/she was listed with. I'd rather choose a child than choose an agency!" Many people don't realize that this is an option because you need to first have an understanding of the different file designations used by China for special needs adoption. China designates files as LID only or special focus. Both types of files can be found on the shared list or designated to a specific agency. Some files designated to a specific agency can be merely designated, or they can come from an orphanage partnership. Some of the files originating from a partnership are "pre-release" files. Confused yet? We will discuss all of these terms in this chapter.

Special focus files

I'm going to start with special focus files because those are the files found on photo listings or waiting child advocacy sites. With this method of finding your child you wouldn't worry about sorting out an agency's match wait times, travel accommodations, or cost sheets. You find a child that you want to adopt and use the agency who has their file. **Special focus files** are files that are open to a wider pool of adoptive families because the child will typically be a little more difficult for an agency to place. China has some pretty strict criteria for adoptive parents including marriage/divorce, BMI, health, and financial guidelines. You can request a waiver if you don't meet some of the criteria, and sometimes with a waiver comes the requirement that you adopt from the pool of special focus files. Special focus files may be matched to a family who has not yet completed a dossier. So when people say that they found their child first, they are referring to special focus children.

At any given time the largest amount of available files in China are special focus rather than LID only files (we'll get to those later) because the majority of LID only files are matched right away. Special focus files encompass a large variety of ages and needs. Young boys with minor needs are often designated special focus simply because fewer people want to adopt boys. I have seen boys as young as 6 months with minor needs designated special focus. Usually the young girls will have more complex medical needs. Special needs such as blindness, Down syndrome, or children who use wheelchairs are almost always special focus regardless of age or gender. Older children are more likely to have minor or repaired needs and are designated special focus because of their age. **It is important not to assume that all special focus files are complex**. Sometimes the child simply hasn't been matched after three months so the designation was switched. If you find the right child and the file is special focus don't worry that you are missing something--you're only missing the opportunity to make a great child part of your family!

Maybe you're now thinking "So if I find a special focus child I'd like to adopt, I can be matched with this child before I ever start the process? Is there a downside that I'm missing here?" Many people prefer to adopt from China by finding their child first, but there are a few downsides. The first is that you do not get to choose the agency. More than likely than not, your child is with a reputable agency, but perhaps the child is with the most expensive agency or when you start reading online you hear only negative comments about this agency. Good or bad, you would need to commit to the agency which has the file that you desire. You might want to consider researching to narrow down your agency choices, look at their waiting child lists to find your child. At the very least, I would suggest that you figure out if there are any agencies you would absolutely not work with. I will help you to know which questions to ask.

The other downside is that the process will seem longer for you this way. Usually you would at least be through the home study process before being matched, and often your dossier would already be in China. During our first adoption we were matched very early in the process and were absolutely in love with our son. Then our social worker took six weeks after the last home study visit to write the report. She took a two week vacation! Next we hit an immigration snag when our immigration officer said our file was on her desk and would be approved by the end of the week. Instead, she went on vacation too! It was so difficult to have seen our son's face and know that he was just sitting in the orphanage getting older as one thing after another happened to delay our process. In the end, our process was very fast, with him coming home in under a year but every adoption will hit snags. It was ten months from the time we were matched until we traveled which seemed like an eternity. With our second adoption we waited to be matched until our dossier was almost ready to be sent to China so our time from match to travel was closer to four months. Before you start viewing all the photo listings try to consider how you will feel about this aspect of being matched early.

If you like the idea of finding a child first and think you are pretty open as far as gender, age, and special needs are concerned, there are several ways to find waiting children. In addition to checking the different agencies' waiting child pages there are a variety of advocacy groups and sites where you can view waiting children from China. See the Additional Resources section at the end of the chapter for links to my favorites.

Maybe you've been looking at special focus children but are really overwhelmed by the needs that you're seeing. Some people will be required to adopt a special focus child if they have received a waiver or if they want to take advantage of the dossier reuse option. Keep in mind that the children who you see on photo listings and through advocacy avenues are the children who are more difficult to place. Agencies have access to a larger pool of children, and they will place those with minor or moderate needs first with people who are already clients in progress with their agency. If you sign with any agency, they will be looking for a child who meets the profile you submitted when you completed the medical needs form. As a waiting client, you will be considered when they receive new partnership files, or they will be on the lookout for new additions to the shared list. So if you are having trouble finding a child through photo listings and advocacy routes alone, you should consider signing with an agency and having them match you. If you are looking for a special focus child because you want to reuse your dossier, you will need to stay with the agency you used previously.

"I saw a little girl on an American-run foster home's blog that I would love to adopt! How can I find her file?"

There are many foster homes in China run by non-governmental agencies (NGOs). Often, they will use social media such as blogs, Instagram, or Facebook as a way to fundraise or raise awareness. The children of the most popular foster homes become almost adoption celebrities, with people constantly asking "Does anyone know who has Cynthia's file? I just love her and we want to adopt her!" The competition for some of these girls is fierce! The ironic thing about this is that many of the people who are interested in adopting a child from one of these foster homes would otherwise tell you that they would like to adopt a child with minor needs. However, these children were selected to be sent to the foster home because they have complex needs and their home orphanage could not provide the care they needed. Most of the foster homes will not give detailed information on the child's medical needs to protect the child's privacy, so this can give the impression that the child's medical needs are minor. In this way, the social media campaign is successful--it is causes people to look at the child rather than all of the scary terms in a file.

NGO foster homes have no input in the preparing of a child's file. Often, they have no idea whether the child has a file prepared. They will know what the child's home orphanage is, but they are prohibited from sharing this information with random people who e-mail them. If you want to adopt a child from a specific foster home, it is best to have your agency contact them directly for information. A few NGOs are known to have partnerships with specific agencies, so that is another avenue for possibly finding a specific file. When one agency posted that they had the file of one of the young girls from such a foster home, they received almost fifty inquiries within a few hours! So while a few people will adopt the child that they've loved since they saw that first photo on the foster home blog, most will go on to adopt other children. If a particular little face has caught your heart despite the mile-long list of needs, maybe you could consider being open to more needs. There are so many more children with the same needs who will wait for a family because they don't have the exposure and beautiful pictures of the ones who are in the well-known foster homes.

Things to consider when choosing your child first

If you've decided that you really like the idea of finding a specific child to adopt, you've probably already visited a few agency websites to view their waiting child photo listings. I mentioned previously that one of the downsides to choosing your child first is that you must use the agency that has the child's file. Here are some things to consider before you start viewing an agency's photo listing. If you find an agency you absolutely don't want to use, focus on the photo listings of other agencies.

Agencies know that photo listings are a good way to get new clients. Sometimes agencies will manipulate their photo listings to make their agency seem especially attractive to new clients. These are some of the tactics to look for which might be a red flag signaling an unethical agency:

- Posting children they know they will place with other families. An agency will post a girl with minor needs and when you inquire they will say that they have another family already committed to her but would be happy to work with you to find another child for your family. China requires that agencies not post LID files to photo listings, but I have seen agency advocates post photos on waiting child groups (away from China's monitoring eyes) saying "So excited that this sweetie's file is being prepared. She will most likely be matched with a family already in process so apply to our agency now if you'd like to be considered!"

- Selectively list a child's needs so that her needs sound more minor than they are. Many of the children now have multiple needs, so they might only mention a minor condition and omit a more serious medical condition. Be aware that profiles typically only mention a small amount of information from the file.

- Mixing in shared list files to make it appear that they receive more files than they do. Remember that the amount of children you see on an agency photo listing does not in any way indicate the amount of files an agency receives. It is always a good sign if an agency continues to advocate for a child after their file has returned to the shared list, but the website should make it clear whether the file is designated to the agency or is on the shared list.

- China has guidelines for agency photo listings. While agencies interpret them in different ways, it is a red flag if you see an agency ignoring multiple rules. Before China's guidelines for agencies changed, there was one agency which used to leave matched children up for a year or longer. Matched children should not stay up on the website for a long period of time. LID files are not supposed to appear on a photo listing. Photo listings are supposed to require some sort of password or security step to make sure they are not accessible to the general public. Agencies are supposed to keep identifying information such as the child's full Chinese name, birthdate, and province private.

- Look at what an agency promises on their website. Be wary of any agency that still characterizes adoption from China as being young girls, or states that most children have needs that are minor, correctable, or already repaired.

- The non-special needs (or "healthy" child) program with China is effectively no more. If you find an agency who is still accepting applications for this program even though the wait is currently 8 years for a referral, I would be concerned.

- Check for the cost sheet. I will talk about cost related issues in another chapter, but be aware that the most ethical and reputable agencies will post not only all of their charges for an adoption through their China program, but will also have a link somewhere to their total operating budget. Some agencies may choose not to post this information because they don't want the cost of adoption to scare off potential clients, but they should make it easy to obtain a full accounting of their China program.

- Some agencies will require you to pay to view a file or have a paid application with them to view a file. There are only a few agencies that require this and most are reputable, but be aware that the majority of agencies will not charge at all for viewing a file. If you are in the "just looking" phase, you can look at files with other agencies without any cost.

- Watch out for pressure tactics. Some agencies that fish heavily for clients through photo listings will let multiple families view a file at the same time and then place the file with the first family to decide to move forward. While this method of placing a child is not unusual, some agencies can turn it into "Hurry and act now if you want this child!" This is a big decision, and if an agency is pressuring you to quickly commit, walk away. It indicates the agency is more concerned about closing the deal than finding the best placement for a child.

- To check any individual agency, do a Google search for the agency name plus the keyword scam or ethics. You can also join the Rate Your Chinese Adoption Agency Facebook group and search for feedback there. Keep in mind that no agency is going to please 100% of their clients. If an agency has a waiting child you are very interested in, don't be scared off by a bad review or two. Just screen for persistent serious problems. There are many great agencies out there!

If you find a waiting child you are interested in adopting, when you contact the agency it is extremely important to ask how the agency matches photo listing children with families. It is likely that you aren't the only one who is interested in the child. There are three main methods commonly used by agencies to decide which set of potential parents will end up with a child on a photo listing. Let me familiarize you with them so that if an agency uses a method you are uncomfortable with, you will know to decline the chance to view the file and avoid their listings in the future.

The most common is **First Come, First Served**. The first family to ask for the file gets to review it, and other people who want to review the file are added to a list. The first couple has a certain amount of time to review the file and decide–maybe a few days, maybe a week or two. (While files pulled from the shared list are only locked for 72 hours, agencies have greater latitude in their designated files.) If they decline the file, it is passed to the next family on the list, and so on until someone is ready to submit a Letter of Intent to Adopt (LOI).

Pros: Only one family views a file at a time, which does not put pressure on the family to rush into a decision. First come, first served is a principle which seems fair to Americans (further on into the process you will realize this is not an Asian view), so it is not as disappointing to not get matched with a child you love. You know it's not personal; you simply weren't first in line.

Cons: This can really drag out the process for the other families and the child involved. If there is a child who is seriously cute but with a serious medical condition, the file could be viewed numerous times before someone is ready to write a LOI. One parent told me their child's file was turned down over 50 times before they accepted it! For children with time sensitive medical needs or who are close to aging out, this method can waste valuable time.

Let's call the second method **Race to the Finish**! Agencies who use this method will allow all interested families to view the file at the same time. The first family who is ready to write an LOI gets the child.

Pros: This more efficient method cuts down on the wasted time of First Come, First Served.

Cons: This method can really pressure families to make a decision before they're ready. Maybe they're still waiting to hear back from a doctor who reviewed the file but they don't want to chance losing the child. Unethical agencies can pressure families to act quickly by saying they think another family is really interested when really, they just want to close the deal and get you to sign.

The third method is **Committee Decides**. All interested families are allowed to view a file at the same time and if multiple families are ready to move forward then an agency committee chooses from among the potential families.

Pros: Committee Decides is the least popular method and it is easy to find people who are angry about it online. From my perspective, I'm not sure how "I saw her first!" is any more fair. Committee Decides is a child-centered method to find the best family for a child. While most of the young children with minor needs would thrive in any loving family, there are often instances where some families would be a better fit than others. If a child has a time-sensitive special need like Thalassemia, isn't it better that they be matched with a family who is already DTC so they can come home six months sooner than if the family who saw the child first was only starting their home study? Wouldn't a better family for a child who is deaf be one that is already fluent in sign language and a part of the deaf community? In cases dealing with older children, wouldn't the best family be one who is experienced with the challenges of older child adoption and who has parented past the age of the child, rather than a family with only younger children and just beginning their first adoption?

Agencies who use this method are committed to placements which give the child the best chance for a successful adoption.

Cons: I will also acknowledge the serious flip side to this method, which is that it is harder on the potential families. It is very common for people to feel emotionally connected to a child from the first moment they see the picture. I can understand how devastating it must be to feel deeply in your heart that this is your child, and now a committee is telling you that there is another family better for the child than yours. Not only is it a loss, but it comes as a veiled insult. If you feel you can't handle the heartbreak of a committee deciding that you aren't the best family for a child, it is important to know which agencies use this method and avoid their photo listings.

Hosting programs

A relatively new method to find your child first is to use an orphan hosting program. These programs have been used in other countries for many years and now China has begun to participate. A variety of agencies have programs and they are set up in many different ways. Usually, the children will travel to the United States for a few weeks during summer or Christmas break. Often, the children are hosted in private homes by families who have a completed home study, but being open to adopting is not a requirement for all agencies. There is a fee for to a family to host the child. Sometimes the host families must be within a certain geographic location, usually within close proximity to the sponsoring agency while other agencies have the children stay at a central location and families participate in organized activities to meet the children. The children who participate in the programs can be as young as three up to thirteen years of age.

Pros: Hosting programs are a great way to find homes for children at ages which are typically harder to place. Many families have adopted a child they never would have considered prior to the hosting experience. Families feel much more comfortable interacting with a child in person rather than reading a brief description in a file. Even if the family who hosts does not adopt the child, they can advocate for the child. Having a person who has met and interacted with the child can ease a family's fears about the child's special need or personality. If the child is adopted by the host family, it will make their transition after the adoption much easier. Children who are not adopted will benefit from the chance to experience family life.

Cons: Many people have serious reservations about orphan hosting programs. Some argue that hosting programs place enormous pressure on the children. While they are supposed to be told that they are going to America for a trip to learn about another culture, the reality is that many of these children will be told by orphanage personnel before they leave that if they are good and behave, they will get a family. Usually, the children will all come from the same orphanage, and it can be hard for children if they aren't selected for hosting while their friends are. Just as in adoption, the younger children and girls are everyone's first choice for hosting, while the boys get left behind. Certainly, for children in the younger ranges of three to five years, it is unlikely that they are able to have any understanding of what they are participating in. Host parents can sometimes get a false impression of the child's personality if they are on their best behavior during the trip. They might be caught off guard if attachment or behavioral issues show up after adoption because they had a false idea that their adoption would be easier because they already had a trial run at parenting the child. Furthermore, it could be difficult if the child gets attached to the host family and the host family does not end up adopting the child. One woman who participated in a program told me that the child she hosted was crying at the airport, begging to be allowed to stay. Although they had already started the process to adopt the child, she was bound by the program rules to not tell him that. It was very difficult for her to see him upset and not be able to reassure him that he would be in their family forever in a few more months.

In the fall of 2015, a different type of hosting program began. Four different agencies sent volunteers to visit children from a particular orphanage. The volunteers who participated were matched with a buddy to advocate for. They participated in a variety of activities with the kids during the week and then returned home to advocate for the kids they met through online avenues. If this program continues, it could possibly be a venue for meeting a potential child to adopt in a way similar to the blind referral system used by some countries. For a family open to a wide range of ages or special needs, spending a week getting to meet children already available for adoption could be a good way to find their child. However, this would have the same negative aspects as mentioned above. It is incredibly hard for children to be in competition for parents. Imagine the rejection they must feel as potential parents show up and always leave after choosing a different child.

It is important that the in-China hosting or camp program you choose to become involved in is focused on providing a fun experience for the child and not a parent-centered trip to an orphanage to "shop" for a child, thinly disguised as a humanitarian trip. These kids are smart. They know what is going on. Try to carefully evaluate the ethics of the organization, as well as how the program is run, to protect these children from heartbreak. Also, keep in mind that it is difficult to evaluate a child's behavior in a realistic way in such a short amount of time. These kids want to please so much. If you take some time to watch videos of older kids available for adoption you will see that they are often shown cleaning the orphanage, playing an instrument, caring for younger children, or other activities designed to show off how much they deserve a family. They feel an enormous amount of pressure to prove that they are worthy of a family. All of these children are worthy of a family! Make your goal be to provide a fun experience for a great group of kids rather than auditioning potential children. If you happen to meet one who you believe is the child for your family then that's wonderful, but it shouldn't be the focus of the trip.

LID files

Next, we are going to focus on another file designation used by China, known as a **LID file**. To adopt a child from China, parents must first compile a dossier of documents required by China to prove that they are qualified to adopt. The dossier is sent to China, where it is given a Log In Date (LID) when it is logged into the Chinese computer system. Children who are designated LID are typically young children with minor needs who are reserved for those who already have a dossier logged into China's system.

You might be wondering, "What is the point in making some kids wait for families to have a Log In Date? Don't they want these kids to find families?" Most of the people who adopt from China will want to adopt a child who is very young and with minor needs. The majority want to adopt a girl specifically. At a certain point, China realized that the young children with minor needs were not going to have any trouble finding homes. In fact, most agencies have a list of parents waiting to adopt them. People would "lock" these files before their dossier was ready, hit a snag with their home study or immigration approval, and the child would be left still sitting around in the orphanage, getting older. By reserving these files for people who already have a dossier logged in, it moves the children through the system faster, getting them out of orphanages and into homes.

It can be harder to define a LID file. What exactly does "young with minor needs mean?" China decides whether or not a file will be designated LID only. Usually, LID files tend to be those of children under the age of 3 with minor needs. Because people overwhelmingly prefer to adopt girls, they will accept a girl who is older and with more involved needs rather than adopt a boy. As a result, even girls of five to seven years of age are often labeled LID only, as are younger girls with more significant medical needs. Fewer boys are given a LID designation. However, there are no established guidelines for this, and it sometimes seems pretty random which files get the LID only designation—I once saw a 6 year old boy with four different special needs listed as LID only. As to what constitutes minor needs, that is a topic we will discuss in depth soon.

If you know that you would like to adopt a young child with minor needs, and especially if you want this child to be a girl, LID only is probably the route for you. You should find your agency first and I suggest one with multiple orphanage partnerships. More on partnerships later.

"Exactly how young is the youngest child I could adopt? Why doesn't China prepare the files sooner?"

According to statistics kept by the US State Department, most parents who adopt from China today are bringing home children between two and three years of age. If you wait until you have a log-in date to be matched, you would travel approximately five to six months later. That means that most people are matched with a child between eighteen and thirty months old. I have seen a few people adopt a child before their first birthday, but that is not a common occurrence. Be aware that if you limit yourself to being matched with a child under the age of one then it will significantly increase your wait time.

According to the Hague convention, China is supposed to make an effort to locate the child's birth family and give a chance for them to be adopted domestically. This means that few orphanages will begin the process of preparing a file before the child is 6 months old, assuming they were abandoned around the time of their birth. The few files I have seen which were ready when the child was around six months old were for children who had needs such as albinism or Down syndrome, which made the orphanage confident that the child would not be chosen for domestic adoption. The process of preparing a file takes about six months.

Each orphanage director chooses which children to make available for international adoption and when to prepare the files. There are a few orphanages known to prepare files really early. If age is the most important factor to you, you can ask around in online groups to find which agencies have partnerships that seem to have many very young referrals. Most orphanages prefer to wait until the child is between one and two before preparing the file. One reason is to see how the child will develop. A child who was born prematurely may or may not catch up developmentally; waiting to prepare a file might make them more adoptable if the prospective adoptive parent can see that they are developing appropriately. I know of one orphanage director who will not prepare a child's file until they are speaking at least a few words for this reason.

Other children may be expected to have surgery which will stabilize or repair their condition, but they will need to be old enough for the surgery. This is particularly the case with heart issues. It is a sad reality that heart issues are a survival of the fittest for children in orphanages. Some children will grow strong enough to have a surgery, make a good recovery, and then the orphanage will begin preparing the file. Other children will die before they are considered stable enough for the surgery. A pragmatic orphanage director will decide that there is no need to waste precious funds preparing a file before knowing which way a child with complex heart condition will go. Children who have a condition which is labeled "repaired" will find families much more quickly than children with unrepaired conditions, so that can be a motivator for orphanages to wait to prepare the files.

People often ask if they can find a LID child that they are interested in adopting and then sign with that agency. This is not possible because you must already be signed with an agency to have a dossier in China. Sometimes families who already have a dossier logged in with China will change agencies in order to be matched with a LID child designated to another agency, but that is a different situation. In addition, according to China's guidelines, agencies are not supposed to post LID designated files on photo listings. As mentioned previously, most agencies do not have any trouble placing LID files, at least if they are girls, and most have a waiting list of families. All the children you see on photo listings should theoretically be designated as special focus.

Files designated LID only will not always remain so. Agencies have designated LID files for three weeks, and then they will return to the shared list. If no one has sent a Letter of Intent to adopt a child after a month on the shared list, the LID only file can be switched to special focus. This opens a wider pool of prospective adoptive families for the child, and hopefully will enable them to find a family.

Partnership and pre-release files

LID designated files are increasingly being designated to agencies through partnerships. **Partnership files** include both LID only and special focus, but they will be designated to a single agency for a specific amount of time. Under the partnership system, agencies cultivate a relationship with an orphanage. The orphanage receives needed resources, such as material aid (formula, crib mattresses), medical supplies, or teaching consultation. In return, agencies will be the first to receive new files which are prepared from their partner orphanage. Agencies can take more time to match children with the right waiting family and the family has more time to review a file than is available if a file is pulled from the shared list. Many agencies will travel to their partnership orphanage(s) to get more information on children, to interact with them, and get video to add to their files. For older children or those with harder to place needs, the agency can advocate for them through newsletters or blog posts with no concern that after they find a family the file will have disappeared off the shared list.

Many people do not realize that files are not prepared for all of the children in an orphanage. In fact, only a small portion of the children will have files prepared. The orphanage must bear the cost of having files prepared, so usually only those children considered "adoptable" will have the chance at a family. Through the partnership system, some agencies are encouraging orphanages to prepare the files of children who might not have been selected initially. During a visit, the agency representative might say "We really think we could place this child." Usually, the agency will pay to have the file prepared, so there are some children who would never have been eligible for adoption if it weren't for a partnership.

If you are already in process with an agency then you might be given a **pre-release partnership file** referral. This is when a partner orphanage sends a copy of the file to the agency at the same time they have sent the prepared file to the CCCWA for final approval. Once the CCCWA has approved the file, the designation will be released to the agency who will submit your LOI. The biggest question people have about pre-release files is how long it will take before the file designation is received. It depends on how far in advance the orphanage notifies the agency, how soon the agency tries to match the file, and how long it takes for the CCCWA to process the file. The designation can come as early as two weeks or drag out for months. The best way to get an idea of how long you could wait for the file to be released is to ask other families with your agency how long they waited for pre-release files.

Most agencies have at least one partnership now, and larger agencies will have over a dozen. The more partnerships an agency has, the more files they will have access to so you may be matched faster, although larger agencies will also have a correspondingly larger number of families waiting to be matched. However, more partnerships mean a greater financial commitment from the agency, which will raise the operating costs of the agency and usually, therefore, the fees you pay to the agency.

Shared list files

The **shared list** is a list of files for children which are available to any agency. It includes children who are designated both LID only and special focus, although at any given time only a handful will be designed LID files. All agencies have access to the shared list, but many will have access to additional files designated to their specific agency most of them due to a partnership agreement. I think the partnership system, while not perfect, is an improvement. Previously, new files were added to the shared list once a month. It used to be that on that day agency representatives would stay up late, rushing to match families with files the instant they appeared, competing against each other for the most desired files. Families had two days to make a decision, which wasn't always enough time to get a thorough review from a doctor. Files are still added to the shared list on a regular basis, but since many orphanages are now participants in the partnership system, there are fewer orphanages whose files are added directly to the list. Any files of young children with minor needs from an unpartnered orphanage do not linger on the shared list. For this reason, the shared list is becoming the place where hard to place children collect.

At any given time, there are about 2000 children waiting on the shared list for families. Of that number, about 300 will be girls and the remaining 1700 will be boys. Many of the harder to place children will be passed from agency to agency for a time so that the agency can advocate for them specifically, and hopefully, after being highlighted at one of these agencies, they will find a family. I know people have concerns that the partnership system is preventing kids from getting families, but the files most are interested in, young girls with minor needs, are not going to languish at an agency. Even the boys will be placed within three to six months, particularly with European families who are not allowed to specify a gender preference by the adoption laws of their countries. I think it is more likely that kids get lost on the shared list as their file stagnates without an agency publicizing it and maybe requesting an update.

Many people want to know if there is a way to view the shared list so they can find a child that way. Only agencies have access to the shared list. There is no website you can go to which will show you which children are currently on the shared list. Some agencies will include shared list children on their photo listings. Because the files on the shared list are constantly being added, locked, or designated, it is too difficult for advocacy sites and groups to keep track of the various files on the list. For this reason, most of the children you will find on advocacy groups are designated to specific agencies, but some agencies will release files if they do not have any interested clients. If you are trying to find a specific child, you can request that your preferred agency keep an eye on the shared list for the child if you have their Chinese name and birthdate.

Transferring files

Many parents who have signed a contract with an agency and are faced with a long wait to be matched with a LID child will begin searching photo listings and advocacy sites to find potential children. When they find children they are interested in who are designated to an agency rather than on the shared list, they often become frustrated that an agency won't release the file to the agency they are working with. The potential parents have already made a financial commitment to their agency and it is understandable that they would not want to lose money by switching agencies. At the same time, adoptive parents need to realize that agencies do need to make enough money to stay in business. International adoption numbers have plummeted in the past decade and there is now a lot of competition for the few families who are adopting. Agencies especially rely on the files of young girls to make enough money to stay in the black. Several smaller agencies have closed within the past few years, so this is reality for the agencies.

When will agencies transfer files? It depends on the agency and for some the answer is never. Other agencies will transfer if they have no families who have shown interest in the file. The greatest likelihood that an agency will transfer a file is if it is not a young girl, or if it is almost to the end of the time that the file is designated to them. Typically, agencies have LID only files for three weeks and special focus files for three months. Agencies are least likely to transfer a partnership file because when they enter into the partnership agreement they commit to placing 80% of the files they receive from the partner orphanage. They make a financial commitment to the partner orphanage and will pay for files to be prepared which the orphanage might not otherwise have done. China will end a partnership if the agency does not live up to this part of the bargain.

One last thing to keep in mind is that while you might feel very sure this child is the child for you, agencies have experienced instances when file transfers have not worked out. A couple has assured an agency that they are committed to this child, the agency transfers the file, and a week or two later the child shows up on the other agency's waiting child photo listing because the couple changed their mind. After agencies experience this a few times, they become less likely to transfer because they know that they will lose the chance to find the child a family if the couple they transfer the child for changes their mind. So while you may be frustrated, there is more involved than the agency not caring if the child gets a family. However, it is true some agencies are better about transferring files than others. It would be wonderful if all agencies would transfer the files of children in danger of aging out and those who have serious medical conditions. If you find an agency that won't transfer the file you are interested in, ask when their designation for the file will end and if they will contact you or your agency if they still haven't placed the child by the end of that time period. It is possible to transfer agencies in order to adopt a specific child, although it will require financial sacrifice on the part of the adoptive parents because agencies will not refund any fees already paid.

Additional Resources

Find My China Child Facebook group, where you post what sort of child you are looking for and people post waiting children who meet that profile.
https://www.facebook.com/groups/Searchingformychinachild/

China Waiting Child Advocacy which is a Facebook group where advocates post children who have not yet been matched.
https://www.facebook.com/groups/chinawaitingchild/

The Advocate for WC yahoo group actually has files which include snapshots of the shared list and folders which are arranged by need. So, for example, you could see all of the children waiting who have albinism.
https://groups.yahoo.com/neo/groups/AdvocateforWC/

Rainbow Kids has information on agencies, special needs, and waiting child listings
http://www.rainbowkids.com/WC/

There are also many different advocacy blogs. Two of my favorites are Twenty Less and Waiting Child Info.
http://twentyless.com/
http://www.waitingchildinfo.com

Rate Your China Adoption Agency Facebook group where you can get feedback on agencies you are considering.
https://www.facebook.com/groups/215308551969138/

"Can I adopt from New Day?" blog post with information on adopting from an American –run foster home which applies to any private foster home
http://newdayfosterhome.blogspot.hk/2014/12/can-i-adopt-from-new-day-and-other.html

6

Choosing the Right Agency for Your Family

Now that we have discussed the different types of files, you hopefully know whether you want to choose an agency first or whether you want to find a waiting child and use their agency. There are still many different issues to consider when comparing agencies; we will discuss some of those variables. I have included questions to ask a potential agency throughout the chapter, but these are all compiled into one list in the Appendix to make it easier when you contact an agency.

When most people begin the process to adopt from China they might choose Local Small Agency that is nearby or #1 China Agency that a friend who adopted raves about. It isn't until you get online later, and maybe join a DTC group on Facebook, that you start to realize how many differences there are between the various agencies. There are many great agencies out there, but let me tell you upfront, there is no perfect agency! You will have to decide which factors are the most important for you and live with the things you find annoying.

I was preparing to discuss the pros and cons of large versus small agencies, but when I polled adoptive parents, I found that people were telling me that they got personal attention and quick responses from a large agency or that a small agency really went to bat for them with the Chinese officials, despite not having the connections or influence of a big agency. I want to give you the tools you'll need to find the agency that is the best fit for your family, independent of big versus small or name recognition.

Whether you are matched before you start the process or after you are DTC, there is still a mountain of paperwork that needs to be compiled before you get to bring your child home. Because international adoption paperwork involves county and state documents as well as documents required by the laws of two different countries, you want to make sure you feel confident that your agency knows what they are doing. Don't be shy about asking how much experience your agency has. While the China program has been around for over two decades, other countries like Guatemala, Russia, and Ethiopia have been the biggest placing countries for most of that time. With two of those programs closed and Ethiopia slowed almost to a halt, more agencies are adding a China program as a way to keep their agency open. Don't assume that just because an agency has 20 years of experience in international adoption that they have been running a China program for all of that time.

Finally, when you are looking at agencies you might run across references about how highly China ranks this or that agency. I looked up the criteria which the CCCWA uses to rank the agencies and found that they are not generally things which would be important to an adoptive family. One criteria is how well the adoption documents were prepared, which is important to everyone. However, criteria such as how many children were placed by an agency or how much they donated to the CCCWA are biased toward larger agencies. While a high ranking by the CCCWA certainly indicates the agency has a good relationship with China and has had a large number of adoptions completed through the China program, I would not let rank alone be a deciding factor.

People who are starting the process often feel more comfortable with an agency that does a lot of hand holding but I think it really depends on the organizational skill of the parent who will end up doing most of the paperwork. Agencies vary as to how much support they offer in compiling a dossier and completing other required forms. Some will do all the paperwork for you and it's included in the price, some will do the work for an extra fee and others basically leave it up to you, with little direction. Once you have compiled the dossier, your agency will review it and mail it to China, but the turnaround time on this will (everybody say it with me now) vary by agency.

The final consideration is how your agency will handle any problems which pop up on the China side of the paperwork. I've talked to more than one person who said that when their LOA was delayed an excessively long time, they were told by their agency that it probably indicated China felt there was a problem. Surprisingly, the agency had been waiting it out because they really didn't know what to do! Some agencies have in-country staff who can visit the CCCWA to check on problems, but other agencies manage to find and fix problems even without in-country staff.

Questions to ask a potential agency:

- How long has your China program been running?

- About how many adoptions did you finalize last year in the China program?

- What support to do you offer in compiling the dossier?

- If the agency compiles the dossier is there an extra fee for this service? Can you get a discount if you do it yourself?

- How long does the dossier review typically take?

- If you have all of the dossier except the I800a sent to the agency, will they review it in advance to save time?

- Are dossiers sent immediately or in weekly batches?

- How will the agency notify you of your log-in date?

- Will you be notified of statuses like "out of translation" or "in review" which can be tracked by your agency in the CCCWA's computer system while you are waiting for your LOA?

- If your LOA wait is long, at what point will the agency check on it?

- Can they offer an example of a time when a client had a problem and how they handled it?

- How will you be notified of LOA?

- Does the agency have any in-country staff or offices?

- What does the agency do for vacation time or other personnel absences to ensure families in process will continue without interruption?

- Are there any holidays where the agency is closed longer than the federal holiday schedule?

Matching

While we will be discussing many different factors to consider when choosing an agency, what is most important to everyone when starting out is getting a match! If you want to adopt a young child with minor needs, you will need to decide on an agency, complete your home study, and send your dossier to China to wait for a match. Let's discuss issues you should consider about the matching part of the process if you have decided that the LID only route is best for your family.

Your agency will find a match for you based on the date your dossier was submitted, basically your place in line. You might think that you'd get matched faster with a big agency because they have access to more files, or faster with a small agency because they have fewer families waiting in line. While either of these can be true, there is no real way to know what the shortest wait is without asking some questions. You don't want to wait until you've already handed over a couple thousand dollars to realize that you are looking at a two year wait for a referral, while if you'd chosen a different agency, you'd have been matched in under six months. Most agencies have more young boys with minor needs than they can place, so this is less of an issue for those who are open to a boy.

The most important question to ask is "How long is your average wait to be matched with a child who matches our profile?" Most agencies will tell you the wait from the date your dossier is logged into China's system. One major agency will give you the wait based on when you submitted your Medical Conditions Checklist (MCC) to them. For most first-time adopters, this will be when they send in their agency application, so about six months prior to being DTC. That means if that particular agency tells you that you should expect to wait eighteen months from MCC to be matched, and another agency is telling you that you would wait about twelve months from DTC to be matched, they would have a similar timeline.

Many agencies will be vague and say "We are able to match most of our couples within a few months of DTC." Don't accept this answer. Ask these specific follow-up questions:

- How many families do you currently have waiting to be matched?

- How many families do you usually match per month?

- What is the current wait time for a child with the profile we are looking for?

- Will we be updated on changes in wait times, or told how many couples are ahead of us in the process?

- Do you have any partnerships? If so, how many?

- What can you tell me about the care the children receive in your agency partnership orphanages? Are any of them affiliated with Half the Sky?

- Does anyone from the agency visit the partnership orphanages and meet children who will be placed by the agency? How often?

- Do you also match from the shared list?

- Do you match strictly from the MCC or will you sometimes give a referral that is outside of what we marked on our MCC?

No agency will be able to guarantee you a set amount of time until you are matched. It varies by how many families are with the agency at the time, how many files they receive, and what special needs you are open to. However, by asking these questions you should be able to get a general idea of the wait times between the agencies you are considering. While there are some agencies who successfully match using only the shared list the majority of LID files are now being matched through partnerships. Choosing an agency which matches parents using both the shared list and partnerships will usually decrease your wait time for a match with a LID only child.

While one large agency uses a computer to make matches based on MCC, most agencies have a human or team of humans to work on matching. Matching is a skill. If you are with an agency where you have developed a relationship with the matching coordinator, she might get a file and say to herself "They didn't mark this need, but they marked these other two and I have the feeling he might be a great fit for them." Sometimes agencies will give a referral outside of the MCC because they know that a couple with a limited MCC is going to have a long wait, and couples will often change their minds about needs if they can put a face to the need. Many people will tell you

"Once I saw her face I just KNEW she was our child! It didn't matter what the need was, I knew we could handle it because she was our daughter." However, it can be emotionally difficult to decline a referral, so if you want your agency to strictly adhere to your MCC then let them know. A good agency will respect your wishes and not pressure you to accept any match you are not comfortable with, nor will you be penalized for declining a referral.

After you are matched, you are going to want to share the news and receive updates about your child. These questions aren't as important, but you still might want to ask an agency:

- When can I share my child's photo on my blog or social media?

- How often can I get an update?

- Is there any cost for an update?

- Can I send my child a care package?

- Can I use a third party vendor to send my child a cake or gift package?

I know this seems like a lot of questions, but I'm only getting started! If you would like to adopt from China, you need to fit three sets of criteria: China's, your placing agency's, and your social worker's. Some of these you can work around and some you can't. Often, choosing your placing agency carefully can help you with these issues.

China's criteria

China really has only one unbreakable rule for their special needs adoption program as regards parent criteria: both parents must be 30 years old. It is written into the adoption law, there are no exceptions. You never knew you'd be looking forward to your thirtieth birthday so much! Some agencies will not let you begin your home study until both parents are thirty while others will let you begin about six months prior to the thirtieth birthday of the younger spouse, so you can mail your dossier to China on your thirtieth birthday. This will shave a good six months off your wait time, so be sure to ask prospective agencies about their policy if age is an issue.

All of China's other parent criteria rules are more like guidelines. They are generous in granting waivers, but some agencies are more willing to ask for waivers than others. It is important to get opinions from multiple agencies before giving up!

Age- In Asia there is a long tradition of grandparents raising their grandchildren while the parents work. For this reason, while China is strict on the lower age limit they will allow older parents to adopt even into their early sixties. It greatly depends on the parents' health, ages, and the age of the child. As of the guidelines issued in December 2014, the youngest parent should be no more than fifty years older than the child.

Health- Mental health issues can be problematic when adopting from China. Recently changes were made to the criteria to differentiate between severe mental illness and more moderate conditions controlled by medication. Similar distinctions were made for health conditions like a history of cancer or organ transplant. There is a lot more flexibility now, especially if one parent is healthy. Sometimes a letter from a physician stating that you are a suitable adoptive parent will be required.

Income and family size- China has traditionally been very generous with these waivers and recent changes stipulate that the cost of living in a family's geographic area is to be taken into account when calculating income. China also did away with family size limitations. If you have a large family, this is more likely to be problematic for a particular agency or social worker, who might have concerns about adding another child to what they consider an already too large family. This issue brings us to . . .

Agency criteria

You might be surprised to find that agencies often have additional criteria beyond what China requires. Some agency criteria is based on the religious affiliation of the agency, while others are based on what the agency feels will lead to the most successful placement outcomes and the fewest adoption disruptions or dissolutions. Here are some issues you might want to enquire about in advance.

Marriage and social issues– It is possible to get a waiver from China if the couple has more than the allowable amount of divorces in their history, but placing or home study agencies may have different criteria. If you are an unmarried female cohabitating with a partner, some agencies may decline to work with you because they feel it is important for children to be placed in families with parents who are married. A few agencies will require a statement of faith, meaning you sign a contract stating that you share the agency's protestant Christian views. If you are not Christian or a non-mainstream Christian (Jehovah's Witness, LDS, etc.) you will more than likely be turned down by these placing agencies.

Family size– There are plenty of large adoptive families, but there are also many social workers, agencies, and even states who want to establish a cap beyond which no family may adopt. If you have a choice of home study agencies, try to preview social workers to see if they are prejudiced against large families. Placing agencies vary, so shop around.

Pregnancy– Some agencies require that you put your adoption on hold if you become pregnant during the process. This means that if you have already been matched with a child, you will no longer be able to adopt that child. Other agencies may be flexible or not care at all. The majority of agencies will say that the youngest child in the home must be one year old at the time the new child is adopted. This is usually presented as a rule from China. However, it is not addressed in the new guidelines, and some agencies have had couples adopt not meeting this guideline, so there seems to be some flexibility if the agency does not have a problem with the placement.

Considering the number of children and age range

You should try to think ahead when your social worker is preparing your home study. It is very common for people to have their home study written for a girl with minor needs under the age of two. And then they decide to be open to a boy, or fall in love with a four year-old girl, or decide to add a second child. Any changes to your home study will involve getting a home study update and filing a supplement with USCIS, costing you hundreds of dollars. You do not want to be out all of this money because you are approved only for "under two" and you accepted a referral who was two years and two months old. Have your social worker write your home study as open-ended as possible. **Be approved for either gender, two children, and as old as your social worker is comfortable granting approval**. This costs you nothing and makes no commitment on your part.

Adopting two at once

Not all placing agencies will allow parents to adopt two unrelated children at once, although China does not have a problem with this practice. If you know in advance that you would like to adopt two children, ask potential agencies if this is something they support. If so, ask if they offer any reduction in fees for adopting two at once. Some agencies do not reduce the fees because there is no reduction in paperwork and working hours on their end, while others do substantially reduce their fees. Even if the placing agency will reduce their fee, be aware that other costs such as those to USCIS, for visas, and the orphanage donations still need to be paid for each child. Your chief savings will be in not having to make a second trip.

If you are approved for two and only adopt one, or even if your agency doesn't allow you to adopt two at the same time, you might choose to reuse your dossier to adopt another child within a year. In that case you are only required to do a home study update instead of an entire new home study, which will save you time and money. If this is something you are interested in ask your agency how quickly you can start the process again. Some require you wait six months or longer before beginning another adoption.

Adopting out of birth order/artificial twinning

Placing agencies might have concerns about the age of the child you are adopting if you have other children at home. If you adopt a child older than a child you already have at home, whether the oldest or the youngest, this is called adopting out of birth order. If you adopt a child who is within a year of age of a child you have at home, this is called artificial twinning, because you will have two children the same age. Because social workers have traditionally considered these practices to have a negative impact on the children, some agencies do not allow them. However, more recently social workers and parents have been questioning whether these rules need to be adhered to in a hard and fast manner. Some placing agencies are now willing to consider adopting out of birth order or artificial twinning on a case by case basis, while others have no problem with them at all.

Expedited adoptions

If you are adopting a child who is in a life or death medical situation, or an aging out child, ask potential agencies how much experience they have with expedited adoptions. If you are concerned that your child's health situation is dire, you can ask your agency if he or she might qualify for a medical expedite. If this is your first special needs adoption, you might not be sure what would constitute grounds for a medical expedite. It might seem very serious to you that your child is two years old with a heart condition that would have been repaired at birth here in the United States or that your child with spina bifida is not being regularly catheterized. Most children who are granted a medical expedite will go straight to the hospital from the airport because their condition is so poor. Please keep in mind that medical expedites are only effective because few people are granted them. It is imperative that you only request a medical expedite in life or death circumstances so the governmental agencies involved do not begin to feel the process is being abused and stop the exceptions. Unfortunately, in January 2016, USCIS began limiting expedites only to aging out children or those who are actively dying because of the large number of families requesting medical expedites.

Some agencies are familiar with this and know all of the steps involved, while others may not be aware this is an option. Sometimes you will not be able to choose the agency, but can connect with other parents online who are familiar with the expedite process and can help walk you and your agency through it. The most common cause for an expedited adoption would be if you are adopting a child who is close to aging out. Because Chinese law requires that the adoption must be completed by the child's fourteenth birthday, time is often a major concern. Be sure to ask if your agency has experience with expediting the adoption of an aging out child. There are many things that can be done to make sure the adoption is completed in time. I have known people who adopted an aging out child in under three months from start to finish, barely making it across the finish line by finalizing the adoption in China before the Travel Authorization had been issued. Most agencies will transfer the files of aging out children, so if an agency is skeptical that they could complete the adoption in time, you could see if they would transfer the file to another agency that is more experienced with the expedite procedures.

No one wants a child to lose their chance to have a family because of finances. For this reason you will find that there are many generous grants available for children who are nearing the end of their opportunity for adoption. Sometimes a particular child will be offered a large grant by a private donor independent of an agency. Some agencies will reduce their agency fee by a significant amount in addition to offering a grant. Finally, many of the orphanages in China will reduce or waive the required orphanage donation in an effort to help these kids find a family. While no one should consider adopting an aging out child because it is cheaper, if you are interested in adopting a child who is close to aging out, you should be aware of all of these available resources.

Special situations:

- Questions regarding your marital status—single parent, cohabitating, divorce history.

- Do you require a signed statement of [protestant Christian] faith?

- If you have a large family, how comfortable is the agency with your family size?

- What is your policy if we should become pregnant during the process?

- If you are in process for a domestic adoption or stalled in another international program, what is the agency's policy on concurrent adoption?

- What is your policy on disrupting birth order?

- What is your policy on artificial twinning?

- Will you allow us to adopt two unrelated children at once through the China program?

- If the agency allows adopting two at once, is there any agency fee reduction?

- How soon after an adoption is finalized can we begin the process again?

- How much experience does your agency have with expedited adoptions for an aging out child or for a life-threatening medical condition?

- What happens if we meet our child in-country and his or her condition is completely different from the information in the file?

- What sort of post placement support do you offer?

- Can you tell me about a recent instance when you had a family struggling with the placement once they were home? How did you help them to find the resources they needed?

Travel questions

If you are reading this book because you want to begin your first adoption it's a safe bet that travel arrangements are the last thing you would think to ask about when choosing an agency. You might be surprised to hear that one of the things adoptive parents can get most contentious about is how an agency handles the travel portion of the trip! If you are an experienced adoptive parent, your blood pressure might be starting to rise at the mere thought of travel groups. If so, remember that you do not have to work with an agency that requires travel groups.

So here's the deal—you compile a dossier, you get matched with a child, and after that long wait for the official letter from China saying that you are all set, you are ready to hop on a plane. But like anything else, agencies all do things in different ways. Some people can be on a plane four days after their Travel Approval arrives, while others are stuck revising their packing list for another three weeks until the next time their agency sends a travel group. I know it seems odd to be asking about travel when you are nowhere near that part of the process, but let's look at the pros and cons of travel groups so you can figure out if you want to rule out an agency based on their travel rules.

Pros: Bring On The Travel Group!

- Your agency will handle all or most of the travel arrangements. You will be met at the airport and someone will help you check into your hotel. If you haven't traveled much or are concerned about traveling to China, you will welcome not having to worry about any of this!

- By sending families in groups, agencies can secure group rates for hotels and guide services, keeping your travel cost lower than if you had booked everything individually. Some agencies don't send groups during the two annual trade fairs or the two weeks of Chinese New Year, when travel costs double.

- Similarly, by booking your airfare two or more weeks ahead, you will often pay less than those who buy tickets at the last minute.

- Many people love the bonding aspect of travel groups. You can swap adoption day stories, ask advice from seasoned adoptive parents, or be the parents who are helping out the overwhelmed new parents. Some travel groups continue to have reunions years after they traveled.

- Some of the larger agencies have an in-country office within the hotel they use in Guangzhou. It can be very helpful to have them available for late night translations, to arrange a medical visit for a sick child, or to use the stockpile of donated medications and other items (sometimes strollers and inflatable mattresses even!) in their office.

- When you realize you forgot to pack something, you can borrow the item from someone in your travel group or from the agency office (if available).

- Often, people need time to schedule work and childcare, so delaying travel for a little while due to a travel group schedule isn't much of a problem, and having fixed dates can sometimes help in the planning.

Cons: I Would Never Use An Agency That Requires A Travel Group! Ever!

- You are an experienced traveler and you like being able to choose your own hotels and flights.

- Agency travel groups will have everyone stay in the same 5-star hotel, and you would rather use a different hotel where you can use some of your travel points on for some free nights. Or perhaps you are a low maintenance traveler who isn't intimidated by stories of strange smells and hard beds–it's only two weeks, people!—and you want the freedom to stay in a 3- or 4-star hotel to save some money.

- Just because your agency doesn't use travel groups doesn't mean you'll be left on your own as far as travel arrangements. Your agency will be able to book your in-country flights and hotels for you or refer you to a travel agency they use.

- You feel comfortable getting around on your own, and you like the idea of seeing the "real China" rather than spending a lot of time in touristy group activities.

- While some agencies use travel groups to save money, others use the opportunity to make some money, requiring you to purchase an expensive "travel package" that costs much more than if you had done the booking yourself.

- The biggest reason to avoid travel groups is that you can leave as soon as possible after you receive your Travel Approval. This is what you've been waiting for and you want that baby in your arms ASAP!!

Probably you had a gut reaction to one or more of the pros/cons while you were reading through, but there are still some questions you can ask to see if you can live with an agency's travel requirements. Even if you don't care one way or the other you might find information on your specific agency's policies helpful, for example knowing which hotel they use if you want to apply for a hotel affiliated credit card and start earning points. Some of these only apply to particular situations, so only ask those that might apply to you:

- Do you require that we travel with a group?

- How often do you schedule the groups?

- Can I book my own in-country hotels and travel arrangements?

- If you don't have parents travel in groups, will we be responsible for getting ourselves to and from the airport and to various adoption related appointments?

- Will I be able to travel during a trade fair or Chinese holiday if I don't mind paying the additional travel expenses?

- Will I be able to receive an itemized receipt for the travel costs?

- If I am adopting an aging out child or a child with a medical expedite, will I still be required to wait for a travel group?

- What is the typical length of time between travel approval and travel for your clients?

- Am I required to stay at a particular hotel or work with a particular travel agency?

- Are the guides used by your agency employees of a guide service or of the adoption agency? For either, ask why they choose to do it that way.

- Are guide fees separate and if so, how much are they? Can we choose to forgo the guide on days when there are no adoption related appointments to save on guide fees?

- Does your agency have an office in the hotel at Guangzhou?

- Can I stay at a hotel other than the one you use?

- Can I use frequent flier miles or hotel points to save money on my travel expenses?

- Do you plan any outing for parents or are we on our own between adoption related appointments?

- Are group trips to destinations such as the Great Wall or the Guangzhou zoo optional or required? If I don't attend, will I still need to pay for it?

- Do you allow one parent to travel alone?

- Can we bring along our whole big family? (My agency said "Sure! We love it when the whole family goes!")

- Does your agency allow us to send the orphanage donation by electronic funds transfer? Only a few do, so this shouldn't be a deal-breaker but it's good to know because it's never too early to start haunting your bank for new $100 bills.

Financial considerations, grants, and understanding the business side of agencies

Finances are probably the number one deterrent to adopt for families, and it can be difficult to compare costs between agencies. When you are beginning to look at agency websites, check to see if their website makes the costs clear though payment schedules, a detailed breakdown of the costs, and resources available for making adoption affordable. When you are comparing the "sticker price" of agencies don't forget to ask about any grants an agency might offer to lower their cost. This can sometimes make a substantial difference in the costs between two agencies.

Somewhere out there someone is thinking "Look, I just want to know how I find out which agency is the cheapest!" That is a surprisingly difficult question to answer.

I reviewed cost sheets for several popular agencies to try to answer that question. You start with the application fee which can range from $200 to $700. All agencies will have the same fixed costs for the adoption such as the fees you pay to immigration and to China. There is also an "agency fee" which should cover all of what you pay to the agency that isn't a fixed cost from somewhere else. However, the agencies all calculate these fees differently on their cost sheet. Some favor one large "inclusive" agency fee while others have an agency fee which seems low but they nickel and dime you with various other fees.

And an itemized cost sheet may or may not be available on the website, just to make it a little bit more difficult to compare costs.

Let's look at two different agency fees using information I pulled from two actual agency sites:

Agency A has an agency fee of $15,000. Agency B has an agency fee of $5500. Sounds like an easy choice, right? But Agency B has the following additional fees:

- Translation and document fee $600

- Dossier registration fee $800

- Dossier translation fee $350

- Professional service fee $1500

- Orphanage donation $5300

- Fees to US Consulate for services $1000

- ——————-Total extra fees = $9550

All of those extra fees for Agency B, which are standard expenses for any adoption from China, are included in the agency fee of Agency A. So if you subtract those out, you are actually comparing an agency fee of $5450 for Agency A to the agency fee of $5500 for Agency B making them essentially the same cost. This is why it is so difficult to compare agency costs!

Let me give you another example of how agencies vary in fees: orphanage partnerships. I discussed orphanage partnerships previously, and because they involve an agency supporting an orphanage financially, partnerships raise an agency's operating costs. Agencies can spread this cost around in different ways. Let me use the same two actual agencies above, and add Agency C.

- Agency A has twelve partnerships and includes any partnership costs in their comprehensive "agency fee."

- Agency B has twelve partnerships and has a "charitable aid and development fee" of $500 which is probably used, in part, to support their partnerships.

- Agency C has twelve partnerships and charges a $600 fee specifically to people who adopt from a partnership orphanage, but also an additional $250 fee for everyone which goes to support their charitable development work.

Another important aspect which few people consider when comparing fees between agencies are the home study and post-placement costs. Sometimes your placing agency will also be your home study agency and in that case, you can't do much about the cost of the home study. If you are in that situation be sure to ask if you would be able to keep your home study if you transfer to another agency later in the process. Most people will use a local home study agency and that agency will send the home study to the placing agency for approval. The placing agency might tell you that you need to use a particular home study agency that they are affiliated with or you might be able to choose any Hague accredited agency. My placing agency estimated the home study cost at between $2500 and $3500, but my local home study agency only charged $1500 so shop around if you have that option.

China currently requires that you submit post-placement reports for five years following an adoption. Unfortunately, some parents are less motivated to complete this paperwork once their child is home. When an agency consistently has parents who do not submit post-placement reports, it reflects poorly on that agency and can affect their working relationship with China. For this reason, many placing agencies are now requiring a security deposit from parents at some point before the adoption is finalized. Many home study agencies are also either requiring a deposit or that all the post-placement costs be paid upfront rather than the old way of paying per visit as you go which means that sometimes you will get hit with double deposits. I spoke with one parent who paid $6000 in post-placement visits before they were allowed to travel.

If you are comparing two agencies and they are $2000-$3000 apart in costs, be sure to ask about their post-placement policies because this can turn a small price difference into a large one.

Here are some questions to ask potential agencies about this part of the adoption process:

- Does the agency require a post-placement report deposit or that all the costs be paid upfront?

- If it is a deposit, what will happen to the money if you move or the agency closes? I can't stress this point enough because many parents have lost their deposit money for these two reasons.

- Does the placing agency charge one post-placement fee that covers all of the reports or a fee per visit for translation and submission of the reports?

- How much does the home study agency charge per post-placement visit?

- Does your agency require that all post-placement reports be written by a social worker or will you be able to self-report the ones allowable by China? Now that China allows some reports to be completed by the parents you can save the cost of the social worker's visit if your agency allows this, which almost all do.

Other financial related questions to ask potential agencies:

- Is an annual financial report showing your operating budget available for clients to review?

- Do you have an independent financial audit conducted? If so, is that report available?

- What sort of aid programs does your agency sponsor in China?

- Do you offer grants for waiting children?

- Do you offer a returning client discount? Military discount?

- If you know you would like to adopt two children at the same time, ask if there is an agency fee reduction for this.

- Are the grants automatic or is there an application process?

- Do you partner with any grant organizations, such as Brittany's Hope?

- If I have funds available through an organization like Reece's Rainbow or Adopt Together, will you count those toward our bill? Do you charge a processing fee for the transfer of these funds?

- Do you have a way for people to contribute directly toward our adoption costs? Is there a fee associated with this?

- If people contribute funds that are more than the amount owed to you, will you keep the extra funds or are those returned to us?

- If I receive notice of a grant after my child is home that is paid directly to the agency, will that amount be refunded to us (since you're already paid the bill) or does the agency keep the grant money?

- Do you require that all post placement fees be paid upfront? If so, will the funds be held in escrow? What will happen if we move or if the agency closes?

Moving to a slightly different topic, when you are comparing agencies, it can be helpful to understand why it is that costs vary so much between agencies. While people sometimes assume that "bad" agencies charge high fees and "good" agencies charge low fees because they only care about finding children homes, this view is missing the basics of how businesses are run. Larger agencies often have higher fees because they have higher operating costs. Supporting a dozen orphanages in China rather than only one is just one of many differences that can add to an agency's operating cost. A larger agency will often spend more than a smaller agency's entire operating cost on humanitarian aid programs alone!

A larger agency will:

- Have multiple offices in the United States (multiple buildings, staff, etc.)

- Operate programs in five or more countries (adds travel to multiple countries)

- Have in-country offices in multiple countries (buildings, staff, taxes to multiple countries)

- Operate aid programs in the countries where they have adoption programs (again requires more staff and travel)

- Sometimes will continue to operate aid programs in countries where international adoptions have closed like Guatemala or Cambodia

Now maybe you're thinking "That's all well and good, but I can't really afford to pay more in agency fees because they have to pay a lot of staff. I'm all for donating to charity, but I can donate money to my own charities after I have this adoption paid off!" Every family will have different priorities when choosing an agency, so it is important to decide what is most important to you and choose an agency based on that. For some families, ethics and humanitarian aid are the biggest priority, while for others, it is keeping the adoption costs as low as possible, or which agency will match them the fastest.

While a smaller agency might have lower fees, smaller agencies can end up with more profit per adoption than a larger agency with higher fees because of the higher operating costs for larger agencies. One large agency told me that they actually lose money per adoption but are able to make up the difference because they have other sources of income such as investments, heritage camps, and major fundraising activities (this information was verified by an independent audit of their finances). However, while smaller agencies might have a greater profit per adoption, they operate on a much smaller profit margin and don't have other sources of revenue to offset their costs.

Generally, smaller agencies seem more likely to use the travel costs as a way to generate more income. Because most people focus on whatever is labeled "agency fee" on the cost sheet and as travel costs vary so much by time of year, it is easier hide some extra fees in that column. Larger agencies can use their travel groups to obtain group rates at hotels or with guide services while smaller agencies aren't able to do this. This is a generalization that doesn't hold true for all agencies, however, because a large agency will sometimes require you use an expensive travel agency to make all of your arrangements. Be sure to use the questions in the travel section figure out if you will be facing unexpectedly high travel costs with an agency that seems to have lower fees overall. One good question to help determine if the agency is padding the travel portion is "Will I be able to receive an itemized receipt for the travel costs?"

Why am I giving you this general information about operating costs? Because there is a lot of money involved in international adoption. When you're running low on funds and feeling stressed it is very easy to feel that the agencies are all about the money. Someone out there probably is getting rich off adoptions, but for most agencies, big or small, the decrease in international adoptions paired with rising overseas costs means that they are doing all they can to stay in business. Agencies can and do close, and the reality is that they need to bring in some money in order to stay in the black. You need to use your financial resources in the most effective manner to bring your child home; similarly, your agency needs to use their financial resources the best they can so that they can continue to help children find families.

Finding your priorities

Now you can see how difficult it is to compare costs between agencies. The conclusion I have drawn from my research on this topic is that it is almost impossible to determine which agency is The Cheapest. There are too many variables to compare. Most agency fees will vary within a range of about $5000. If you narrow it down to two agencies and their costs are within $2000-$3000, I would consider what factors are most important to you as you make your decision. Everyone needs to think about what they would pay more for, because as I pointed out, there is no perfect agency.

It is probably difficult to remember all the issues I have discussed in this chapter, so let me summarize the main factors to consider when comparing agencies. You might want take a moment to rank them in order of importance to help you in making your decision:

- How much an agency charges for the adoption, including grants they offer

- The ethics of an agency, including how much humanitarian work they do

- How quickly you could potentially be matched with a child

- The travel arrangements used by an agency

- The post-placement costs, requirements, and resources of an agency

Let me give you some examples of how this works in practice. Unlike when I gave examples comparing program costs, these are not actual agencies, just composites of typical experiences.

Big Agency is big, but you didn't realize how big until you waited three weeks for your dossier to be reviewed so it could be mailed to China. Then you waited nine months more than all of you friends on your DTC group to get a referral, even though you all sent your dossiers around the same time. But because you had been logged in so long, you got your LOA in a week and made up time there, Also, you split the difference on the travel group issue because your agency is so big that they send groups weekly enabling you to travel two weeks after your Travel Approval arrived. Your agency is one of the cheapest options even though they don't offer grants, and you feel like you got great service, but part of you wonders if next time you shouldn't pay a little more to go with an agency that will get you a referral sooner.

Small Agency is pretty small, and you loved chatting on the phone with your agency rep. It felt as if you were part of a family. In fact, you still have the agency rep's number on your mobile phone. Their fees were a little higher, but they offered a lot of grants making it basically the same price as some of the cheaper ones. They don't really do much humanitarian work outside of their orphanage partnerships, but that wasn't really a priority for you. You had to do most of the paperwork yourself, but the ladies from your DTC group were a huge help with that. It was so exciting that your agency mailed your dossier to China the day after it arrived! The only thing you didn't like was that they required you to use a particular travel agency to handle all of the travel arrangements. Yes, you got to leave a week after your TA arrived, but you feel that they really jacked up the price, and you could have saved money by booking your own hotels and flights. You also got really mad that they charged you a daily guide fee even on days when you didn't use the guide! You were a little jealous of the great day trips and guide service that your friends with Big Agency enjoyed. You hate to leave the agency family, but you're thinking that next time you might find an agency that won't charge so much for travel.

Middle Agency is a mid-sized agency. Their fees are a little higher, but you felt you got a lot of perks for the money, such as a dossier preparation service. They included a lot of those little fees in their price, so you weren't always being asked for money. You were disappointed that they only send dossiers to China on a Friday, but at least they reviewed it in two days, so it went out the same week they received it! You had to wait three or four months for a referral, but it was so worth it once you saw her picture, and besides, you know lots of people on your DTC group with Big Agency that waited much longer. You didn't even mind the travel groups, because your agency got great group rates on the hotel and guide service so it seems you paid less than the people who booked their own travel. You especially love all the humanitarian work this agency does and their sterling ethical reputation. Unfortunately, your agency only sends a travel group to your child's province once a month, so you had to wait over a month after your TA to travel!! Yes, you saved over $2000 on your airfare by waiting so long, but it seemed like everyone else left within a week of getting their TA. You loved your agency, but you think that next time you might shop around a little to see if you can find one that is not quite so pricey and will let you travel sooner.

All three of these people had good experiences with their agency, would recommend them wholeheartedly to friends, yet had a major issue that they weren't quite happy with. Would you pay more to shave six months off your referral time? To leave right away after travel approval? That's what you need to decide when choosing an agency. If you have taken the time to talk to a few agencies and you've narrowed down the list, thinking about the priorities for your family will hopefully help you to make the final decision.

In conclusion

I know this is an almost overwhelming amount of information, and it's overwhelming to consider where to begin. I suggest you take some time to read through all of the information in these two chapters and decide which factors are most important to your family. Narrow down the agencies to three or four which are the best. Contact the agencies and ask them questions. I've given you plenty to ask, so contact them a couple of times—both call and e-mail. How quickly did they respond? Did they give you vague answers or specific ones? Did they ever act annoyed in any way with your questions? Cross any agency off the list that didn't return calls, acted insulted that you asked about finances, or wouldn't give you a straight answer to any question. An agency that doesn't make a potential client a top priority is going to make even less effort when you've already given them money. Choose the agency that you felt a connection with, or that best matched your priorities. Remember, there are many great agencies out there!

Additional Resources

China Adoption Questions group, a general group for adoption from China where you can people questions about any topic or be

directed to a group with a more limited focus such as the ones below.
https://www.facebook.com/groups/1445220415746574/

Rate Your China Adoption Agency Facebook group
https://www.facebook.com/groups/215308551969138/

Reusing Your China Dossier Facebook group
https://www.facebook.com/groups/457341644284151/

Adopting Out of Birth Order From China Facebook group
https://www.facebook.com/groups/655497011138092/

China Adopt 2 Questions Facebook group for those considering adopting two unrelated children
https://www.facebook.com/groups/1445817295682845/

Considering Older Child Adoption From China Facebook group
https://www.facebook.com/groups/1512734842274229/

7

Boy or Girl?
Talking about the adoptive parent
preference for girls

When you and your spouse started discussing adoption, I'll bet there is one thing you agreed on right away-- that a little girl would be perfect for your family. Wondering how I know? Because 90% of adoptive families feel the same way. Although everyone has their own personal reason for choosing to adopt a girl, they are usually surprised to hear that everyone else wants to adopt a girl, too. Adoptive parents overwhelming prefer girls to boys to the extent that 75% of the children in China waiting to be matched with a family are boys. One major agency shared that for every forty dossiers they have logged in for families wanting to adopt a girl they will have only one family open to a boy. That's a huge imbalance! Another agency shared that when they post a girl to their photo listing they will receive an average of twenty-five inquiries about her while most boys on their photo listing receive zero to one inquiries. It takes a boy three times as long to find a family as it does a girl. For this reason, there is a saying among advocates and agency personnel that "boys wait for families while families wait for girls."

Maybe you are thinking "But everyone assumes that only girls are abandoned in China, so that's probably why people who adopt from China are thinking girl." Nope. This preference holds true whether you are talking domestic infant adoption, adoption from foster care, or adopting internationally from any country in the world. A few countries have tried to counter the girl preference problem by setting criteria for requesting a girl. If you are a European parent, you aren't allowed to choose the gender of the child you adopt. But for the most part, if you are an American couple who wants to adopt, you can choose to say that you will only adopt a girl, and most will do so.

Why is it that adoptive families prefer girls? I have been active on adoption groups and reading blogs for quite a while now, and the one theme that really keeps popping up is that women really want to have a daughter. Because women are usually the one in the couple who suggests adding to the family, they will often drive the adoption discussion. Don't men want sons? Well, maybe, but perhaps they feel some inward reluctance to have a son who isn't genetically related pass on the family name. Or it is also possible that men feel if they adopt a girl they get to take a pass on more of the responsibilities. One woman shared that her husband felt that by adopting a girl he wouldn't have to worry about getting a call that his teenage son was in jail, until a neighbor pointed out that a daughter might tell him that she's pregnant! And of course, if you are adopting as a single mom, you probably feel better equipped to parent a girl than a boy.

Perhaps the two most common reasons given are that a woman has one or more boys but has always wanted a daughter, or has a single daughter who really wants a sister. These are perfectly reasonable desires, and adoption can certainly be a way to fulfill those desires while giving a family to a girl who doesn't have one, as long as you keep in mind that you will be adopting a girl who is a unique individual and may or may not meet your expectations. After all, sometimes sisters are best friends and sometimes they are worst enemies. Not all daughters have any interest in wearing skirts accessorized with bows as large as their head and taking ballet lessons. These sorts of family dynamic issues are faced by all families, biological or adoptive.

I'm not at all surprised when women who have two or three boys decide to pursue adoption to have a daughter. What surprises me is how persistently people will choose a girl regardless of their family composition. While each family will make an individual decision as to which gender is the best fit for their family, in the end most of them will decide on a girl. Interestingly, people give the same justifications over and over. Families with a single daughter will say "She needs a sister" while families with a single boy will say "We want to have a daughter." A family with two boys will say "We really want a daughter" while a family with two girls will say "We always dreamed of adopting a girl." Families with three girls often say "We only have three bedrooms, so we have to adopt a girl." While families with three boys and three bedrooms say "We really want a daughter." When you hear from families with four or more of the same gender, you hear "We wouldn't know what to do with a boy if we had one" from families with all girls while once again it's "We really want a daughter" from families with all boys. I have never heard anyone say "We really want a son" or "He needs a brother." It's kind of like a flow chart which gives every possible family composition but they all lead to the girl box in the end.

This really makes me scratch my head. Why are bedrooms an issue if you have girls at home but not boys? Why is it so important for a girl to have a sister but not a boy to have a brother? Why do families with several girls say that they wouldn't know what to do with a boy, while families with several boys don't seem to worry about the learning curve for a girl? It's really quite an interesting sociological phenomenon. Probably the reason no one dreams of adopting a little boy from China, or adopts because they want a son is because the general perception is that there are far more girls available for adoption than boys. When you see all the adoptive families with girls, you assume that's what is available and maybe more families with only

104

daughters would adopt a boy if they knew that boys need families too.

Many people share that a major motivation for them to adopt was an awareness of the discrimination against women in other countries. People who are adopting now grew up hearing news stories about China's one child policy and the widespread abandonment of unwanted girls. They feel they can make a difference in one girl's life by adopting one of those "unwanted" baby girls and letting her know that she is wanted and loved. I've heard women say "I've known I wanted to adopt a little girl from China since I was six (or nine or eleven) years old!" They feel that girls raised in China will face discrimination and a life of hardship if they are not adopted. This is usually based on an outdated view of attitudes in China. In fact, an agency representative shared that one of their partnership orphanages has a waiting list of over two hundred Chinese couples who want to adopt a healthy baby girl.

While I can understand this point of view, I am uncomfortable with how much adoptive parents discriminate against boys in their desire to make up for the discrimination against girls. In countries where there is a preference for boys, it is unlikely that a boy raised in an orphanage will have any advantages in life. For many of these boys, their lack of education and family connections will cause them to always struggle. They very well may not be able to have their own family because they cannot hope to be well off or well-connected enough to attract a wife. Any orphan is at a disadvantage and all of them need homes.

To make things yet more uncomfortable, let's look at another reason no one would dream of listing as motivation–race. Let's assume that a woman dreams of a daughter. Little dresses and giant bows, tea parties and dolls. But what about when she grows up? Well, there's always the big white wedding dress. The one thing you can count on is that children will grow up. What do you think of when your internationally adopted child grows to adulthood? Let's look at the most broad stereotypes out there. The sort of two-dimensional characterizations that show up on TV shows and comedy routines.

Eastern Europe:
Men- tall, alcoholic
Women- tall, great supermodels

Africa:
Men- tall, violent, uneducated
Women- tall, dignified, gorgeous, smart

Asia:
Men- short, nerdy, effeminate
Women- petite, sexy, submissive, smart

Latin America:
Men- short, lazy, sexist, uneducated
Women- sexy, fiery personality

Caribbean:
Men- lazy, druggies, uneducated
Women- sexy, bikinis

How can so many negative stereotypes of men compete with the attractiveness (pun intended) of the women? And even leaving aside the topic of race, boys are perceived as more violent, more impulsive, not as good in school, and more likely to have autism. Perhaps these fears keep people away from boys while the thought that girls would be more compliant (a loud ha ha from those of us who have girls) makes a girl sound safer. I heard one adoptive parent say that they were afraid a boy would be more likely to sexually abuse one of their biological children, even though they wanted to adopt a child under the age of two!

Girls can also act out sexually if they have been abused, behave violently, not perform as well in school--really any of those negative stereotypes. I understand that adoption can be scary because of the unknowns, but choosing a girl over a boy will not rule out any of the possible negative outcomes. The idea that girls are somehow easier than boys is just wrong. There is no easy way out in parenting!

Okay, so the gender preference begins to become understandable. But then I become confused yet again when you start to bring in the religious angle. While the media has recently discovered the Christian adoption movement and several controversial articles have been written on the subject, it is impossible to deny that many people cite religious reasons for adopting. Over and over again people say that they felt called to adoption in light of James 1:27, which reads "Pure and genuine religion in the sight of God the Father means caring for orphans and widows in their distress and refusing to let the world corrupt you." One might assume that those adopting out of religious motivation would be less biased against adopting a boy. To the contrary, if I had a nickel for every time I've heard someone say "God called us to adopt a little girl", I'd have enough money to fund another adoption!

Now, I should say upfront that in my religious tradition, we talk a lot about discernment, but it is less common than in the evangelical churches to discern a clear specific message from God. My husband and I felt that God was calling us to adopt, but we did not get a lightning bolt message regarding race, age, or gender. I do believe that God calls people to specific tasks, but when I look at the sheer number of people called to adopt a little girl, I have to wonder why God isn't calling more people to adopt boys or older children or children with big special needs? The cynical side of me thinks that some of these people are reading their own desires into God's message because it is hard for me to understand why God would call families with three, four or five girls to wait in line for months to adopt a girl when there are so many boys waiting for families. When Jesus said to welcome the children in His name, I'm sure that included boys, who are "the least of these" in the world of adoption.

But in charity, I remind myself that it is always easy to obey God's call when it aligns with your desires. Perhaps the families being called to adopt boys, older children, and children with big special needs are trying to ignore their calling. I know that when we first considered adoption, a girl is exactly what sprang to mind for us. And with three boys and a lone daughter, who could blame us? But when we learned how long the boys wait for families, it tugged at our hearts because we love our boys so much. Yes, we wanted a daughter, but we already have one. Was having another really so important? After a lot of prayer and discussion (both between ourselves and our children), and yet more discernment, we decided that we couldn't choose when we had biological children, so why should it matter when you adopt? Adoption, for us, was about welcoming a child into our family, not about trying to create our personal idea of the perfect family.

I don't expect all families to make the same decision as us, or to come to the same conclusions. I'm not trying to berate those who adopted or hope to adopt a girl, nor am I trying to make you feel bad. This is not about asking people to justify their choice or to choose a boy out of guilt. It's about asking people to take a moment to consider their reasons for marking only the girl box. I hope that families, and especially women, who are usually the driving force behind the adoption decision, will take a good look at their motivations. Maybe a few more people will realize that they have a place in their homes and hearts for a boy after all. Perhaps after consideration more people will be open to either gender. Why limit yourself? Check both boxes and see what referral you receive. If you are adopting because you hear God's call, then try leaving that opening to see if he is using this tug on your heart to lead you to your son. Consider the *child*, not the gender. You can always decline a referral, so you've really got nothing to lose. If you take a chance, you might realize all of the fun that a boy can bring to your life!

Additional Resources

Snips & Snails v. Sugar & Spice: Gender Preferences in Adoption
http://creatingafamily.org/blog/snips-and-snails-vs-sugar-and-spice-gender-preferences-in-adoption/

New York Times: Black babies, boys less likely to be adopted
http://economix.blogs.nytimes.com/2010/01/25/black-babies-boys-less-likely-to-be-adopted/?src=twr

Love Without Boundaries: The adoption of boys
http://www.lwbcommunity.org/the-adoption-of-boys

Love Without Boundaries: What about the boys?
http://www.lwbcommunity.org/what-about-the-boys

Personal experience- A family with two boys writes about deciding to be open to either gender
http://holtinternational.org/blog/2016/01/saying-yes-boy-one-adoptive-familys-story/

Personal experience- A family with three girls writes about deciding to be open to either gender
http://holtinternational.org/blog/2016/02/blessed-with-a-boy/

8

More Big Decisions
Which age? Should we adopt two?

After you have checked one or both of the gender boxes, you will need to select an age range for your child. The greatest number of people will want a child under the age of two. The age range you list will be the upper limit you accept. So if you mark "under two" and your agency has the file of a girl who is twenty-six months old, they will most likely not refer the file to you. On the other hand, you also need to consider the amount of time it will take to complete the adoption. If you are not matched until after your dossier is in China then it will only be between three and five months before you travel. However if you are matched with a waiting child before you ever begin the process then your child might be a full year older before you meet her on adoption day.

For girls, many people will be open to a daughter up to the age of five, while the number of couples open to a boy will steeply decline once a boy reaches the age of three. On more than one occasion, I have seen boys on agency photo listings who were three years old and had no special need at all because their medical need had resolved or been corrected. Yes, completely healthy three-year-old boys waiting several months before a family decided to adopt them. Therefore, by opening your age range up a little higher, the number of files available for you to consider will probably greatly increase.

One factor which holds many people back from considering older children is the concern that older children will have more problems attaching. This could certainly be the case for older children, but there is no major difference in attachment between a one-year-old and a three-year-old. One positive for adopting a child in the three to seven year age range is that they have a far greater understanding of what is happening to them when they are adopted. If they have normal verbal development, they will pick up English quickly. While you might have missed out on first steps and first words, you will find that adopting a child three or older there is still plenty of magic in new experiences. You will be amazed at how excited a child will be at having their very first birthday party, experiencing a trip to the zoo, and participating in American holidays. You will see through their eyes how weird the idea of Halloween actually is (we dress up in a costume and people give us candy?) and how magical all of Christmas can be when experienced for the first time.

You might be surprised to hear that many people have adopted a child under the age of two and found that they had attachment difficulties. So much of attachment will depend on what sort of care your child received, trauma your child might have experienced, how many placements they have had, and their own personality. I have a friend who adopted about the same time as our first adoption. She and her husband were matched with their daughter when she was a little over one year old. She came home well before her second birthday. I heard recently that they dissolved the adoption because their daughter was diagnosed with reactive attachment disorder. After months of intensive therapy they decided that having a certified therapeutic family adopt her was the best decision. Perhaps having gone from birth family to orphanage to foster family to adoptive family within eighteen months was too much for their daughter. By all accounts she had been very attached to her foster mother so maybe the trauma of losing her caused her to refuse to form an attachment to her new family. Whatever the reason, her adoption failed despite her young age. This is rare, but it does happen. I'm not telling you this story to scare you away from adopting. I simply want you to know that there is no magical formula for guaranteeing attachment. If you find yourself interested in a child who is three but you thought that keeping your age range under two would make attachment problems less likely, then go ahead and request that file because a three year old could be a wonderful addition to your family.

I will also share a positive story with you. One of my sons stayed at the same orphanage for over a year, but in the six months before the adoption he was moved to foster care, then that foster family decided to stop fostering, so he was switched to a different foster family. That's orphanage, foster family, new foster family, then to us, a total of four placements in six months! But our son was absolutely fine. He is a laid-back easy-going guy. He attached well to us, although it was not an instant process. He was adopted less than a month before his second birthday. Our other adopted son joined our family the week he turned three, after having lived in a large orphanage from a few months old. He also had a smooth transition. If anything, his adjustment was a little easier because of his personality.

The same will be true for many children, even if they are four, six, or eight. When you are considering your age range, you might want to look at other factors. If you do not have any children, you may feel it is best to start out with as young a child as possible to gain parenting experience. Many couples who already have children want to adopt a child who is younger than their youngest. If your youngest is five or seven, then a 3 or 4-year-old might work as well in your family as a toddler. If you begin to consider adopting out of age order, perhaps because your oldest is a girl followed by two younger sons, and you think a girl between the two boys would be ideal, then you are considering something called disrupting birth order. Similarly, if you are in your forties and beginning a family, you might think it would be best to start off by adopting two children at the same time--after all, you aren't getting any younger! These are both practices which are permitted by China but not allowed by all placing agencies.

You might assume that if China allows a practice, such as adopting two unrelated children at once, your agency will allow you to do so. This is not always the case. All placing agencies determine their own guidelines for adoptive families. Sometimes, even when a placing agency will allow something, the social worker who writes your home study might not approve your family for that situation. For example, a placing agency might not have a problem with you adopting an aging out child who is older than your oldest child, but if your social worker opposes disrupting birth order, she can refuse to approve you for a teenager in your home study.

"You mean agencies or social workers think their rules are more important than finding these kids a family!? I'm going to choose an agency that understands that each family knows what is best and what they can handle!"

Before I discuss these situations, it is important to understand the reason behind these rules. Generally, the older the agency, the more likely they are to stick with what are called "best social work practices." These are guidelines such as only adopting one unrelated child at a time, keeping birth order, avoiding "artificial twinning" (ending up with two children of the same age), and never adopting a child older than the oldest child already in the family. In most other countries these practices are not allowed, but our American independent streak rebels at those sort of absolute guidelines. However, many agencies now are allowing these practices, at least in some situations.

Why would any agencies not allow these things? Because agencies that have been around for decades have seen a lot of failed adoptions. I spoke with a representative of an agency often characterized by adoptive parents as being "conservative" and "having a lot of rules." I was told that their top priority was finding the right family for a child. They wanted to make sure that the adoption was successful and they didn't want to risk the child's placement by matching them with a family with the potential for disruption. A future chapter offers a longer discussion as to why you need to keep this possibility in mind as you decide whether or not these special adoption situations are right for your family.

I see people asking about these three situations extremely often in online adoption related groups. As I have mentioned previously, it is important to remember that these groups are full of people who are happy with their experience. You will most likely not hear from people who would tell you that they had a bad experience adopting outside of the best social work guidelines. You can hear from many people who disrupted birth order in their family, adopted two unrelated children at the same time, or adopted an older child who was aging out and will tell you how amazing it was for their family but that does not help you to know what YOUR family's experience might be; you are a different family, adopting a different child or children. That doesn't mean I'm trying to talk you out of it; I'm trying to make sure that you've seriously considered all aspects of the situation. I might sound too negative, but thinking about the hard aspects of adoption will only give you more tools to succeed. If you read through the negative aspects that I mention and think to yourself "We could absolutely handle that!" then go right ahead! Educated and informed families are the best families for children. We will now look at the three most common issues on which parents clash with agencies. I've included links to resources on all three situations in an extra-long Additional Resources section, so please take the time to read those as well before making any decisions.

Adopting out of birth order

Best social work practice would say that you should adopt a child who is at least nine months younger than your youngest child based on the theory that this would be the closest naturally occurring spacing between siblings. I know someone who spent several months convincing her agency that it would be acceptable for their family to adopt a child who was a mere eight and a half months younger than their youngest child, so some agencies hold very strictly to these guidelines.

If this is something you want to do, you will need to discuss it with your social worker and placing agency. They will probably want you to consider your family dynamics. How would you handle it if you had an extended period of conflict between the adopted child and the child who was upset from their place in the family? Unfortunately, adopting out of birth order is a common theme in adoption dissolution. When the adoption of a child leads to turmoil in the family, it is never the biological child who needs to find a new family. Most children who have experienced trauma will do best as the youngest child in the family.

If you are considering adopting out of birth order, take some time to look at the roles of all the children in your family. Most social workers consider not displacing the oldest as an unbreakable rule. Although one aspect to consider in this regard is that most children who are adopted will be at a younger age emotionally, so a child might be older than your oldest on paper but fit in as younger than your oldest. Adopting a child younger than your youngest is considered ideal because this is the natural order of adding to a family. However, if your youngest has been "the baby" for seven years or longer, than he or she might find it difficult to give up that special place in the family. For this reason, if you are adopting out of birth order, adding children into the middle often seems to be the most successful. Gender can be another factor in adopting out of birth order. A child might not be the oldest, but if he is the oldest boy, that is still a special role.

Frequently, parents adopt a same-gender sibling specifically because their son doesn't have a brother or daughter doesn't have a sister. If your daughter has been the only girl in your family for a long time, she might not want to give up being your princess. Even when a child thinks they want a same gender sibling, they can be unprepared for the reality of that sibling. A child does not understand that their dream sister who is a best friend might turn out to be a rival instead. As an adult, you should understand this better than your child and spend some time preparing her for this. If you are adopting because "she always wanted a sister", be prepared that she might say "I don't like her! Give her back!" while you are in China. This happens with biological siblings as well, but somehow adoptive parents seem less likely to prepare their children for the negative aspects of a sibling. This may be related to the fact that you can't choose the gender when you add a biological sibling, so it seems less like ordering up a ready-made playmate.

A child who was more recently adopted into a family will not necessarily be as set in his place as a child who has been the oldest his entire life, so your agency might consider the situation of an adopted child differently than that of a biological child. Much of the success will be determined by the personalities of the children involved; unfortunately you won't know your new child's personality when you are making the decision. Discussing all of these factors with your social worker as you decide consider how your new child will fit into your family is a good idea.

Adopting two unrelated children at once

The second issue is adopting two unrelated children at once. Adoption involves a huge amount of stress and upheaval for a child. When you adopt two at once, the theory is that you cannot give each child the amount of attention that they need to bond with your family. Because China's adoption program involves special needs, you need to consider that you will also be dealing with double the amount of doctor visits. I am sometimes concerned that there can be a subtle form of peer pressure to adopt two at once on online adoption groups, with many people asking "Are you going to go for two?!" Deciding to adopt two unrelated children at once should involve careful consideration.

- How much parenting experience do you have?

- How much adoption experience?

- Do you have a plan for the medical care the two children will need? What if they have unexpected medical needs, for example both end up needing surgery at the same time?

- How much of a local support network do you have?

- Can you afford to double the fees? Likely spend three weeks in China instead of two?

- Have you thought through the worst case scenario? What if one or both have unexpectedly worse medical issues? What if they are both having attachment issues?

- Be aware that you might be tempted to favor one child over the other. Children react so differently to the adoption experience. If you have one who is seamlessly attaching to your family while the other is acting out and constantly causing stress in your family, it can be very easy to unconsciously favor the "easy" child. As much as you know that you shouldn't compare the two children, it is almost unavoidable especially if they are close in age.

- Are you doing this because you think it will be cheaper or make your life easier? I have seen multiple people actually say "I'm not going to go through all of this trouble twice. I'm just going to get two at once and get it over with all at the same time." I'm going to be completely blunt here and point out that you need to consider the impact this will have on the children involved and not your convenience.

If you are seriously considering adopting two children at the same time, you probably have a lot of questions about how it works and the best way to go about it. First, be aware that it does add significantly to your cost. If you know before you begin that you would like to adopt two, ask prospective agencies about their fees. Some charge double the agency fee with no discount, while others charge very little more if you adopt two. Your US and China fees will be doubled, but you will save on travel costs because you will have only one trip. It might be possible to have the orphanage fee reduced depending on the child and orphanage. Those who have adopted two at once a few times have found that it added $10,000-$15,000, which is significantly less than two individual adoptions. If you are eligible for the adoption tax credit, that is PER CHILD so that will be helpful. Employee adoption benefits vary.

Next you might wonder if adopting two at once will extend your trip. The answer is usually, but not always. If you are adopting children from two different provinces, the most common scenario is that you would travel to one province, finalize that adoption, travel to the second province and finalize that adoption, then travel to Guangzhou to finish up the visa process. However, you could have each parent go to a different province and meet up in Guangzhou. Or you could ask the provinces to expedite the adoption so that you spend about half a week in each, then have a Thursday consulate date in Guangzhou making the trip more like 2.5 weeks. If you adopt two children from the same province, perhaps through an agency partnership, then it would not add any additional time. Adopting one or both children from Guangdong province, where Guangzhou is located, could also cut down on the time a bit if your agency will schedule the medical appointment sooner rather than waiting for the group Saturday appointment.

Another question people frequently have is how to go about deciding which special needs to choose for the children. When you adopt two at once, one can be a LID only with minor needs, while the other is required to be special focus. Because it can take longer to be matched with a LID child, many people choose to find a special focus child after they are matched with a LID child so that the process isn't delayed for the special focus child. However, because you can be matched with a special focus child before your dossier is ready, others will find a special focus child early if they feel their wait for a LID child will not be too long with their agency. If you are looking for two young girls with minor needs then it could be tricky to find two with whose needs you are comfortable. There are far more young boys or older children with minor needs designated special focus.

Some people choose to have one child with a special need which requires little medical intervention, such as a limb difference, paired with another child who will require a lot of medical intervention, such as a complex heart condition. Others will seek out children with the same medical condition so they can double up on specialist visits. I do know of one family who adopted boys with the same special need who both had the same surgery scheduled on the same day within two weeks of coming home! Probably the majority of parents choose two children individually that they feel are their children rather than trying to plan out the specifics to that degree.

Age is a final consideration. Some people choose children the same age and artificially twin them. A downside to this is the tendency to compare that I mentioned earlier. Even within the same orphanage, children of the same age can get radically different care. With older children of the same age, they could see each other as competition rather than be the best friends you imagined. Especially if you are adopting two older children from the same orphanage--consider that they might already have roles within the orphanage that would make being adopted together a negative. For example, if one was a favored child and bullied the other. This dynamic would continue within your family instead of the scenario you imagined, which was allowing two friends to remain together.

Most people adopt two children who are at least a year apart in age. Often, having one child two or three years older works well. Caring for two toddlers is intense, especially if you are also dealing with it while traveling in another country! Having one child who is able to walk starts you off ahead. Having children with a decent spacing interval also decreases the tendency to compare them. One negative to adopting one older and one younger is that if your older child was given a caregiver role in the orphanage, he or she might fall into that role with the younger child. You will need to work extra hard to make sure both children understand that you are the parents and will take care of parenting both of them.

There are many different ways to adopt two children at the same time from China. The best combination of age, special need, and location will be different for every family. Ultimately, the success of the placement will depend on the personalities and life experiences of everyone involved, and that is almost impossible to know in advance. Hopefully I have given you many possibilities to consider and discuss with your agency.

Adopting an older child

The third issue is older child adoption. The definition of an "older child" can vary, but I am going to focus on the age range of ten to thirteen, the time period where a child is close to "aging out" in China. China does not allow children to be adopted past their fourteenth birthday. There are no exceptions to this rule, even if a parent is in the process of adopting a child. For this reason, you will often see advocates publicizing children who are close to aging out. "URGENT! This is the child's LAST CHANCE for a family!!!" Maybe these pleas tug at your heart and you wonder, is this something that your family should do? Here are some things to consider when making this decision.

One import aspect when you consider adopting an older child is that at the age of ten, the child must consent to the adoption and sometimes they say "No thanks, I'd rather stay here!" There are no refunds in this scenario, and there have been couples who have returned home without the child they intended to adopt because he or she could not take that leap of faith and sign the documents. These kids are so incredibly brave. I know that I wouldn't be able to leave everything I know behind to live with random strangers on the other side of the world! However the orphanage director, nannies, your translator, and even your agency staff will put immense pressure on the child to sign. This can be both good and bad. It is good because many children get last minute nerves and they turn out to be very happy that they were talked into signing. It is bad when the child really was not interested in being adopted but was coerced into it, which makes for a very long, painful attachment process.

Is your primary motivation in adopting an older child that you want to save the child? I have seen many instances where people have been told that an orphanage kicks a child out onto the street on their fourteenth birthday. As far as I am aware, this is not the case. On our first adoption trip, when we visited our son's orphanage, I asked the director what happened to children who aged out. She said that those who could live independently would be given some education or vocational training and they would try to find them a job. They continue to live at the SWI until they turned eighteen. It is my understanding that while children are no longer eligible for adoption at fourteen, they remain in state care until they become legal adults at age eighteen. Those who cannot live independently will live there for life because as a social welfare institution they house adults as well as children. However, every orphanage is run independently so every director will handle things differently. While children who have aged out will face many challenges in life, it is not necessarily so dire as being kicked out onto the street. Organizations such as Love Without Boundaries are working to give these children more educational opportunities, and at least one agency has a similar program as well. Sometimes, if a child is able to obtain a university education through the assistance of a charity, the orphanage will allow them to return "home" on holidays and vacations. Yes, adoption will give these children more opportunities, and more importantly, a lifelong family. However, it is important to understand the challenges before taking this step and not rush in to "save" someone, expecting that happy ending.

One question to ask yourself is why adopt an older child from China rather than the US foster system? Since I adopted from China you might wonder why I ask this question. I support both adoption systems and I think that you need to find the best fit for your family. But if you are considering adopting in the ten to thirteen year age range, this is an age where there are many children available here in the US. Sometimes people have the mistaken idea that a thirteen- year-old from China won't have any baggage, unlike a teenager in the US foster system. If you are feeling called to adopt an older child from China, you need to make sure you understand that there will be challenges including additional challenges specific to international adoption. Among them:

- Care varies widely in China. Older children have lived over a decade with their family, with a foster family, in an orphanage, or any combination thereof. They could come to you having experienced malnutrition, a lack of necessary medical care, neglect, and physical or sexual abuse. Sexual abuse is a concern of any child, regardless of age, so I have included the link to a .pdf on how to make a sexual safety plan for your family in the Additional Resources section of this chapter.

- They may have years worth of ingrained orphanage behaviors.

- Related to orphanage behaviors, you should expect your child to be immature for their age and behave accordingly. You should have zero expectations of your child acting like their same-aged American peers.

- The information in their files might be incorrect, and not only medical information. Your child is might be older or younger (but usually it's older) than indicated in the file. Or they might have biological siblings you didn't know about until you got to China and your child told you about them.

- It is much more difficult to learn a new language after puberty, even if you are immersed in it.

- Your child may have received little or no formal education. Mixed with the language issue, this means that they may not ever achieve reading fluency. Adopting older children will bring many educational challenges and you will need to be prepared to be an advocate for your child and make sure their educational needs are met at school. You need to have the ability to celebrate the progress that your child makes, even if he is never a college-bound honor student.

- They will have unrealistic expectations of their own. Children are often told that everyone in America is rich and they will be given anything they want. They may be terrified of you because they were told that you plan to sell them for organ harvesting (yes, really!). Your child may be on her best behavior for weeks because she was told that you would send her back if she misbehaved.

- Older children may not even understand what adoption is. Love Without Boundaries interviewed older children in orphanages and they struggled to come up with answers to questions about what adoption is, why a foreign couple would want to adopt a Chinese child, or what they thought life would be like after adoption.

If you have considered all of those points and read through the information in the Additional Resources section and still feel that you are called to older child adoption, there is still a little more information to be imparted. First, no one wants a child to lose their chance for a family because of finances. For this reason, you will find that there are many generous grants available for older children who are reaching the end of their opportunity for adoption. Sometimes, a particular child will be offered a large grant by a private donor independent of an agency. Some agencies will reduce their agency fee by a significant amount in addition to offering a grant. Finally, many of the orphanages in China will reduce or waive the required orphanage donation in an effort to help these kids find a family. While no one should consider adopting an aging out child because it is cheaper, if you are interested in adopting a child who is close to aging out, you should be aware of all of these available resources.

Because the adoption must be completed by the child's fourteenth birthday, time is often a major concern. It is important to ask if your agency has experience expediting the adoption of an aging out child. There are many things which can be done to make sure the adoption is complete in time. I have known people who adopted an aging out child in under three months from start to finish, barely making it across the finish line by finalizing the adoption in China before the Travel Authorization had been issued. Most agencies will transfer the files of aging out children, so if an agency is skeptical that they can complete the adoption in time, you could see if they would transfer the file to another agency more experienced with the expedite procedure. If the agency is unwilling to transfer or is offering a generous grant which you need, you can find online support to walk your agency through the process.

Finally, if you are considering adopting an older child from China, it important to know that this is an area where child trafficking occurs. Unfortunately, some people bring home older children only to find that they have a family back in China. Usually, their family has received money in exchange for letting their child live at the orphanage to be adopted. They are told that their child will receive a wonderful education in America and return home once they graduate. Sometimes the kids are threatened to make them cooperate. They can be understandably angry when they learn that they do not have the ability to return to their family in China and aren't even Chinese citizens any longer. There are many older kids in China who need homes, and you want to make sure that you make one of them a part of your family rather than someone who has been coerced into coming to America with you. While most of these false orphans come from one particular orphanage, the problem isn't limited to only that orphanage. There are often red flags that will help you spot these kids. Allow me to break out the bullet points one more time.

- Abandoned at an older age under fishy circumstances. Found wandering the streets at ten or twelve but can't remember their own name, parents' names, or address.

- Came into state care at an older age because their entire family died tragically. Often comes with fake death certificates to aid the story.

- Looks older than twelve or thirteen. Many of these kids are closer to seventeen, so if your son has a five o'clock shadow in his pictures, beware.

- Not only are completely healthy, but excel academically. Often are accomplished at playing a sport or instrument.

- For more information Google "China aging out fraud."

I don't want to leave you on that negative note, especially since this chapter has been focused on the negative more than usual. I would like to highlight the story of Jasmine. Lisa and her husband Dan decided rather last minute to adopt Jasmine, even though they had previously discussed older child adoption and said it was something they would never consider. When they arrived in China to adopt Jasmine, they realized she had muscular dystrophy rather than spina bifida, so her special need was a much worse diagnosis than they had been prepared for. Despite this, they completed the adoption.

As Jasmine grew comfortable enough to begin sharing her story they learned that she had been mistreated by both her father and her orphanage nannies. She was abandoned by her grandmother, the only relative who had treated her with kindness. She hadn't received any education in her orphanage and had been told that the American couple coming for her would surely mistreat her or abandon her in America. This sounds like everything I've been warning you about, right? Certainly the biggest challenges Jasmine's family have experienced have been rooted in her mistreatment at the orphanage. They struggle to teach her that she has value, that she is loveable, and that they will never abandon her. One of the most difficult moments was when they had to tell Jasmine that there was no surgery in America to help her walk, despite what she was told in China.

However, Jasmine is thriving in a loving family. She is so appreciative of "simple" things like hot showers and being able to finally receive an education. Jasmine lives to encourage more people to consider adopting older children. She and her family have raised money to help others adopt. In fact, before a surgery, the anesthesiologist told Jasmine that sometimes the medicine would help you to have wonderful dreams. The doctor asked her what she was going to dream about and Jasmine replied "No more orphans in China." This is why some families will educate themselves about all of the negative aspects of older child adoption and decide to go ahead anyway. Because it's worth it, and it makes all the difference in the world to kids like Jasmine.

Additional Resources

Creating A Family's Nine Rules For Adopting Out of Birth Order
http://creatingafamily.org/adoption-category/top-ten-rules-for-successfully-adopting-out-of-birth-order/

Creating A Family podcast on Adopting Out of Birth Order
http://creatingafamily.org/adoption-category/disrupting-birth-order-in-adoption/

Disruption: A failed mom's look back
http://anymommyoutthere.com/2008/07/disruption-failed-moms-look-back.html

Creating A Family's Pros and Cons of Adopting More than One Child at Once
http://creatingafamily.org/adoption/resources/artificial-twinningvirtual-twins/

Creating A Family radio show on Adopting Two Unrelated Children at the Same Time
http://creatingafamily.org/adoption-category/adopting-two-unrelated-kids-time/

LWB Wisdom Wednesdays: Adopting Two At Once
http://www.lwbcommunity.org/wisdom-wednesdays-adopting-two-at-once

Characteristics of families who have successfully adopted two at once
http://creatingafamily.org/adoption-category/cut-adopt-one-time/

Post-Orphanage Behavior in Internationally Adopted Children
http://www.bgcenter.com/BGPublications/OrphanageBehavior.htm

Creating A Family's resources on Older Child Adoption
http://creatingafamily.org/adoption/resources/adopting-older-children/

Workshop on creating a child sexual safety plan from Florida's Center for Child Welfare
http://tinyurl.com/z5q75gm

Keck, Dr. Gregory. Parenting the Hurt Child: Helping Adoptive Families Heal and Grow. Colorado Springs, CO: NavPress, 2009.

Facebook group Considering Older Child Adoption From China
https://www.facebook.com/groups/1512734842274229/

Vickie at Just a MINute Mom has a must read post called You Shouldn't Adopt A Teen.
http://wwwourchinagirl.blogspot.com/2014/07/you-shouldnt-adopt-teen.html

A Little Advice From the Front Lines For Parents To Be gives an honest account behaviors in country with newly adopted older children
http://whereyouwantmetogo.blogspot.com/2015/09/a-little-advice-from-front-lines-for.html

You might have used Adoption Learning Partners for your required education hours. They have a variety of educational modules on older children. You might look at the <u>Tough Starts Matters package</u>.
http://www.adoptionlearningpartners.org/catalog/courses/toug h-starts-matters-package.cfm

If you want to read more about Jasmine, visit the <u>Ellsbury family blog</u>.
http://www.seriouslyblessed.com/category/jasmine-shuang-shuang/

9

Which Special Needs?

When you decide to adopt through the China special needs program, you will be able to choose which special needs you are open to accepting. Most agencies will present you with a medical needs checklist, and you check all the needs you will consider. A typical form will have over fifty different medical conditions listed. The conditions range from familiar scary medical diagnoses like spina bifida and HIV+ to unfamiliar yet still scary sounding medical conditions like as thalassemia or Tetralogy of Fallot. It can be daunting sifting through the medical conditions list or looking over photo listings trying to decide where to begin. When you are unsure of the idea of adopting a child with medical needs in the first place, it's especially hard to know what to sign up for. Many people are left wondering "What are the easy special needs?" Answering that question can be difficult, because everyone's idea of what needs are "easy" is different. You know you've found an easy need for your family when you learn about what care or management is involved in the special need and find yourself saying "Okay, we can handle that, no problem! Is this a big deal for some people or something?" Here are some considerations to get you started.

What are you familiar with?

Sometimes the best place to start is what you know. A family who adopted through my agency was motivated to adopt a child with a limb difference because the husband is a prostheticist.

Many people who choose to adopt a child with Down syndrome say that they started on that path because they have a close relationship with a friend or relative with Down syndrome. Often, parents are inspired to adopt a child with the same special need as a biological child. One advocate in the Chinese adoption community decided to adopt after her biological child was born with a rare form of dwarfism. She and her husband went on to adopt four children with dwarfism and she is frequently the first person within the China adoption community that people turn to when they are considering dwarfism as a special need. Teachers and medical professionals probably have experience with a variety of medical needs, but everyone can ask around among family and friends.

How is your insurance?

It sounds obvious, but you should check your coverage before you decide which needs you are open to, especially if finances are a concern. If you are open to hearing impairments will your insurance cover hearing aids or cochlear implants? Insurances often limit coverage on durable medical equipment like prosthetics and wheelchairs. Speech therapy is frequently not covered by insurance but children with cleft palate can need extensive speech therapy. Care for children who have special needs requiring regular transfusions, such as hemophilia or thalassemia, can be particularly expensive. How is your out-of-network coverage if you choose to travel to have your child treated by a specialist? Many states offer services to help make medical treatment affordable or make up for insurance coverage gaps. Some states grant this medical coverage to any child born with a disability, regardless of income level. It is best to confirm coverage on a medical need you are considering before you send a Letter of Intent to adopt a particular child.

What resources are available in your area?

If you don't already have a child with special needs, you might not know the strengths of your geographic area regarding treatment for that need. Do some asking around to see what is available. If you have a school for the deaf or blind, you might feel more comfortable adopting a child with those special needs once you see how much they can help you. If you live in Boston, which is home to the premiere pediatric cardiac center, you might feel more confident adopting a child with congenital heart disease. Shriner's Hospitals provide excellent care, often at no cost, for children with cleft lip/cleft palate and orthopedic issues. We didn't realize until after we were matched that there was a Shriner's Hospital specializing in orthopedics near us. Your social worker will probably be a wonderful resource, but don't forget to also ask your local pediatrician.

What sort of time do you have?

You should expect the time immediately after returning home with your child to be full of doctor visits and surgeries, therapies, or other procedures. Once that stage is over, how much time do you have available for medical needs? Some special needs require a lot of maintenance and with weekly therapy visits. Perhaps you expect the child to be in and out of the hospital during times of illness. Other special needs are the sort where you only check in with a doctor once a year or so. How easy is it for you to get time off work? If you have other children, what sort of commitments do you have with them? Living in a rural area can present unique challenges. How far away are the medical facilities you'll be using and how often can you make that drive? Is there anyone in your area with experience with some of the less common special needs, such as thalassemia?

How good is your support system?

Having a good support system can make all the difference in the world. Maybe you already have children, but you live right next door to Grandma and Grandpa, who love to babysit. Perhaps you have a church with an active meal ministry. But if both spouses work jobs with little flexibility, or you already have children and no reliable babysitter, you should be realistic about that when you choose to be open to some special needs.

Have an honest conversation about looks.

Many adoptive parents are uncomfortable with visible special needs like limb differences or dwarfism. However, children with these special needs are often physically very healthy and require little in the way of medical care. It is natural to feel a connection with a child who is especially cute, but take some time to consider whether a child with a visible special need might be a good fit for your family. Once you have a relationship with a child, you don't see their need, no matter how visible it is–you simply see your beautiful son or daughter!

On the other hand, many people are moved to reconsider special needs that they thought they couldn't manage after being drawn to a child's picture. I have heard so many people say "Once we saw that picture, we knew we could handle whatever the need was. We just knew she/he was our child." After having the file reviewed by a doctor and hearing what sort of medical care is necessary, you will probably find it is not as daunting as you thought. If you find yourself drawn to a particular child on a photo listing, don't rule him out because he has a scary special need. Use it as motivation to learn more about the need.

Educate yourself about special needs you are considering, and maybe some of those that you aren't.

Once you begin to do a little research, you may find your that perception of what is involved in a medical need isn't correct. I, like many people, assumed that a cleft palate could be repaired with a single surgery. In reality, it is a special need that is more involved than that, often requiring two or three palate surgeries, lip or nose revision procedures, bone grafts, throat surgery, and years of speech therapy. Many families are caught off guard by the amount of involvement necessary for this need. Cleft lip/cleft palate is still a manageable need for most families, but you don't want to be surprised by what is involved after you get your child home.

On the other hand, you might be more open to reviewing spina bifida files if you learn that in mild cases the child is able to walk. More people are considering needs such as spina bifida or anal atresia when they learn that people with these issues can achieve social continence through self-catheterization and a bowel management program. The category of limb differences can be huge, and maybe you would be open to a few missing fingers (or extra ones), but not a child who is missing both arms. Most children with a particular special need might be more than you think your family could handle, but you could be open to milder cases. Not all agency medical conditions checklists will have a way to indicate the degree of seriousness. If your agency checklist doesn't have options for minor, moderate, or severe then you should handwrite it in if it makes a difference in your openness to a particular need.

Finally, make sure you aren't deciding based on an outdated understanding of what a special need involves. Through medical advances, children with hemophilia can lead active lives. Drugs are available to strengthen the bones of children with osteogenesis imperfecta (brittle bone disease). Similarly, through new pharmaceutical advances, children who are HIV positive can live completely normal lives with the viral load at undetectable levels in the bloodstream. Hearing about the difference that new treatment options make in the care of certain needs is often a decisive factor in parents changing their mind and deciding to be open to a need.

Consider the worst case scenario

Finally, remember to take the worst case scenario seriously. Files from China are generally accurate, but often minor issues are not disclosed. Sometimes children are misdiagnosed. Heart issues are rather notorious for "minor" being more "major" than was thought. A few people will find they have adopted a perfectly healthy child, but many more will find they are dealing with a need that is far more complex than they thought when they accepted the file. If you have a file reviewed by a doctor it can be easy to focus on the positives, especially if you have already fallen in love with the photo. Be sure to spend some time asking yourselves how your family will cope with the special need being worse than presented, if the situation turned out to not be correctable, or if the "institutional delays" turned out to be true cognitive delays. There are no guarantees in adoption, any more than there are in life. You have to have a certain amount of flexibility and the ability to be comfortable with unknowns when you choose to adopt a child with special needs.

Along the same lines, it is common to have feelings of guilt about not being open to some needs, or having to decline a referral. When filling out the medical needs checklist, it is common for couples to struggle with the feeling that they are being asked to judge the worthiness of the children. For some people it can feel as if every box you leave unchecked is a child you are saying doesn't deserve to be in your family. Remember that the best family for a child is one which can meet their needs. If you know that your family honestly cannot meet a child's needs, medical or otherwise, try not to feel guilty about it. Families will answer all of these questions differently and a need that is too much for one family will be another family's "easy special need."

If you're looking for an "easy" special need, consider adopting a boy

Because adoptive parents overwhelmingly prefer girls, many boys who are young and have minor needs will wait much longer to find a family than girls with the same age and need. For this reason, I've heard adoption advocates say that the most common special need is being a boy. Take some time to consider how important each of the factors of age, need, and gender are to you. Usually, boys and older children will be available with more minor needs or even no known medical condition at all.

Worrying about "what if?"

I started this chapter discussing how to find the "easy" special need. Don't we all want an easy special need because we're scared about the how our life could change? So much of special needs adoption is facing the "what if" and realizing that it doesn't matter anymore. What if you take a leap of faith, and you realize the child you adopted is so much more than their special need label? It can be very easy to focus on the diagnosis in a file. Try to look past the labels and see each of these files for what they are-- a unique child who needs a loving family. That is the biggest need for each of these children, and it is the same for each of them.

Categorizing the special needs

Now that you've taken some time to consider what resources you have in your area, what sort of time commitment you have, and other practical factors, let's look at some other considerations. For the majority of people, the question might be "What are the easiest needs?" However, other people might want to adopt a child who is considered difficult to place so they might be asking "Which are the needs few people are willing to accept?" Here are a few different ways of categorizing the special needs found in files:

"What are the most common needs people are open to when they are looking for a child with minor needs?"
• Birthmarks

• Cleft lip and cleft palate

• Club feet

• Minor and correctable heart conditions

• Missing or extra digits

• Treated congenital syphilis

These represent special needs which are correctable, do not affect intellect or mobility, and are generally less visible once corrected.

"What are the most common special needs in the files made available for adoption?"
• Anal atresia

• Cerebral palsy

• Cleft lip/cleft palate

- Down syndrome

- Heart conditions

- Hydrocephalus

- Limb differences

- Spina bifida

This list is pretty much a list of the most common birth defects in any human population, with the exception of anal atresia, which has a higher incidence in China than in the US.

"What special needs do the children have who are most difficult to place?"

- Being a boy

- Any intellectual/cognitive delay

- Urinary or bowel incontinence

- Uses a wheelchair

- An identified syndrome

- Visual impairment

- Disordered Sexual Development (ambiguous genitalia or intersex disorder)

- HIV+

- Cancer, or a history of cancer, such as retinoblastoma

Other than being a boy, these are all things that cause people to go "I just couldn't handle that!" We will discuss some of these needs later on because often they are not so scary if you have a better understanding of what is involved in the need.

"Which special needs are matched fairly quickly for girls but cause boys to wait for families?"

- Albinism

- Age[1]

- Giant congenital nevus

- Deafness

- Dwarfism

- Skin disorders like ichthyosis or epidermolysis bullosa

- Microtia

Girls with these needs are so easily matched that their files are often labeled LID only if they are young. What is interesting about this collection of needs is that with the exception of deafness they are all visible needs. In some ways you might expect this to have a greater impact on girls than boys. Perhaps similar to the impulse people feel to adopt "unwanted" girls as a way to show that they have value, people also decide to adopt a girl with a visible special need because they want to teach her that she is beautiful in her own way as a reaction against society's emphasis on beauty in girls.

"Which special needs will lead to a shortened life expectancy due to the limitations of health care available in an orphanage if the child is not adopted?"

- Cancer

- Congenital heart conditions

---

[1] Older girls are not matched quickly in the way that young girls with the medical needs listed are. However, it is substantially more difficult to find a family for an older boy than an older girl. There are twice as many boys as there are girls over age 10 on the shared list.

- Hemophilia
- HIV+
- Spina bifida
- Thalassemia

These conditions really have nothing in common. Children sometimes receive heart surgery or chemotherapy in China, but the quality of medical care is usually much better in the US. However, congenital heart conditions and cancer are still potentially lethal for the children even if they are adopted and receive the best treatment available.

Chronic blood shortages mean that children with Thalassemia are not transfused as often as needed causing their life expectancy to be only age ten in China, while life expectancy in the US is now sixty-four. The clotting factor given to people with hemophilia in the US is not available in China, so the life expectancy of a hemophiliac there is only to age twenty-four.

Children with spina bifida or other diagnoses which can cause incontinence who are in orphanage care in China are often left in diapers rather than using a catheterization routine. This can lead to routine bladder infections and over time cause the kidneys to stop functioning.

China has a strong stigma against HIV positive individuals. Medication may not be as readily available and HIV positive individuals, even children, are often turned out of hospitals when they are ill because of their status. While the long term life expectancy of children living in the US who are HIV positive is uncertain due to how recent the medical advances have been, those whose viral load remains at the "undetectable" level is currently assumed to be the same as the general population.

What parents want you to know

This final section should not be considered medical advice. Rather, I'm going to pass along some information shared by parents of children who have some of those "I could never do that" special needs. These are the needs I often hear people asking about, saying "I never considered this need but there is a child I am drawn to who has it. Can you tell me what daily life looks like?" If this information helps you to think a need might be a possibility for you, I would encourage you to do more research.

Blindness/Vision Impairment- More people are open to albinism as a special need than to other vision impairments, which is a confusing phenomenon when you consider that most people with albinism are legally blind. Most parents find any special need associated with vision to be very scary because they can't imagine what their own life would be like without sight. What parents who have adopted visually impaired children want you to know is that they find it so easy, they feel it really shouldn't be a special need at all! These kids compensate in so many other ways for their loss of vision. Most attend public schools and will grow up to marry and lead productive lives. I had a friend in high school who was blind. He taught me to play chess, was the marching band drum major, walked across four lanes of traffic every day to take calculus at the university near our high school, and is now a professor of music. However, children with VI who are adopted from China will need time and therapy to overcome the delays they experience due to caregivers who don't understand how to give them the non-visual stimulation they need to grow and develop.

Deafness- Surprisingly, what I heard from parents who have adopted children with this special need was kind of the opposite of blindness. Parents want you to know that communication is a greater challenge than they expected, but it is worth the effort. It is vital that you have access to resources to learn ASL, something you should consider doing before you even meet your child, because she will soon surpass you. Ideally, your entire family would sign all the time, even conversations which don't include your deaf child. This is because they often miss out on those side conversations. Imagine that every time you came across people conversing and tried to join in by asking "What was so funny?" you received the response "Oh, I'll tell you later." Being unable to take part in routine conversation, even indirectly, will over time cause your child to feel excluded. While hearing aids and cochlear implants are helping children hear, they rarely provide full hearing. They also fail at times, so having the ability to sign will ensure that he or she always has a way to communicate. Finally, be aware that there is a deaf subculture and topics such as whether or not to implant children, or send them to a school for the deaf versus mainstream education are all very loaded topics. As with any special need, it will be up to you to educate yourself and be your child's advocate.

Disordered Sexual Development- This is a very large category of special needs encompassing abnormality in the systems that affect a child's sexual development. Some of these children have hormonal abnormalities such as Congenital Adrenal Hyperplasia (CAH) while others might have physically ambiguous genitalia, often labeled by the antiquated term "hermaphrodite" in Chinese files. These files will often be listed as "sensitive special need" on advocacy photo listings. Parents who have adopted children with these special needs want you to know that these kids are healthy and normal! Their greatest need is for a loving family who will support them as they develop a sexual identity as male or female, protect their privacy, and help them to navigate peer and romantic relationships as they grow. Being within traveling distance of a specialized DSD clinic is important to make sure your child is getting the most modern treatment options. Be aware that surgery to assign a gender to a child at a young age is not medically necessary. The current recommendation is to wait on surgery until the child is old enough to want it, and many adults with DSD have chosen not to have surgery at all because they are happy with their bodies intact.

HIV positive- Parents want you to know that dealing with people's ignorance is the greatest challenge about adopting a child who is HIV positive. Thanks to new medications, the virus can reach levels so low they are "undetectable" in a blood test. This means that as long as they are taking their medication twice a day (sometimes dropping to once a day after age twelve) they can expect to have a normal life expectancy. Many HIV positive adults are married and have biological children with an HIV negative spouse. Insurance companies will pay for the medication and there are many programs available that will even cover the cost of the copayment. Most families pay only $30-$60 per month for their child's medication. China currently considers HIV positive children to be unadoptable, so few files are made available. This will change if more families request HIV positive children, so let your agency know if you are open to this need. Be aware that the few HIV positive kids available for adoption are usually older and sibling groups are not uncommon. Most have come into care after the death of their parents. These files will often be listed as "sensitive special need" on advocacy photo listings.

Hydrocephalus- This diagnosis literally means "water on the brain" and it is a condition in which there is excessive fluid in the brain. It is sometimes the result of brain damage or occurs in conjunction with spina bifida. Hydrocephalus is most commonly treated by a surgical procedure to shunt the excess fluid away from the brain. Hydrocephalus can cause brain damage if left untreated but it is typically not a condition which affects intelligence. Parents of children with hydrocephalus find this condition to be very manageable.

Incontinence- Parents want you to know that yes, you will deal with pee and poop. However, this doesn't mean your child will be attending prom in diapers! There are many modern medical advances that make it possible for people with incontinence to achieve "social continence", which means they wear normal underwear. Urinary incontinence is usually managed through a catheterization routine. Children are able to self-catheterize by age eight, sometimes younger. Bowel management can mean routine enemas or surgical methods to ease the process. Social continence isn't achieved instantly, so you should have a flexible attitude and a good sense of humor as you work with your child's doctor to find the management system that works best for your child.

Spina bifida- This is a very common birth defect with a wide variation. The most common associated conditions would be reduced mobility, incontinence, and hydrocephalus. Please refer to the entries related to those conditions. Club feet is another associated condition, so if you are open to club feet as a need you might want to research spina bifida as well, because you could learn once your child is home that they actually have a mild form of spina bifida. Spina bifida is not associated with cognitive deficiencies and children with spina bifida grow up to live independent and productive lives.

Wheelchairs- Parents want you to know that children are not "limited" by a wheelchair. It gives the child mobility they are lacking! If you are adopting a younger child, you probably do not need a special house or van, although many parents find these helpful once the child is too heavy to lift. Depending on their special need, your child can probably get him or herself up and down stairs, into a vehicle, in and out of their wheelchair, and live a fully independent life as an adult. Most parents say the most difficult aspect is visiting private homes that do not have a wheelchair ramp to enter, but portable ramps can be purchased to take along when you visit friends and relatives.

Additional Resources

Podcasts from Creating A Family you might find to be helpful: Should you adopt a child with special needs? (8/13) https://creatingafamily.org/adoption-category/should-you-adopt-a-child-with-special-needs/

Evaluating special needs to see which one is a good fit (12/12) https://creatingafamily.org/adoption-category/evaluating-special-needs-to-see-which-one-is-a-good-fit/

Health issues to consider when reviewing an adoption referral or potential match (12/09) https://creatingafamily.org/adoption-category/health-issues-to-consider-when-reviewing-an-adoption-referral-or-potential-match/

Other good resources are the Rainbow Kids website and the No Hands But Ours blog, where you can get information on various needs and read personal experiences of families who have adopted children with those special needs. http://specialneedsadoption.rainbowkids.com/ http://www.nohandsbutours.com/special-needs/

Bethel China is provides an education to orphans in China who are blind. They have several resources on their website about adopting visually impaired children, and you can also see which children at Bethel are available for adoption.
http://www.bethelchina.org/adoption-information/

Video profiling the Ayers family in Cincinnati who decided to adopt a child with dwarfism because both parents have osteogenesis perfecta, a type of dwarfism. It a wonderful illustration of how a life can be lived fully from a wheelchair and you will find Kara's comments on the discrimination that parents with disabilities face eye-opening.
http://www.cincinnati.com/videos/news/2015/07/26/30691111/

Blog post from a mother who adopted a child with a facial deformity. A great read for those considering a visible special need.
http://ordinary-time.blogspot.com/2013/12/adopting-child-with-facial-deformities.html

10

When it is Time to Review a File

The matching part of the adoption process is never easy. Not that any of it is easy, but since this is the point of the entire ordeal, things are especially high stakes when they involve identifying the child who will be yours. Some people can't handle waiting and want to see that face as soon as possible. They scour photo listings--both their agency's and others--plus advocacy sites until they find their child. Other people are completely uncomfortable "choosing" a child. So many children need homes, and it feels wrong somehow to single out one from so many to give a place in your family. People who feel this way prefer to have their agency select the child who seems to be the best fit.

No matter whether you find your child first or wait to be matched by your agency, there will be a point where you will have a file in hand to review. How do you know if this is the one? For many people, there is no question. "I just knew she was our child" is a common refrain. "You will just know when it's the right one." If you have that magic moment, issues like their medical need or the quality of care at their orphanage is less relevant. It's more of an issue of preparing for **what** you will need to deal with when you get your child home than an issue of asking if you **can** deal with it.

It is also important for you to understand that **it is okay if you don't have that magic moment**. Adoption is very romanticized, and you will find when you meet your child that the reality rarely matches up with the dream. It's not that it's always bad, simply that the child you imagine is not going to be the same child you meet. If you are referred a child who meets your criteria, but you don't feel an emotional connection there is nothing wrong about accepting the referral. Your attachment to the child will come in time. In fact, probably before you travel to meet him.

If you are being matched by your agency, you will most likely receive one file at a time to review. It should be one which fits the criteria you submitted to them. If you are trying to find your child through photo listings or advocacy sites, it is possible for you to review more than one file at a time through different sources. I suggest you refrain from doing so. If you feel you have identified more than one child which would possibly fit well in your family, you will be placed in the position of choosing between them. This is difficult for people. It also isn't fair to the children to compare them to each other. They are all worthy of a family. Rather than comparing files to each other, choose only one file at a time to review, looking at the child as an individual. If you feel you cannot meet the needs of that child or that he isn't a good fit for your family, for whatever reason, decline that referral. You can then move on to request the file of another child which you feel has potential for your family.

How accurate are files from China?

For most people it is the medical information that is the main concern when reviewing a file, so that is the main focus of this chapter. When you get to the point where you are ready to review the file of a referral, you might start to wonder just how accurate the information in the file will be. Files from China are generally accurate, but no one wants to bring up the minority of instances where the file is radically different from the child's actual diagnosis because no one wants to scare people away from adoption. As I've mentioned before, we love the happy endings, and if we scare people away from adoption, some of those children needing families will never get their happy ending. However, wishful thinking does not guarantee a happy ending. Prepared adoptive parents are the best way to create "forever families."

There are many factors to consider when discussing file accuracy. First, how are we defining what "accurate" means? Most people refer to a file as accurate if the listed special need is correct, but I have seen people say that their child's file wasn't accurate because it said their child was drinking from a cup when in reality they were still taking a bottle. If you adopt from Korea, which is the gold standard of the international adoption community, you will get a mountain of medical information. You will know the exact number of cigarettes and alcoholic beverages the birth mother reported consuming. Your child will have regular medical care and check-ups in a country with a world class medical health care system. You should not expect this sort of detailed information from files in China.

Consider the care you might receive in the United States in rural Appalachia compared to a teaching hospital in a major city. In China, the health care situation varies even more widely. When a child's file is prepared in China, the doctor examining the child may not have the experience to correctly diagnose a complex medical condition or rare disorder. A child often has only the most cursory exam in order for their file to be prepared by a doctor who has never seen the child before. Some orphanages have enough funding for children to receive regular and expert medical care equivalent to what we have in the United States, while other orphanages are underfunded and the children will have little access to health care other than the required medical exam. Similarly, with each orphanage in China being independently run, some will produce files that are highly accurate while others are pretty sloppy in filling out the forms.

Due to these factors, while files from China are generally accurate they are rarely completely accurate. It is a fairly typical occurrence that the main special need is accurate, a "repaired" need might be more involved than expected, and additional minor needs were undisclosed or undiagnosed in China. It is very common for children to have minor conditions which are not listed in the file.

- For those adopting very young children, keep in mind that the child might not have been old enough when the file was prepared for an accurate diagnosis to have been made. If a child is only six or nine months old, it is impossible to know yet whether the child will have delays in walking or talking, which will be evident by the time you meet your now two-year-old on adoption day.

- Some conditions such as tooth decay are not considered major enough to be worth noting. Dental hygiene in China is not the same as it is in America and few orphanages have the nannies brushing the teeth of every child twice a day. Both of our sons seemed completely unfamiliar with a toothbrush when we adopted them and that is the norm for most. You should assume your child will have at least some tooth decay. It would not be unusual for your child to need teeth extracted, enough fillings to require a surgical suite so the work can be done under anesthesia, or dental work to the tune of thousands of dollars.

- Some conditions might not be noticed in a quick medical exam. The doctor doing the exam might not notice head tilting that indicates a vision problem, mild facial asymmetry, or other indicators of an underlying problem. These would more likely be noticed by the nannies who work with your child, but they are not directly involved in preparing the file.

- The sort of standard tests and developmental checks that we have here in America are not routine in Chinese orphanages. Hearing tests are rarely performed so children can often have up to moderate hearing loss go undetected if they have enough hearing to compensate. While head circumference measurements are important to American doctors, it is not a standard used in China so the measurements provided for files are often incorrect because they are not measured properly.

• Your child's condition could have worsened since the file was prepared, or they could have developed a new condition such as a hernia. In boys, testicles can wander around in the first year so your son might have developed an undescended testicle that was in the correct place when the file was prepared. Because you are not the legal parent until after the adoption is finalized parents are NOT usually notified of changes in the child's health such as a surgery or a burn scar from an recent accident.

• The most common undisclosed conditions include: tooth decay, hernias, undescended testicles, spinal anomalies such as mild scoliosis, facial asymmetry, mild to moderate hearing or vision issues, mild heart conditions or murmurs, and positive Hepatitis B status despite negative result in file.

The only statistics I am aware of regarding file accuracy are found in the Donaldson Institute adoption study from 2013. They studied 271 children adopted from China, a mixed group composed of children adopted through either the original non-special needs program or the special needs program. As a whole, 50% of parents said that their child's file contained accurate medical information. Of the children who were adopted with identified special needs through the special needs program, 32% were diagnosed with an additional special need once home. The most common diagnosis received was that of developmental delay

Most parents indicated that they felt the issues were due to the poor quality of medical records. Translated medical records were found to contain less detail or were less accurate than the original language reports. Some parents indicated that poor medical care in China was the reason for the discrepancy between their child's condition and diagnosis. A few parents felt that China had lied or been misleading in the reports which were issued.

While this study sounds concerning, keep in mind that this study has a very small sample size. The dates of the adoptions were not included, but as half of the adoptions were from the non-special need program it is not likely they were recent. Keep in mind, a decade ago the children did not receive good orphanage care in China and were adopted at younger ages. It is not surprising that a girl adopted at nine months of age, who had spent most of her life confined to a crib or chair, would be diagnosed with developmental delays. In addition, because no other diagnoses were listed besides developmental delays, we have no way of knowing whether these were minor needs like a heart murmur or more serious medical issues. The data is certainly interesting, but not detailed enough from which to draw any concrete conclusions.

International adoption specialist file review

The best thing you can do to make sure you are maximizing accuracy is to have the file reviewed by a doctor who specializes in international adoption. This can cost several hundred dollars, so many families are tempted to skip it in favor of having their local pediatrician review the file or sometimes no doctor at all. Even if you are certain that this is your child, having a doctor review the file can give you more information to be prepared to meet the child's needs. International adoption (IA) doctors have experience interpreting files from China and understand how Chinese doctors typically diagnose and how orphanages typically prepare files. Remember that the language difference can also cause translation issues. An international adoption doctor can tell you "When the file says _____ what it usually means is _____." For example, Treacher-Collins syndrome is not recognized in China, so those children are usually listed as having Down syndrome. Dwarfism is often listed as hydrocephalus in younger children (children with dwarfism have a disproportionately large head) or short stature for an older child.

When you have the file reviewed, it is important to include the Chinese language file as well as the English translation. Even if you or the doctor does not read Chinese, there is often additional information included. Sometimes additional photos are attached the end that aren't also included in the English translation. The developmental section has an area where the person submitting information checks boxes for developmental milestones which are dual Chinese/English. The English transcription the boxes checked is not always accurate. In addition, seeing which boxes were not checked can be informative. In the English transcription, only the information from the checked boxes is included.

Two issues that frequently come up when reviewing files are head circumference measurements and developmental delays. Head circumference is not used as a development marker in China so orphanage personnel are often not skilled at taking accurate head circumference measurements. The head circumference measurements from one of my sons went from off-the-chart small to off-the-chart large in a six month time period, which is a good indicator that whoever was taking them was not taking them correctly. A good IA doctor will be aware of this and should look at the overall picture the measurements paint, taking into account not just one problematic set of measurements, but also their overall development and whether or not their head looks proportionate in photos.

Not all IA doctors are equal. It is important to remember that a good IA doctor will only go over the information in the file, giving you various scenarios so that you can make the decision as to whether or not the child is a good fit for your family. Any IA doctor who tells you that you should not adopt a particular child or describes the child in a derogatory way, saying, for example, that the child would be lucky to get a job bagging groceries, is not being professional, and you should seek a second opinion. The doctor's job is not to make judgments about the child, but to give you the information they see so you can make the right decision for your family. It is also important if you have a solo doctor rather than a clinic review a file that you use someone who specializes in adoptive medicine as a career rather than someone from another specialty who moonlights reviewing files to bring in a little extra money. If a doctor isn't seeing as patients any of the children whose files they have reviewed, they are only seeing half of the file picture. Check with your agency for IA doctor or clinic recommendations.

The fee for an IA doctor or clinic review will often also cover writing prescriptions for the trip and support in-country which can be helpful if you need to consult the doctor about concerns you have after meeting the child. I want to really underscore the importance of viewing an IA medical review as an investment. It is very frustrating for me to see how many people feel that paying for a review is too expensive, but a few months later the same people are upgrading to economy plus plane seating or booking executive suites in hotels because "it's worth every penny." I think part of the issue is that the file review cost comes earlier in the adoption process when you are still counting every penny. By the end, you are bleeding out funds so quickly that adding on a couple hundred bucks seems hardly worth mentioning.

Children who are in institutions do not develop at the same rate as children raised in families. A general rule of thumb is that the child will lose one month of development for every three months in an institution. This would mean that it is not at all unusual for a child in an orphanage to not be walking at a year old. An international adoption doctor should be adept at sorting out what are typical orphanage delays and what are true developmental delays due to an underlying condition or syndrome that may not have been diagnosed in the file. They are also aware of which special needs can have correlated developmental delays. Children with heart disease, for example, are often delayed both physically and developmentally because their body puts every available resource into compensating for the heart problem. Most children with orphanage or special need related developmental delays make rapid progress once they are home and their needs are addressed. However, there are never any guarantees that the delays will be overcome. You should also keep in mind that a "developmental delays" label in a file typically indicates that the child is even more delayed than their same-age peers in the orphanage.

Considerations outside of the file

Some of the factors which will make the most difference in your child's behavior, health, and adjustment to your family will never appear in their file. Those factors would be how much trauma they have endured, if they have been abused, the quality of care they are receiving, and whether or not they have experienced malnutrition. Experiencing trauma or not having connected with a particular caregiver early in life can cause lifelong changes in the brain. Science is only now starting to understand how the brain is impacted by these experiences and adoption therapists are developing a wide variety of methods to help children who have come from hard places to overcome trauma and learn to connect to other people. While malnutrition is sometimes listed as a special need, there are many orphanages in China where children will routinely go hungry, and those children will not have malnutrition listed as a need in their file. I mention this because you can wait to be matched with a child who has a very minor need in your eyes, have the file reviewed by an IA doctor, meet the child and find that medically all of their information was correct, but then be caught off guard by attachment or trauma issues. Your child's orphanage name should be listed in the file. You can try to connect with parents who have adopted from the same orphanage online through Facebook groups or an Internet search to get an idea of the condition and care from that orphanage.

Another important aspect of file evaluation is how informed and objective adoptive parents can be. Parents having unrealistic expectations is far more common than inaccurate files! It is so very easy for parents to fall in love with a picture. I have heard many people say "We didn't have the file reviewed because we knew it wouldn't matter–she was our daughter!" This is not necessarily a problem unless the reality doesn't meet up with the fantasy in a way the parents are completely unprepared for when they meet their daughter. Tales abound in the adoption community of parents choosing not to finalize an adoption for reasons which indicate that they were inadequately prepared. She walked with a slight limp, one of his eyes was droopy, etc.

It is especially important to be well informed about the special needs to which you decide to be open. Many people have the mistaken impression that if the file indicates that the child's need is repaired or the child has had surgery, no further medical intervention will be necessary. For many common conditions, such as anal atresia, spina bifida, heart conditions, and cleft palate, an initial repair does not completely resolve the issue. At other times the repair may not have been done well or done optimally so further surgeries are necessary to correct the work done in China. If you think that albinism is just a matter of extra sunscreen and sunglasses (as I have seen people say online), you may be caught off guard when you are handed a child with significant visual impairment. I have a friend who advocates for children with heart issues and has talked to parents who seem to believe that their child's heart condition will be completely repairable despite clear advisement to the contrary by doctors who have reviewed the file. When you are in love with a picture, it can be easy to fall into denial about the true state of the child's health.

Photos are an important evaluation tool. One of our son's orphanages did a great job of sending photos with our updates that showed his developmental status. In the very first update we requested, they sent a series of photos showing him going from a sitting position to a crawl, then crawling toward a toy a nanny had enticed him with. I corresponded with Shecki who adopted a son whose special needs were much greater than she and her husband expected. In fact, it took over a year of intensive testing and evaluation before he was accurately diagnosed here in the United States, as his case is extremely rare. Still, Shecki shared her experience because she feels that people have a tendency to be too optimistic, especially if a file is labeled with delays. She told me, "We missed things. Looking back, we can see that Luke wasn't sitting independently in any of his photos. He was either contained in a chair/stroller or there was a hand holding him up, although one picture showed him standing, leaning against a wall, which was hugely misleading. Luke has never pulled himself to stand, but can bear weight (sometimes) when placed in a standing position."

As Shecki said, sometimes it can be easy to miss warning signs from the photos. At other times, they can be misleading in the other direction. I have known people who worried because they only received photos where the child wasn't smiling or making eye contact, but after the adoption they received photo files from the orphanage (this is common practice with OneSky orphanages) that showed the child happy and engaged. We experienced that ourselves when we only received photos of one of our sons walking with the assistance of a toy. Although the update said that he had begun to walk, we weren't completely sure he really was walking. When I uploaded the files from my One Sky disk, I found several photos of him chasing other children around the room. It would have been reassuring to have those ahead of time!

Unfortunately, parents do not have access to this additional information from private charities until after the adoption is finalized. This is to protect the child's privacy, but there are times when having access to those quarterly reports or updates would make a difference in a parent's decision. Shecki wrote: "After we got home, I requested and received quarterly reports from the NGO working with his orphanage. Had those reports been part of his referral file, we would not have submitted LOI for him. Let me say that again. Had we seen those reports prior to the adoption, we would NOT have adopted him. That's where I get resentful. The first report shows a very, very sick baby, who looks nothing like the little butterball we saw in the referral pictures. And *every* single report lists him having cerebral palsy, which was NOWHERE in his referral file. We were not approved for cerebral palsy in our home study, and we would not have pursued him, had we had that info."

While access to information from private charities is not available, it is becoming more common for parents to be provided with video, and this can certainly be more informative than photos. It is also possible to ask questions of the orphanage, to try and follow up on things that a doctor feels might be problematic. However, there is no guarantee that the questions will be answered. Some orphanages are better at communicating than others. Generally, you want to ask as few questions as possible and word them carefully. You can ask for testing, and at times you can pay for more expensive tests the orphanage would normally have done. Sometimes the answer will be no. We asked for a hearing test on one son, as well as photos showing his ears so we could try to determine if his malformed ear had an ear canal. The provided photos were not from an angle that showed his ear canal and the orphanage replied that there was no need for a hearing test because they felt his hearing was fine. We had assumed that he would not have hearing in that ear and so were comfortable going forward without the additional information we had requested. In our case, the reality turned out better than our expectations because he did have an ear canal and only mild hearing loss in that ear.

You should also be prepared that sometimes the information listed in files or given in updates is confusing or conflicting. For example, we had some concerns about the verbal development of one of our sons, so we asked a few different questions to try and get additional information. Between the various questions we learned that he did not speak much--only two words (at age two and a half)—and that they considered his verbal development on par with his same-aged peers. In case this information wasn't contradictory enough, they included a list of twelve different words and phrases he said on a regular basis for good measure! As there was no way to reconcile any of these answers, we kept our expectations low for his verbal development. At times similar confusion is caused by translation issues, so you should try not to read too much into the phrasing used. One mother wondered if she should be concerned because an update described her daughter as being "off in her own world" when she played. It is doubtful that is a literal translation of the Chinese. In English, being off in your own world has a connotation that can bring up fears of autism. If the translator had chosen "is very focused" or "concentrates intently", would it seem as worrisome or more like a positive trait for a child?

Sometimes it is possible to get additional information on children from other avenues. There are American run foster homes in China which post pictures or videos. They cannot directly provide information to parents before the adoption is finalized but if you know that your child is in a home that has a blog or Facebook page, you can often get unofficial info from those sources. Many adoption advocates request updates or keep track of files as they pass from agency to agency. Unfortunately it sometimes happens that one agency will have video or photos which are not passed along with the file when it leaves their agency. Files that come from an agency partnership will have access to more information than those from an orphanage with which an agency has no relationship. Often, if you are adopting from an orphanage with which your agency is partnered, you will find agency personnel have met with your child, or the child might have been evaluated by an American doctor during an agency visit to the SWI. It is very common for parents to be able to get updated photos from other parents who are adopting from the same orphanage and travel sooner. The only picture we received of one son standing unassisted was taken by a family who traveled to his orphanage to adopt a few months before we traveled. We received no pictures of him standing unassisted in official updates.

Having access to this additional second hand information can be a mixed blessing. Often advocates can use supplemental information to successfully find a family for a child who has a file which is outdated or inaccurate. Many children have languished because their file indicates that they have low intelligence, maybe from an "intelligence test" performed when they were a toddler, but people at the foster home or someone who worked with them at a summer camp say that the child has normal intelligence and is a joy to be around. Or over a number of years their special need has improved and they are basically healthy, but the file doesn't reflect that because it is years out-of-date. Advocates do incredibly good work in helping these "hidden gems" to find homes. However, sometimes advocates can minimize a child's needs by being overly optimistic about how much a child can improve once home. They encourage families to step out in faith, saying "She will just thrive once you get her home. All she needs is a loving family and she will catch up!"

Many children do make incredible improvements once they are part of a family and receiving regular medical care and therapy services, but there are never guarantees about the future. Going back to the previous point about having realistic expectations, be sure to ask yourself if you would love and cherish this child as a part of your family as they are right now, as presented in the file, or if you are really only comfortable with the potentially improved child. To quote from Shecki again: "When considering any special need, you should think of the worst case scenario, and determine whether your family could handle that or not. When I considered 'delays,' tacked on to the end of Luke's primary special need (which, ironically, aside from one specialist appointment has been a non-issue), I thought 'worst case scenario' would be that he'd still be a little behind when he was school age, and would need an IEP to help him get through school with his peers. Never in my wildest imaginings did I think that 'delays' meant he would not walk, speak, or toilet train, and that he would not be in a regular classroom at all. The long and the short of it is, we took a risk, never really believing, or even suspecting, things would turn out as they have."

Making the decision

In the end, you will need to decide whether to accept the referral or decline it. Sometimes you will know immediately if the child is a "yes" or a "no". Perhaps he is exactly what you are looking for and cute as a button to boot, or she could have medical needs far beyond what you are comfortable with parenting. It can be very difficult for parents to make the decision to decline a referral, even if they know they cannot parent a child with those medical needs. Often, parents will want to know if they can be informed if the child finds a family. It is hard to say "no, we will not parent this child". It can haunt you. Try your best to remember that if you do not have the resources to address that child's medical or emotional needs, you are not the best family for that child. Every child belongs in a family who can meet his or her needs, and one family's "no" will be another family's "easy need--yes!"

It is very common for a couple to disagree about a referral. Usually, one parent is more comfortable with the child's medical needs than the other. It is very important that both parents be fully committed to the child they will be adopting. This is a lifelong commitment. It is best to agree in advance that both parents will need to feel no hesitation about going forward. If one is unsure, it is fine to take some time to consider but the other parent should not pressure the hesitating parent. You do not want to get to China and have a parent get cold feet. There should be no opening for "I didn't even want to adopt her in the first place but you talked me into it!" accusations.

If you find the decision to decline a referral too difficult, you should discuss your child criteria with your agency's match coordinator or matching team. While no agency is guaranteed to get it right the first time, they can try to minimize the chances of a poor match by sticking very closely to your medical conditions checklist. If you were searching for your child yourself, you could choose to wait for your agency to match you rather than continue looking at waiting child files. The matching experience will be different for every family. Some will adopt the first file they review while others will review a dozen or more before finding the right child. Although you are anxious to see your child's face, try not to worry—the right match will happen in the end.

Additional Resources

A listing of all the OneSky (previously Half the Sky) affiliated orphanages
http://halfthesky.org/en/node/4712

A listing of Love Without Boundaries foster care locations. If your child was a part of a LWB program you can receive their reports after the adoption is finalized.
https://www.lovewithoutboundaries.com/programs/foster-care/locations/

Agency provided list of IA doctors and clinics
http://www.bbinternationaladoption.com/adoption-medicine

Donaldson Institute adoption study
http://adoptioninstitute.org/old/publications/2013_10_AChangingWorld.pdf

You can read more of Shecki's experience adopting Luke at the Greatly Blessed blog
http://grtlyblesd.blogspot.com/

11

Adoption Dissolution
Begin with the end in mind

I am not sure I will ever find the right place in this book to discuss a hard topic. I am talking about adoption disruption and dissolution. For the sake of clarity, an adoption disruption is when the adoption is not completed, such as when a couple travels to China but decides not to finalize the adoption once they have met the child. An adoption dissolution is when a legal adoption is dissolved, although this is commonly referred to as disruption as well. I thought this might be the best place because now is the time when you are making decisions about your adoption. We've touched on this when discussing adopting out of birth order, two at once, or an older child. Now it's time to have a more direct discussion.

When your child is not who you expected

Unfortunately there are no statistics available about the rates or causes of disruptions and dissolutions specific to the China adoption program. Anecdotally, the main cause of disruptions which happen in China are a disconnect between the medical needs of the child and what medical needs the parents feel they can address. In the previous chapter, you might have been left wondering what would happen if you, like Shecki, arrive in China to find a child that does not match up with what you were

164

expecting? That is the exact scenario which can and does lead to a disruption of the adoption, so let's discuss it first.

I spoke with another parent, who wished to remain anonymous, who reviewed the file of a girl who had some markers that could indicate a potential syndrome. Initially they decided not to submit a Letter of Intent to adopt, but later found sources of additional information. The girl was enrolled in a program of one of the American charities, so they were able to find blog posts about her and communicate with people who had met her. With this new information they felt confident enough to move forward with the adoption. However, once they arrived in-country the girl was extremely delayed and not the active and engaged child they were expecting.

At this point, adoptive parents are faced with a difficult decision. You have 24 hours to decide to finalize the adoption. When you have a child who is not making eye contact, who is not communicating, and who is not doing things you have been told they can do, such as walking or crawling, you must quickly decide if this is medically relevant or if they are reacting to the trauma of the adoption. These children have just been taken from everything familiar to them and handed over to strangers. It is not unusual at all for children to cry for hours, to sit limply and not make eye contact or react to your voice, or to stop walking and talking. When parents reach out to other adoptive parents in that situation, they are frequently reassured that the child is in shock and will come around.

One thing which will not help with these feeling of panic is that the orphanage director very well might try to talk you out of the adoption. This is especially the case if your child has a life-threatening condition, is extremely malnourished, or has very obvious delays. I have heard this from multiple parents. You need to not let this sway you. If you make the decision not to adopt your child, please do not let it be because the orphanage director told you that this baby was no good, you don't really want her, and that you should come back and get a better one.

There are a few practical things you can do if you are in this situation:

- Request a delay before you finalize the adoption. It can be possible to add an extra day for you to gain extra information and for your child to adjust.

- Try to contact a doctor at home to get their advice. While it can be difficult to arrange in 24 hours with the time difference, if you describe the child's behavior and send photos or video, it is possible to get a medical assessment.

- Try to talk to the child's nanny or foster parents. It is not always the child's primary nanny who accompanies them to the civil affairs building, but it is possible that the people who accompanied your child knows them well enough to discuss their usual behavior. Your guide may have the orphanage director's phone number so questions could be asked through your guide.

Ultimately, you will need to decide if you want to finalize the adoption. A friend who wrote on her blog that she was scared but finalized the adoption anyway said she was bombarded with messages from people who said they had felt the same way. If you are scared, know that you are not alone. So many families are scared to death when they sit down to sign that paperwork. Probably for this reason, families who decide to disrupt the adoption and leave the child in China can be harshly judged by the adoption community. Certainly, we have all heard stories where the potential adoptive parents seem to behave as if they received a defective product and returned the child for the most superficial of reasons. But for most parents (hopefully), this is a heartbreaking decision that is not at all easy. They love this child and they wonder if he or she will receive good care if they leave them in China. Sometimes, children who are rejected are deemed "unadoptable" by China and their file is pulled so that they do not get a second chance for a family. However, if a family truly knows they cannot provide the care a child needs, and they did not have the information to know that ahead of time, it is the best decision to not finalize the adoption.

For the anonymous family I wrote about earlier, this is how their story ended. They were able to delay the adoption by a day. They sought a doctor's evaluation and asked other adoptive parents for input. In the end, they decided that their family could not provide the long-term care she needed and did not finalize the adoption. A year later, she was still in China, available for adoption. As Shecki wrote of her experience, "If you get to China, and you disrupt because you're afraid there's bigger issues going on, you get roasted alive online because, 'How can you know after only one day what progress that traumatized child would make, given the chance?' and then you're accused of ruining their chances of getting adopted by some other family. If you bring them home and then you're overwhelmed, you get tons of people telling you, 'You should have known better! You knew he was delayed, but you brought him home anyway!'"

Shecki and her husband found another family to adopt Luke after struggling for two years with his placement. After six months the family declined to finalize the adoption so he is once again back with their family. Shecki's family shows a very average time frame for an adoption dissolution. Usually, the family tries counseling or other avenues to make an adoption work for two to five years before deciding to dissolve the adoption. It is not a quick or easy decision for families.

One final topic to discuss is the frequent suggestion I've seen that a family should bring the child home anyway, even if they know they cannot parent the child, because "there are people here who will adopt them." I want to point out that this is completely unethical. This child is under the guardianship of the Chinese government and the Chinese government has given your family, and only your family, permission to adopt them. On all of the documents you sign for China and when you take the oath at the US consulate, you are promising that **you** are adopting this child forever. It doesn't matter if you think they will be better off in the US than in their orphanage in China. It doesn't matter if you think you know a family who can handle the child's needs better than yours. If you knowingly adopt the child intending to turn them over to a family when you return to the US, you are committing fraud and could be considered guilty of human trafficking.

Other factors in disruption or dissolution

People in the adoption community love the happily-ever-after ending. People who aren't in the adoption community love it too— just look at the movie *Annie*. We all want to believe that every adoption ends with a child being united with their "forever family." And the vast majority of adoptions are successful—over 90% according to several studies. However, we need to acknowledge that there are times when adoptions fail. People who have had a failed adoption usually do not stay within the adoption community, so you rarely encounter their experiences in your online groups. You will only read about the happy endings. When you are trying to decide if you should pursue an adoption, you might ask in an online forum "Has anyone else done this?" Keep in mind that the responses are already pre-selected to be favorable. When it works out for people, they are happy and want to encourage others. When the outcome was not good, they do not want to be condemned by the adoption community, so they leave.

Although I have been in the adoption community a fairly short amount of time, I have already encountered three different families who complained about how their social worker was making them "jump through hoops" before approving the match they wanted and then a year later when the child/children were home, they were writing on their blogs that their adoption was failing. My intention in writing about the negative aspects of adoption in this book is not to scare anyone away from adoption. I only want to stress the importance of making an educated decision and having realistic expectations about the difficulties involved in making such adoptions successful. You will not be set up for the best possible ending if you don't start at the beginning by educating yourself in order to have realistic expectations.

What happens to a child when an adoption is dissolved? Here is a common scenario. Try to imagine for a moment an older child, who has grown up in an orphanage in China. One day an American couples arrives–the Mama and Baba they have always dreamed of--but a few months or years later things aren't going well. There could be any number of reasons why, most of which I discussed in the chapter on adopting an older child. Will the child go back to the familiar orphanage in China where he or she has spent most of his/her life? No. Now an American citizen, this child will stay in this strange land, where they may or may not speak the language. What happens to this child now?

- He might end up in the US foster care system. Often this is a last resort for parents because they fear they might lose other children in their home or that it would rule out the possibility of adopting again.

- She might end up re-homed. Sometimes this is done informally through online networks, or another official adoption may be facilitated through an agency, such as Wasatch Second Chance adoptions.

- The child has a tragic ending. It is a sad reality that every year children who were adopted are abused or killed at the hands of their "forever family."

When things like this happen people inevitably say "Why did the agency let that happen? Why weren't these parents prepared? We need more education, better screening!" It's the complete opposite of "Each family knows what is best and what they can handle." Hopefully, you now have a better understanding of why some agencies have placing criteria for families. It's because not every family does know what they can handle until they get there. We need to acknowledge that people on both sides of this issue are working for what they see as best for the adoptive child. One side says "They need a family, disruptions are rare and it's better to take the chance to get them a family" while the other says "Disruptions are real and we need to wait for the best family for a child rather than chance putting them through the trauma and upheaval of a disruption."

When discussing China adoption in particular, disruptions and dissolutions seem often stem medical needs differing from what the parent was expecting, which we just discussed extensively. It is very difficult for parents when they travel to China and are presented with a child who has medical needs they did not expect. Of course, it is even harder on children who expected to have a family and instead find themselves back at the orphanage. This scenario, adoption disruption, is far more common for those adopting from China than dissolution after returning home to America. I remember when the news that a little girl was left in China swept through the online adoption groups. In her case, the news was especially upsetting because there was concern that she might not live long enough to find a new set of parents due to her heart condition and extreme malnutrition. I'll be brutally honest–that happens. Fortunately for her, because of how much this disruption was discussed online, a new family stepped forward almost immediately and the adoption was finalized. It is also not unusual for older kids who are brought back to the orphanage to age out before they find a new set of parents. Or the orphanage decides not to list a rejected child for adoption again. This is why adoption advocates argue so strongly against dissolution ever being considered a possibility.

However, a major factor in in-country disruptions is that the parents have unreasonable expectations in two areas: what the medical needs they were open to involve in reality and how children react to the trauma of adoption. While it is sometimes the case that the child's medical condition is radically different from what was written in their file, many parents are uneducated about the medical need they signed up for. Parents have returned a child with albinism because they were surprised at the extent of her visual impairment, a child with dwarfism because his legs were bowed, a child with cleft palate because food came out of his nose, and a child with cerebral palsy affecting her legs because she walked with a limp. While these examples might be difficult to believe, they serve as an illustration of how many people can put on rose-colored glasses or listen selectively when given medical information.

The other area of unreasonable expectation is that the parents were panicked by the child's immediate response to the trauma of adoption. They might be completely unprepared for the behaviors that an older child can come with. This is the sort of thing that should have been well covered in pre-adoptive training, but it is so easy for parents to forget when it is staring them in the face in the form of a child who is screaming for hours, or is almost catatonic in reaction to being taken from everything they've known and handed to strangers.

One comment I hear a lot is "If this child was born into your family with special needs, you wouldn't have the option to disrupt. You would learn to deal with it because they're your child." I don't think that's exactly accurate. Americans abort 50% of pregnancies with major birth defects and 90% of pregnancies with Down syndrome. Many people are scared when confronted with the possibility that their child is less than perfect and reach for abortion as a solution to this fear. Even when the child is born parents can choose to not parent them. This is the case with the youngest children listed on adoptuskids.org who usually have serious medical needs. The National Down Syndrome Adoption Network matches adoptive parents with birth parents who have chosen to make an adoption plan for their child. Adopt America Network does the same for children with any special need.

Disruption is the adoption equivalent. You might point out that if someone is adopting from the China special needs program, they should be open to parenting a child with special needs. However, I have seen countless parents ask "What are the most minor needs you have seen listed in China?" or "What are the easiest special needs?" Many people who adopt are clearly uncomfortable with parenting a child with special needs and have decided they can accept a limited range of possibilities. If they meet a child in China who falls outside of that range then they panic. And honestly, for some couples there seems to be an aspect of ordering up a product and then return it if it doesn't meet their expectation.

What we all hope will happen here is that when the panic wears off and things calm down, and when the child starts receiving necessary medical care, therapies, and love, then the parents will bond with the child and feel that fierce love that makes a parent do anything they can to save their child when their child is in danger. It is these feelings that cause adoptive parents to react so strongly to the idea of adoption disruption or dissolution. So many families have continued with an adoption despite being confronted a child who has unexpected medical needs, or who was malnourished or one acted out with disturbing behaviors. I have shared many of their stories throughout the book. However, we also need to consider the range of outcomes if the parents adopt the child and don't bond with the child over time.

Parenting a child with special needs can bring a lot of stress. When you add adoption to the special needs mix, we are creating a high stress situation for these parents. I know, you're thinking, "But what about the children, this isn't about the parents!" Bear with me. What I am saying is, I think that high stress parents with no attachment to the adopted child can be a lethal mix. How many times have you seen headlines about a child who died of shaken baby syndrome at the hands of a babysitter or was abused by a cohabitating partner of a parent? Statistics show a clear correlation about abuse and lack of biological relationship to the child. When you do not feel a bond to a child, you are less patient and more frustrated with the challenges of parenting.

Would Lydia Schatz's parents have spent hours methodically beating a biological child to death, or is that something that takes a feeling of detachment? What about Hyunsu O'Callaghan, whose father said he wasn't bonding well with him, then was charged with beating his son to death while caring for him and his other son when his wife was away for the weekend? An internet search will bring up their stories or you visit the Pound Pup Legacy website for a full page of adopted children who died at the hands of their parents, if you have the stomach to read them. Of course, these stories don't always end in death. The Harrises in Arkansas were recently in the news for keeping the two daughters they had adopted through the foster care system locked in separate rooms before eventually passing them along to a friend who sexually abused them. Amy Eldridge, who founded Love Without Boundaries, tells of a similar instance of abuse which occurred in the absence of parental bonding in her post on disruption.

I think when adoptive parents write that when someone adopts a child they should be committed forever, it is because it is impossible for them to imagine not feeling that bond with their child, of not having the fierce Mama Bear protective instinct kick in. I think that in an ideal adoption world all but a few parents would bring their child home with them from China. Take some time to see what the child is really like when the panic wears off-- both the parents' panic and the child's panic. Get their medical needs correctly assessed. Try faking it until they make it in the attachment area and please absolutely seek help from their agency, social worker, attachment therapist and anyone else they can think of. For some children dissolving the adoption and finding a family who is better equipped to meet that child's needs is the best course of action. Am I saying that if we don't let parents disrupt when they're scared, all of the kids will end up abused or dead? No, but when you say that disruption or dissolution should never be an option, you are condemning some of these children to a family where there is no love, and the entire point of adoption is to give them a loving family. When you say that if you aren't prepared to parent any child with any need or you shouldn't adopt from China, you are limiting an already extremely small group of potential parents.

I am glad we are discussing adoption disruption and dissolution more now. I would like to see more people discussing the challenging aspects of adoption so people are not so surprised when adoption day is not a blissful dream come true. I think it is unrealistic to think that adoption will have a 100% success rate when biological parenting does not have a 100% success rate. Prepared prospective adoptive parents are the best way to create "forever families". I think we need to keep working to help parents in the adoption process to be informed and to have realistic expectations, and we need offer them support when they are home deep in the trenches.

It is very easy for adoptive parents to have unreasonable expectations. This is often because they have a rose-colored view of adoption and expect their child to act like their same-aged peers who grew up in families rather than institutional care,

174

especially when adopting an older child. They might underestimate the amount of work involved in adopting two children at once, or the stress and conflict that adopting out of birth order can bring to a family. None of these people deserve to be demonized. They all set out to adopt a child forever, never expecting things to turn out as they did. For most families, dissolution only occurs after several years of trying everything possible to make the placement successful.

Sometimes the parents can dissolve an adoption without any real problems at all. One adoption therapist stated that she found older, first-time parents to have a high dissolution rate because they simply could not adjust to parenting. One couple who adopted a three- year-old boy when in their early fifties decided to seek a new family for him because they felt they didn't have enough energy to parent him. They felt he deserved younger parents. Author Joyce Maynard adopted two older girls from Ethiopia when she was fifty-five, and their adoption was dissolved two years later. While the specifics of that situation are not known, Maynard wrote in an open letter that she knew the girls would do better in a two-parent family with other children in the home.

No one thinks they are unprepared for their adoption. It's one of those things you think you know until you suddenly realize you had no idea. One mother wrote, "We talked to our social worker. We thought we understood the challenges and pitfalls. We heard words like reactive attachment disorder and post-traumatic stress disorder and post-institutionalized behaviors and we thought, naively, optimistically, tragically, that we could handle it. The deep truth, though, is that, like birth defects, like miscarriage, like fatal accidents, we never considered that these lurking horrors would apply to us." You can read the full account of her adoption dissolution in the link provided in the Additional Resources section. Reading through these stories can be very scary if you are only starting to consider adoption. It's scary for people who have adopted. Please be assured that for most people, the adoption is successful and the ending is a happy family. But love will not solve every problem. Please take the time to read through a full range of adoption stories, not only the happily-ever-after ones. Ask yourself some hard questions. Try to cultivate a flexible attitude and have zero expectations for your child. Not only will your child then amaze you instead of disappointing you, but you will find that you are capable of far more than you give yourself credit for.

If you are reading this as a potential adoptive parent, you might be scared out of your wits now. I can only assure you that while these situations do occur, they occur in a minority of cases. I have tried to give you advice to help avoid these situations in advance, but there is never any guarantees in any adoption, any more than there is in giving birth. My agency will often write on a child's photo listing that a child would do best with parents "who are comfortable with the unknowns." Adoption is a leap of faith, and even when you adopt a child whose medical file matches perfectly with their physical condition, you can find that you were unprepared for the child's emotional needs, as they act out of trauma or neglect. You have to learn to be comfortable with the unknown, and be prepared to face the future together, no matter what it brings because that is what you do for your child.

Additional Resources

Love Without Boundaries' Realistic Expectations: Post Adoption Struggles
http://www.lwbcommunity.org/realistic-expectations-post-adoption-struggles

Reuters investigative series The Child Exchange on rehoming
http://www.reuters.com/investigates/adoption/#article/part1

Giving away 'Anatoly Z.' is a very long article which focuses on dissolution though Cindi Peck's Second Chance Adoption service. *Warning: graphic and disturbing content*
http://news.yahoo.com/giving-away--anatoly-a---200851799.html

Amy Eldridge of Love Without Boundaries who gives her perspective on disruptions which she has encountered through her years in Chinese adoption.
http://www.nohandsbutours.com/2015/03/26/disruption-3-things-for-parents-to-consider/

Casting Out Demons the story of the Justin Harris case in Arkansas
http://www.arktimes.com/arkansas/casting-out-demons-why-justin-harris-got-rid-of-kids-he-applied-pressure-to-adopt/Content?oid=3725371

Blog post - Disruption: A failed Mom's look back - Adoption ending in dissolution
http://anymommyoutthere.com/2008/07/disruption-failed-moms-look-back.html

Blog post - When it isn't harmonious - Unexpected medical needs but successful adoption
http://www.nohandsbutours.com/2015/03/13/when-it-isnt-harmonious/

Blog post - Was Our Adoption A Mistake? - Unexpectedly difficult older child adoption but after several years the adoption is successful http://www.rainbowkids.com/adoption-stories/was-our-adoption-a-mistake-179

Blog post - I Was Yours and You Were Mine - Unexpectedly difficult adoption day
http://redthreadadvocates.org/2015/08/20/i-was-yours-and-you-were-mine-the-day-we-met/

Letter from Joyce Maynard
http://www.joycemaynard.com/Joyce_Maynard/LETTERS/Entries/2012/4/4_LETTER_FROM_JOYCE.html

Creating A Family has a radio show discussing adoption disruption and dissolutions
http://creatingafamily.org/adoption-category/adoption-disruptions-and-adoption-dissolutions-highlights/

12

After You're Matched

Now that we've gotten the depressing stuff out of the way let's move on to the exciting part—being matched with a child! For many people, the first emotion they feel once the Letter of Intent to adopt is submitted is fear. Yes, there's the "What did we just do?!" fear, but what I am referring to is the fear that China might say no. Very frequently people ask "How often does China not grant provisional approval?" or "If we have PA, is there any chance that China won't send a letter of approval?" You should rest easy that these steps are mostly formalities. In fact, it is far more common for parents to withdraw from the adoption process before it is completed due to lack of finances, loss of job, or some other circumstance. There have been a few instances where China has said no, but those are rare. Here are some of the circumstances of which I am aware where China declined the proposed match:

- The information in the dossier was substantially different from what was submitted with the LOI. This would have been for someone matched with a special focus child before they even began the home study. What the parents self-reported to the agency didn't match what their actual financial or legal documents said once gathered for the home study.

- The parents did not fit China's criteria and asked for a waiver. Often an agency will suggest that you submit LOI for a particular child because China can be more generous with waivers if it is for a child who is hard to place. Sometimes China says no anyway, but you would already be aware if you don't fit China's criteria.

- The file was very old and the child is no longer available for adoption. The times I know of this happening, the child was adopted domestically but someone didn't update the paperwork. Most agencies will want you to request a file update before submitting LOI to screen for problems like this.

- Similarly, I have heard of a few instances where parents were waiting for a pre-release file to submit LOI for but were later informed that the child was adopted domestically before the file was completed.

So, if you know all of the information in your dossier is correct, if you are qualified to adopt from China or have been granted an official waiver, and if you are adopting a child who has a completed new file or one updated recently then YES this will be your child! It might seem like the process is taking forever but one day your letter of approval will show up at your agency. Now you can get excited and I'll bet you are so excited that you will want to tell everyone you meet about your new son or daughter.

This brings up many new issues for you to consider. Should you keep the child's Chinese name or give them an English name? What about their special need? Is this something you should keep private or begin to educate people about? You will also realize that people will have questions for you, lots of questions. Not only close friends and relatives but your pediatrician, teachers at school, coworkers, and random people in the grocery store, will start to ask you about anything and everything. It's good to start thinking about how you will handle this in advance so you don't have regrets later about what you shared.

Let's begin with the naming issue. When you receive your child's file, there will be three names listed. I'll use Wu Yu Liang for an example. In Chinese the surname is listed first, so Wu is the last name. Yu Liang is composed of two characters which together give a meaning for the name. It is more like one name with two halves rather than the two separate names used in the American naming convention. Often the second half is doubled as a nickname, so our example child is probably called Liang Liang by the nannies. If you have a chance to ask questions, ask what your child is called by their caregivers or foster parents. It is especially helpful if you can record someone from the orphanage saying your child's name on adoption day so you will always know how to pronounce it correctly.

Names are chosen for Chinese children who are wards of the state by methods that differ by locality. It used to be common practice for them all to be given the surname "orphanage" (Fu) or "state" (Dang), as in "ward of the state", to indicate their status. Children who were given these surnames and grew to adulthood in China would be stigmatized for fear that their bad luck in becoming an orphan would rub off on their friends or place of employment. The Chinese government banned the practice in 2012, requiring that only surnames from the one hundred most common Chinese names be used for orphans. Like many laws, it is generally ignored, especially in provinces further away from the reaches of Beijing.

Orphanage directors have many methods for choosing a surname. They might give every child who enters their care in a year or month the same surname. In smaller orphanages, the children might always be given the same surname. Surnames are often based on the geographic location of the orphanage. For example, children from Bao'an will be named Bao or children from Wuhan named Wu. These names are also on the list of 100 most common names, so they would theoretically blend in more easily than a name like Dang.

The meaning of your child's name will likely be included in the file. If you would like to look up the meaning yourself, you will need to find the actual characters rather than using the pinyin written using the English alphabet. This should be at the top of the Chinese language version of your child's file. Mandarin Chinese has multiple words with the same sound. The syllable "ma" could be many different words, all of which are represented by different written characters. I have included a website in the Additional Resources section where you can enter in the pinyin and be presented with the many different character options. You choose the one that is used in your child's name to see the meaning. Unfortunately, I haven't found any resource that would give the meaning of the two characters together. You will need to find a native Mandarin speaker to help you with that. Interestingly, for both of our sons the translation given by a Chinese friend was different from the translation provided in the file.

Whether or not to give your child an American name or keep their Chinese name is a very controversial topic in the adoption community. Those who argue for keeping a child's original name say that renaming is trying to erase their past. A name is part of a child's identity, and you need to respect that identity, including their name. The opposing side says that adoptive parents choosing a name for their child is a way of showing that they are truly part of the family now. People point out that most Americans can't pronounce Chinese names correctly and even Chinese-Americans will go by American nicknames. For children from China specifically, parents argue that they have no way of knowing what name would have been given to the child by their birth parents and being assigned a name by an orphanage official isn't meaningful.

For most parents, choosing the name of your new child is one of the most exciting parts of becoming a parent. Most parents who adopt from China will choose to give their child an American name. Often, they will choose to keep some or all of their Chinese name as a way to acknowledge the child's past and honor their

Chinese heritage. Wu Yu Liang will often become Aidan YuLiang Smith or Aidan James YuLiang Smith. Because the two parts of the Chinese given name have the same meaning when written as one word, choosing to do so will cut down on the amount of middle names. Other options parents have chosen include keeping the child's Chinese name, adding their full Chinese name to an American first and middle name, or choosing their own Chinese name for the child. The latter is best done by consulting a native Chinese speaker to make sure that you aren't missing some nuances of the language. Mei and Meili are especially popular choices for girls.

The biggest question for most parents is how to go about transitioning their child to the new name. It usually works best to call the child by their Chinese name or nickname for the first few days, then start to add on the new name. After a few days of using both you can begin dropping the Chinese name as they get used to responding to it. Most parents find the transition goes quickly and easily but many find it easy to keep using their Chinese nickname affectionately on occasion. After a few days of using it, it won't seem quite as foreign as you thought initially!

Parents who are adopting an older child usually give more consideration to keeping their Chinese name. Older children will have an opinion. Some prefer to keep the name they have been called all of their life while others request an American name. They might feel it gives them a fresh start or they want to embrace American culture. If you have the opportunity you might want to ask in advance if your child has a preference or give them a few choices. You are supposed to choose the name before travel but it can be changed once you are back in the US if needed. One family gave their daughter an American name while keeping her Chinese name as the middle name but they chose an American name which could have several nicknames. This way she could choose to keep being called by her Chinese name or she could have a few choices of which American name to be called.

This is an excellent option which gives a lot of flexibility while minimizing the odds that you'll have to complete name change paperwork later.

Telling the world

Usually the very first thing everyone wants to do after being matched is tell the entire world the news. Being able to see your child's face is the most exciting part of the adoption process! Well, short of the part where you get to meet them, of course. Showing pictures to friends and family in person is one thing, but most agencies have guidelines about posting this information to social media. Some agencies allow it after you have been given provisional approval, others say to wait until after the official letter of approval, and a few do not want you to post any pictures at all until the adoption is finalized. Sharing the child's full Chinese name, location, and date of birth are also frowned upon. This is mainly to guard the child's privacy. Your child is not officially yours until the adoption is finalized and there are many instances when a family will end up not completing the adoption process. Check with your agency if you are not sure about their guidelines.

In your excitement, you will probably find yourself telling people all about your new child. How old she is, her special need, where she is from, where she was found, etc. It is important for you to take some time to consider what you are going to share and who you share it with. In your adoption education you were probably told that your child's story is theirs to tell. People are very curious and will ask you many personal questions about your child. It is best to keep the information you share general, especially if the person who is asking is a casual acquaintance or even a random stranger in the grocery story. Especially if your child has a sensitive special need, you will want to carefully consider what you share and who you share it with. Remember that you can always share the information but once it is shared it can't be undone. If you are unsure of the best way to respond to a comment or question, remember that "Why do you ask?" or "That's personal" are good all-purpose replies.

Updates and care packages

If you were matched with special focus child, you might have many months before you travel. Even if you are matched after LID you've got a good two to three months to wait. Most people like to get an update on their child during this time. An update would typically allow you to have a few questions answered, give you current measurements for the child, and receive a few recent photos or videos. Agencies are required to pay for officially obtained updates. Some charge you per update to cover this cost while others include it in their general agency fees. Typically updates can be obtained every three or four months, but recently there was some indication that China would like to have the number of requested updates decreased. Your agency can tell you how often they will request updates.

When you receive updated photos or videos, if you are adopting a boy you might notice that he is wearing girl clothing. While you wouldn't usually find a boy wearing a dress, other than that, most clothing is considered gender neutral in China. I received some photos of my son in a very nice new outfit that was pink with butterflies and matching pink flowered shoes. Just have a chuckle over it--you can get him in blue once he's home. If you are adopting a girl, you might sigh over her orphanage buzz cut. It is possible to request that they not cut her hair until adoption day the next time you request an update; sometimes these requests are granted and other times they are not. Keep in mind that there are practical reasons for the orphanage buzz cut. First and foremost, lice are always a problem in an institution. The orphanage also will not have air conditioning so it is cooler in the summer. Finally, long hair takes much more time to care for and caregivers never have enough time to care for a large amount of children. You should decide how important it is for you to see her with long hair on adoption day before you send the request.

Most parents like to send care packages to their child during the wait. As with anything else, agencies vary in how they handle this. Some will let you send as many as you want at any point in the process, some say you can send only one and only after LOA, and at least one agency will not let you send anything other than a photo album and letter. Even if you are with an agency without any care package rules, please give serious consideration to waiting until late in the process to send a care package, especially for an older child. There are times when people are unable to complete the adoption, and it is disappointing and confusing for the child if they thought they had a family. Also, time passes slowly for children. Do you remember the wait for Christmas when you were a child? Sometimes, children will ask their parents on adoption day why it took them so long to get them when the parents might have sent a care package only a few weeks before travel!

You might wonder why agencies would discourage care packages. Because agencies work closely with orphanages, they understand the negative side of care packages. Orphanages typically have hundreds of children but only a small percentage will be adopted. It can be discouraging for children to see others getting care packages and families but not ever receive any themselves. It can cause jealousy or bullying, especially among older kids. Some orphanages solve this problem by not giving the child the care package. It might be returned to you on adoption day because the orphanage workers did not want the items you sent to get damaged, or it was too much work to keep track of clothing for particular children separated.

If you do choose to send a care package, keeping it simple is probably the best plan. If you are adopting a toddler, they really aren't even going to understand that it is their future parents sending gifts. Small items that can be shared, like stickers or lollipops, are a better choice than clothing and stuffed animals. The most important item to send is a small photo book with pictures of your family and home. Parents feel that it really does make a difference if the child has seen your pictures in advance and can recognize you in some way on adoption day. Both of our sons still have the photo albums we sent to them and look at them regularly.

Some parents choose to get updates or send care packages through a third party service. This is prohibited by some agencies because they do not go through the official channels. Nor will all orphanages cooperate with these services. Parents particularly like the option of sending a cake to be shared with their child and other children at the orphanage. Usually the orphanage will send photos or video of the cake being shared and it is always fun to see those happy faces. The two main services used by adoptive parents are:

Ladybugs and Love from Above
http://ladybugsnlove.com/

Anne at Red Thread China
http://www.redthreadchina.com/

Birthday cake packages are particularly popular when the child you are matched with has a birthday while you are in process. It can be difficult to miss a major holiday or milestone such as a birthday. Besides the birthday cake package, some parents choose to have a cake or cupcakes at home and take pictures so they can show their child in the future that you were celebrating with her even though she wasn't yet home. You can include your child in holidays in similar ways. For Christmas, you could go ahead and put out a stocking or perhaps buy an ornament to place his photo on the tree. If you are feeling that hole where your child should be during a special occasion, thinking creatively can help you find a way to include him.

Some people like to use a private service to receive a copy of their child's finding ad. The finding ad is part of how China fulfills the Hague requirement that the birth family be searched for. While your child's file probably includes a short line stating that the parents were searched for after the abandonment, an advertisement will also be run in a newspaper. Often this is not done until the child's file is prepared for international adoption. This saves money on running ads for children who will never be adopted for one reason or other. Many parents receive a copy of this ad on adoption day but it is often a small, poor quality black and white copy. The service provided by Brian Stuy will give you a full color scan and it includes the entire page, so you can see the other children whose files were prepared at the same time.

Brian Stuy's finding ad service
http://www.research-china.org/findingads/index.htm

My child doesn't look Chinese

Now that you've seen that picture of your child and are totally in love, some of you out there will have the thought "I know this sounds silly/crazy/strange, but my child doesn't look Chinese." Fairly regularly in an online adoption forum or group, a parent will post this and then usually goes on to ask if other people have children with the same look or to take a poll on possible minority heritage. So if you've had this thought, you aren't alone. I think we can all have a little chuckle at the irony that adoptive parents, who are often very sensitive about any perceived racial stereotypes, can have the idea that there is a particular way to look Chinese when China is a country of over 1.3 billion people and takes up 9.6 million square kilometers of landmass. Do we really think they all look the same? But at the same time, this idea certainly isn't limited to non-Chinese because while you are in China with your child, you may find that your guide or other Chinese people you meet will comment on your child's appearance, saying that the child doesn't look Chinese but Vietnamese/Thai/minority.

I thought it might be helpful to discuss some of the factors that play into appearance, because while you will probably never be able to fully know your child's genetic heritage, some of the confusion might be cleared up with a better understanding of China's history and contemporary life. Many adoptive parents seem to have the default assumption that their child's birth parents are married Chinese farmers, of Han heritage, who have lived in the same area for centuries. That is certainly possible and it was the most likely scenario during the first decade or two of China's adoption program. However, as you have learned, Chinese culture and attitudes are changing fast. China has a booming economy and is no longer isolated. Millions of Chinese people of childbearing age are leaving the farms behind to work in major cities, saving up so their children can attend university. This creates a melting pot effect that is not unlike what we have in America.

First, let's look at regional differences within China. Here in America, we have pockets of people from the same area in Europe in different geographic areas. You are more likely to find people with Hispanic heritage the farther you go southwest, or if you go to areas of the north, you can find a lot of people with Polish or Norwegian heritage. Similarly, you can find some general appearance characteristics which are influenced by geography in China.

The upper northeast of China, which used to be known as Manchuria, borders Russia. Generally the farther you go north the taller and more fair complected the people are. Yao Ming, the famous Chinese basketball player, is from the municipality of Shanghai, which is located in one of the regions where people tend to be taller. Shanghai Municipality is within Jiangsu province, where one of our sons was born. Neither my husband nor I are very tall and we joke that our children are the kids who fill out the bottom of the growth charts. This Chinese son is larger than any of our biological children were at his age. Of course, nutrition plays a role in height as well. In the Additional Resources section you can find a study which found that in all areas of China, people in rural areas where malnutrition is more common are shorter than those in urban areas.

As you travel south in China, you reach the areas that are near to the Philippines, Vietnam, and Laos. In these areas, people tend to be darker complected, as you would expect in semi-tropical regions. To the west, the area closest to the Indian border, is where you find the plains of Tibet. Finally, in the northwest corner, there is a confluence of Eastern European and Middle Eastern culture. This particular area is where the Uighur people live. The story of the Uighur people and their constant state of tension with the Chinese government is a sensitive one. In fact, the Uighur population has never considered themselves a part of China, so if you adopted a child from the Uighur minority group, celebrating Chinese New Year or other Chinese holidays would likely not be a part of their cultural heritage.

Having brought up the Uighur, we are now firmly on the topic of minority groups. There are fifty-five recognized minority groups other than the Han majority within China. Besides the Uighur and Tibetan, you might have also heard about the Miao, Bai, or Dai people. Some of the minority groups reflect the national borders I mentioned previously. For example, Korean is a minority group, as is Mongol and Kazak. When you travel to your child's province you probably will have been informed by your guide if it was an area with a large minority population. Additionally, if your child was found in a minority village, that likely points to minority heritage.

Statistically, most of the foreign adoptions within China take place in the areas where the Han majority live. However, just because you adopted from an area that tends to be Han majority doesn't mean that your child's parents were Han. You also need to consider that the world's largest human migration is now occurring in China. Young people of childbearing age are migrating from the central areas of China, the areas with minority populations, to the urban cities of the east coast. There are many factors why these migrants might choose to abandon a child. Living in poverty, unable to afford medical care for their child, problems with hukou, and the stigma against single mothers are all likely factors. So your child might be of minority heritage even if you didn't adopt from one of the provinces where minority populations are settled.

Now let's look at the married part of the original assumption that all children have married Han Chinese parents. Premarital sex is becoming more common in China, but the stigma against single mothers is unchanged. Many female college students may end up pregnant while they are studying at school and some will choose to give birth and abandon the baby. If the women are students in large urban areas, they might have a foreign boyfriend. Even in rural areas, many foreigners take a job at these universities to teach English for a few years. Foreigners have a certain mystique in Asia, just as Asian women can seem exotic to Caucasians. A college girl goes out clubbing with her friends, has a few drinks, the foreigner starts flirting with her ... you can draw your own conclusions. The same situation can occur for the many female migrant workers in the urban areas. Many of these workers leave home at age sixteen or seventeen for the big city, where they are living thousands of miles away from friends and family. I recommend reading *Factory Girls* by Leslie Chang for an in depth view of life for these young migrant women.

So in conclusion, if your child doesn't look Chinese, there could be many reasons why. Perhaps your child is biracial or is from a minority ethnic group. He or she could be Han Chinese but fair-complected and tall because they are from a northern province. Some adoptive parents choose to have genetic testing through a company called 23andMe to try and find more definite answers. Ultimately, you can be assured that there are many ways to look Chinese and your child is no less Chinese because of his or her appearance.

Additional Resources

The MDGB Pinyin to English dictionary
www.mdbg.net/chindict/chindict.php

Published article on a survey of average heights in China by geographic area
http://www.krepublishers.com/02-Journals/T-Anth/Anth-13-0-000-11-Web/Anth-13-2-000-11-Abst-Pdf/Anth-13-2-103-11-631-Ying-Xiu-Z/Anth-13-2-103-11-631-Ying-Xiu-Z-Tt.pdf

23andMe genetic testing
https://www.23andme.com/

Article on China's young migrant population from the Migration Policy Institute
http://www.migrationpolicy.org/article/chinas-young-rural-urban-migrants-search-fortune-happiness-and-independence

Photographs of all the Chinese minority groups in native attire
http://www.chinahush.com/2009/12/06/family-portraits-of-all-56-ethnic-groups-in-china/

Chang, Leslie T. Factory Girls: From village to city in a changing China. New York: Spiegel & Grau, 2009.

13

Tips for Completing Your Home Study and Dossier

I remember how overwhelming and confusing the home study and dossier requirements were with our first adoption. I think I e-mailed our agency or social worker daily with questions. I found a lot of support online from adoption friends in my DTC group as well. It was all so much easier the second time around, not only because I knew what I was doing, but because I knew where to look if I needed some help. Here are some tips for those of you who are starting out in your first adoption and want to move the home study along as quickly as possible.

Gathering your supplies

- Make sure you have access to a copier (with ink refills) and scanner.

- Have a designated area to organize all of your paperwork. I used an accordion folder and I switched out the tab labels when I transitioned from gathering home study papers to gathering dossier papers. Other people prefer a binder with tabs and folders, or a box with hanging files.

- Keep all of your adoption related receipts in a designated location to prepare for filing the adoption tax credit or employer adoption benefits. There were a lot of audits when the tax credit was refundable. This is less of an issue now that it is not refundable, but it is best to be prepared.

- Find a notary. You're going to be seeing him or her a lot, so preferably one you won't have to pay for services. Check your local bank or see if your employer has one on staff. Using the same notary each time can make the certification/authentication process a little bit easier in the future, but it is not required.

- Decide how you are going to organize all of your e-mails from your agency, social worker, USCIS officer, courier, etc., so you can find what you need easily.

- If you have a smart phone, you might find an app like Tiny Scan, which allows you to turn photos into .pdf files, to be useful.

- Consider how you are going to transfer sensitive information. Most people attach files such as copies of their tax returns or medical records to e-mail but e-mail is not actually very secure. Consider using a platform like Dropbox to transfer this information to your social worker or agency.

- Get a Fed-Ex account (or your preferred carrier) and learn how to use it. You will be mailing a lot of important documents back and forth. You will want to be able to provide pre-paid mailers to people like your social worker or USCIS officer and be able to track the shipping.

- Protect your documents. Any number of important documents have been caught in machines or left out in the rain. When you are mailing items put them in a manila envelope before placing them in the mailer to add extra protection. If you are mailing passports always put them in a zip lock bag before placing them in the envelope.

Prioritizing

The next thing you need to decide is where to start. The requirements for the dossier are the same for everyone, but what you will need for your home study will vary by state. During our first adoption, I lived in a state which was low regulation but required county certification of documents. During our second adoption, we lived in a state which was high regulation but with no county certification requirement, so the experience was quite different between the two. On our first visit in the high regulation state my social worker handed me a list of over thirty-six items we would need to provide! It was quite daunting and much of it seemed like bureaucratic redundancies. So, how do you decide where to start?

- Background checks can take a long time, and you will need them for every state you have ever lived. Make those a priority, especially if you have moved around a lot. If you can use an FBI channeler like FieldPrint, the process is much faster than mailing in paper fingerprints.

- If you or your spouse doesn't have a passport, apply for one now. A copy of your passport is necessary for the dossier, so don't think you can wait until closer to travel.

- If you already have a passport, check to see when it expires. If it expires in less than a year, you should renew it now.

- If it takes a while to get into your doctor, be sure to schedule your physicals early. Some doctors may not complete the forms while you are there, but tell you they have up to fourteen business days (or whatever their office policy is) to complete them for you.

- Similarly, if you need an outside inspection such as a fire inspection, or well water testing, do this sooner rather than later in case scheduling or waiting for results is a problem.

- Get your references lined up. Some people really procrastinate when it comes to writing the letters. If you will need one from a teacher (required by China if you have a school aged child), try to get that done before summer vacation. Some agencies will let you ask an extracurricular instructor, such as a music teacher, scout leader, etc. Using the same references for both home study and dossier will make things easier, so try to find people that will satisfy everyone's requirements. They can print and sign two copies of the same letter. One goes to your social worker and the other to yourself or to your placing agency for the dossier.

- Don't wait too long to work on the personal essay questions you will need to complete for the home study. They usually aren't the sort of thing people can write out in an hour and some people find them emotionally exhausting to work on for long periods of time.

- You should try to think ahead when your social worker is preparing your home study. It is very common for people to have their home study written for a girl with minor needs under the age of two, but then decide to be open to a boy, or fall in love with a four-year-old girl, or decide to add a second child. Any changes to your home study will involve getting a home study update and filing a supplement with USCIS, costing you hundreds of dollars. You do not want to be out all of that money because you are approved only for "under two" and you accepted a referral who was two years and two months old. **Have your social worker write your home study to be as open-ended as possible. Be approved for either gender, two children, and as old as your social worker is comfortable approving.** This costs you nothing and makes no commitment on your part.

Miscellaneous requirement tips

- Remember that if you are unsure of a requirement you should check with your social worker or agency first rather than asking the internet. You can have twenty different people telling you if they were required to have a fire inspection of their home, get their well tested, or take the entire family for TB tests, but it still won't tell you if your particular state or agency has that requirement.

- Be sure you have the most up-to-date information and forms. During our first adoption, one of our background checks was held up because I had sent an outdated form. Rather than informing us that the form was no longer used, the government agency simply tossed it in the trash. If we had called sooner to check on the hold-up we wouldn't have lost as much time.

- For your physical, you will likely need to use separate forms for China and your state, so make sure you have them both on hand. Bring extra copies in case the doctor does not fill the form out correctly the first time. The China physical form will need to be notarized and this is a big problem for people if there is no notary on staff. Some agencies will let you have a copy of the form notarized and send that to China instead. While China does accept this other agencies will not allow you to do it. Instead, ask if the doctor could have the form notarized by the hospital notary when he or she is doing hospital rounds. If all else fails, you will have to try to find a traveling notary.

- Beware of the tendency of American doctors to be overly comprehensive. Stress to the doctor that China does not want a comprehensive medical history. **They should complete the forms from the perspective of noting only issues which could shorten your lifespan or impair your ability to parent**. Think heart attack, not acid reflux.

- You will need multiple copies of "passport style photos", which can be expensive. Some people have had success taking their own passport photos at home. Other people find it to be tricky to get no shadows and everything lined up in the correct proportions, so another option is to pay for one professional passport photo, scan it, and print six copies of it onto a 4×6 photo sheet.

Making copies

You will need to make several copies of all of your dossier paperwork. One to keep for yourself, one for the Chinese consulate/embassy during the authentication process, and one to send with your dossier to your agency. Your agency might take care of this for you, and if so you can skip this next section. However, it is still a good idea to make a copy of everything you send to them for your own records. A digital copy of everything is now required by China. It is a common mistake to leave the copies and scanning step until last. Not only is this a significant amount of labor to do all at once but you cannot remove any of the staples, grommets, or fasteners which office personnel place during the certification and authentication process. Chinese consulates have refused to authenticate documents which have stray staple holes. Waiting until all of these items are attached to begin making copies will require you to develop some serious origami folding skills.

- You should be provided with multiple copies of the home study. You can NOT remove the staples on the one you will have authenticated. Remove the staple from your personal copy to make two additional copies then you can re-staple it.

- As you accumulate the documents make three copies and a scan, keeping the copies all separated in different folders or filed according to your preferred method before starting the certification/authentication process.

- After you add a certification page, make the copies and scan of the certification before moving on to the next authentication step.

Authenticating your documents

After your home study is complete and you have compiled all of the documents needed for your dossier, you will need to have them certified and authenticated. Some agencies do this for you, some do not, and some will for a fee. My agency is one which offers it as a service for a $500 fee and people often ask in my agency group if it is worth the cost. Half the people will reply that it is totally worth it for peace of mind knowing that it was done correctly. The other half (I'm in this camp) say it really isn't that difficult, so you might as well save yourself the money for some other part of the adoption. Such as all the mailing, courier, and authentication fees you're getting ready to pay! Doing this yourself can also save a lot of time. We are an east coast family with a west coast agency. I had the county and state authentications done in two days, which would have taken my agency a substantially longer amount of time with all of the mailing back and forth. Ultimately, the decision about whether to use a dossier service is best considered in light of how organized you are, how many states you've lived in, and how much time you have for the process. You can read through the process below to see if it seems feasible to you.

If your agency doesn't offer dossier service but you'd really like someone else to do this, there are couple of businesses you can use:

- ABC Dossiers at http://abcdossier.com/

- Ladybugs 'n Love <u>dossier prep service</u> at http://www.chinadossierprep.com/#!dossier-prep-info/c5ro

Here are instructions on how to complete this simple 572-step process yourself:

- MAKE COPIES OF YOUR DOCUMENTS FIRST.

- If you are not in a state that requires county certification skip down a few steps.

- If you are in one of the handful of states that requires county certification (Alabama, Georgia, Kentucky, Maryland, New York, and Tennessee as of the time of writing), you will need to figure out which county every notary is from. This is one reason I suggested you try to use the same notary as much as possible.

- Call the county secretary office and ask what you need to do to get notarized documents county certified, how much it will cost, and what forms of payment they accept.

- Drive or mail your documents according to the instructions you received. I had documents from three different counties in our first adoption, so living in a county certification state can add quite a bit of labor.

- MAKE COPIES OF THE COUNTY CERTIFICATION SHEETS.

- After county certification (or start here for most people), contact your state Secretary of State's office and ask what you need to do to get notarized documents state certified, how much it will cost, and what forms of payment they accept. Often, they will do this while you wait if you come in person but take up to two weeks if you do it by mail. This is where doing the authentication yourself can save time.

- Make it very clear to the state secretary people that you do not want an apostille. China does not accept the apostille, despite being a Hague country, so you want a "great seal" instead. If you are certifying by mail, it is not unusual to receive the documents back with an apostille, which will cause you to have to send them through a second time. If you make your request by mail use lots of capital letters and bolding to make it clear YOU DO NOT WANT THE APOSTILLE!!!

- MAKE COPIES OF THE STATE CERTIFICATION SHEETS.

- Figure out in which Chinese Consulate jurisdiction you are located. If you have documents from multiple states, you can send them all through the Embassy in DC. However, those who use the Embassy will need to first send documents through the US Department of State for authentication, which will add more time and money.

- Find a courier for your jurisdiction, call them up or send an e-mail, and they will explain everything that you need to do. This will involve paying the courier, a G1 form or two, and payment to the Chinese Embassy/Consulate for authentication fees, as well as the US Department of State if you go the Embassy route, plus an extra copy of everything, and a return mailer. *whew*

- When you receive your envelope full of completely certified and authenticated documents, do a happy dance and rejoice that you have survived this part of the process. Then MAKE COPIES OF THE AUTHENTICATION SHEETS!!

Immigration

Here is a basic breakdown of the immigration process:

- You mail a notarized copy of your home study to a lockbox in Texas with the required forms, documents, and money.

- The package is opened and you are assigned a receipt date. If you filled out the form for electronic notification, you will get a text letting you know it was received, but maybe not for a couple of days. They then mail all the documents to Kansas. Don't ask.

- About a week after your package is received, you will receive a letter in the mail notifying you of a date for FBI fingerprinting. Yes, this will be your second set of FBI fingerprints. You will have no input on the date or time. It is usually one to three weeks away.

- You will get fingerprinted.

- At some point you will either receive a Request for Further Evidence (RFE) or an approval. An RFE will always delay your approval time. Sometimes officers will be nice enough to e-mail you what is needed so you can get a jump on sending it without waiting for the notification to arrive in the mail.

- The approval is sent by regular postal service, so I recommend including a prepaid mailer when you send in the initial application. With our first adoption, we lived four hours away from the office and it took TEN DAYS for our letter of approval to arrive. The officer may choose not to use the mailer, but most will do so and you will have a trackable shorter wait.

- Notarize a copy of the approval, have it certified and authenticated, and you will have a complete dossier to send to China!

When you send in your I800a application be sure to read all of the instructions carefully, both those on the USCIS site and any your agency may provide. Be sure to include ALL of the supporting information required. It can be quite extensive. Failing to receive even one piece of paper will get you an RFE that will set you back two weeks, because what you send in response to the request will have to be sent through the lockbox again. People particularly have trouble with page nine which you leave blank unless someone else filled in the application for you. YES, send in the blank page!

The final piece of paper you will need for your dossier is your immigration approval (I800a). Some people are not sure if they should wait for the immigration approval to have all of their documents authenticated at the same time or to send them in batches. If you have documents that are approaching six months from the notarization date, you should authenticate them without delay so you don't have to redo the document.

I chose to have everything authenticated while waiting for the I800a. My agency is one which will review the dossier in advance. This gave me enough time so that if they determined one of the documents needed to be redone I could fix it and send the corrected document through the authentication process with the I800a. Not all agencies will review the dossier in advance, so check with your agency. Couriers have different pricing structures, and often one courier will be cheaper for sending a large amount of documents while another courier is cheaper for sending one or two documents. If you are authenticating in batches, check the pricing for more than one courier.

Walking in early for fingerprints

One part of this process which people have a lot of questions about is whether or not walking into an FBI office to get fingerprinted early will expedite the process. When we adopted the first time, this was a common practice. This is not permitted by all branch offices, but if you were able to do so, it seemed to get an earlier approval. At that time, you were assigned an officer with your receipt date. However, in immigration, like any office, some officers are more productive than others. If you were assigned to an officer who got through a lot of files, they would probably make time to get you approved if you had let them know you were already fingerprinted. If you were assigned to an officer who did not get through files as quickly, your file might languish on their desk. In fact, you might get fingerprinted on the same day as someone else and hear that someone else got approved that very day by their officer. But when you called your officer, you kept being told to try back next week. Every week. Until you eventually learned that the officer went on vacation without approving your file. Ask me how I know this.

Anyway, at some point in 2013 immigration changed the way the files were processed, presumably to try and fix this discrepancy in timelines. The current process is that the files are kept in order by receipt date. When an officer is ready to work on a new file they take the next one from the stack, it is assigned to them, and they approve it. Usually on the same day it is assigned, but sometimes within a day or two. This means that the files are approved strictly in order of receipt date. Walking in for early fingerprints should not speed up your process, because your file is not assigned to an officer until after your appointed fingerprinting date. It sometimes happens that if the workload of the officers is low, going in early will lead to an earlier approval. This will only happen if you call to let them know you have been fingerprinted. Often you will merely be told that you have not yet been assigned an officer. You can ask online to see what the current processing times are when trying to decide if you should walk in early. You can also ask to see if your location is one which allows this.

How long will it take from the time you have a receipt date until your I800a is approved? The good news is that while immigration can take up to ninety days it is rarely that long. Wait times vary greatly depending on how many applications are received at a time and how many immigration officers are on hand. Around holidays or before school starts, officers like to take vacation time just like at any other office. Average times are somewhere between forty and sixty days. Someone at the defunct China Adopt Talk Forum used to keep track of current times. This old chart will give you an idea of the wide variation in approval times.

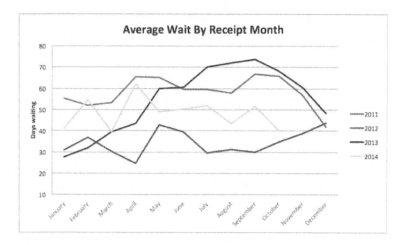

Once you have completed your home study and assembled your dossier, you have finished the most labor intensive part of the adoption process. Sending that dossier off to China is a huge milestone! Most of the rest of the process involves waiting for various government agencies to issue a piece of paper, so you can send it to a different agency so they can issue a different piece of paper. The second half of the process is more trying in many ways, because waiting for other people to do work doesn't keep you nearly as occupied as the first part. But hang in there, you will get to the end of the waiting eventually!

Later changes

Many people have questions about how major life changes, such as a new job or moving, will affect their adoption process. Changes such as a new address or income will need to be reported to USCIS by filing a Supplement 3. A home study update will be required for some changes like a new home or if you change the profile of the child(ren) you are approved to adopt. If you move to another state, you will fall under the laws of your new state of residence. Some states will only need a home study update while others will require an entire new home study. It is best to contact your social worker as soon as possible if you are considering any of these changes to find out exactly what would be involved so you can continue to move your adoption process along as smoothly as possible.

Additional Resources

List of FBI approved channelers
https://www.fbi.gov/about-us/cjis/identity-history-summary-checks/list-of-fbi-approved-channelers

Adam Walsh list of state contacts for child abuse clearances
http://www.ccld.ca.gov/res/pdf/Revised_AW_Contact_List.pdf

Chinese consulate jurisdiction listing
http://www.china-embassy.org/eng/zmzlglj/t84229.htm

ePassportPhoto for taking passport pictures at home
http://www.epassportphoto.com/

123PassportPhoto for printing six copies of a scanned passport photo on an 4x6 photo http://www.123passportphoto.com/

USCIS webpage with lockbox information including a lockbox e-mail address
https://www.uscis.gov/about-us/directorates-and-program-offices/lockbox-intake/lockbox-intake-processing-tip-sheet

USCIS I800a application form page. Complete the G-1145 to receive a text notification that your form has been received.
http://www.uscis.gov/i-800a

For more detailed information about the immigration process, you find additional information which I received when I was allowed to submit questions to USCIS to be answered by an immigration official in this blog post:
https://mineinchina.wordpress.com/2016/05/03/immigration-information/

14

Collecting Your Letters from DTC to CA

Once your dossier is complete and your agency has reviewed it, it will be mailed off to China and the wait for a log-in date (LID) begins. Whether you have been matched or not, everyone's wait begins with a LID. If you are waiting to be matched with a child with minor needs who has the LID only designation, you cannot be matched until you have that LID, even though your dossier has been sent. If you have already been matched, you will begin counting the days from your LID until you receive your letter of approval. How long will you wait for LID? It could be a few days or two to three weeks. It really depends on the method your agency uses to send the dossiers to the CCCWA. Agencies which have an employee in Beijing who can walk the dossiers into the CCCWA tend to get faster and more predictable LID times than agencies that do not.

If you have already been matched then begin counting days from your LID. Count every day, even weekends. If you have not yet been matched, then your count begins when you submit your Letter of Intent to adopt. Now you're waiting again, only now the wait for approval begins. The million dollar question is, how long will you wait? No one wants to join the dreaded "100 Club" of people who waited longer than one hundred days for their LOA. For a long time, the "how long" question was a very difficult one to answer. Some people got approved quickly while others waited much longer than three months, which was supposed to be the longer end of the range.

What happened was that once the dossiers were logged in, those already matched would be sent to translation, while those which weren't matched were set aside. The translators did their work, and in slow times they would grab one of the unmatched dossiers. If you were matched close to your log in date, someone would have to sort through the stack of unmatched dossiers to find yours to take to translation. So usually, those who were matched prior to DTC would have approval times that were shorter, say forty to sixty days, because they moved directly to translation and approval. Those who were matched within a few weeks of LID had longer approval times, around sixty to eighty days. If you had a really long wait to be matched and your dossier had already made it through translation, you might get approval in under a month because you were really only waiting for someone to hunt up your dossier and take it to be approved. However, this formula was a generality. There were always people who seemed to get an extra fast or extra-long approval. Probably, their dossier was on top of the stack, or someone went on vacation, or it got lost on the bottom of the pile. Remember that 'first come, first served' isn't a Chinese principle. The dossiers were processed more by whichever one was grabbed first than by LID date.

But that was then, this is now! Why did I spend time explaining that? Because you might have adopted a few years ago, and can appreciate that there seems to have been a new system implemented. Around January 2015, when the CCCWA put some updated rules into effect and a new computer system was rolled out, there was also a change in how the dossiers are processed. Now, all dossiers go directly into translation. There is now not any difference in approval times for those who are matched prior to DTC and those matched immediately after LID. Approval times are currently far decreased from what they used to be, with most people receiving approval in the forty to sixty day range. If you were not matched until your dossier is through translation (forty to sixty days is a general estimate) then when you send LOI you will probably receive approval in under a week. Sometimes as quickly as the next day. However, current time lines do not predict the future, which can and will change. The general timeline for LOA remains thirty to ninety days.

Your agency should be able to see certain milestones in this process by computer. They should be able to see when you are in translation, in review, match review, and the final designation which is "seeking confirmation", meaning your LOA is on its way! This is known as "soft LOA" online. Some agencies will check on these milestones for you, while others will only check upon request. The system seems to be erratically updated so if you have been sitting at "in translation" for an unusually long time, it might mean that you are further in the process but your status was not updated.

Back to immigration

After you get your Letter of Approval, it is time to file your I800. The I800a was to determine that you were eligible to adopt a non-specific child from China. The I800 will now grant you approval for the specific child or children that you and China have agreed upon. Once again you or your agency will send the forms to the Texas lockbox so they can be opened and mailed to Kansas. The I800 process takes right around two weeks, but most of that is mail processing time. I800 approvals are prioritized by USCIS, so once your file is on your officer's desk, it should be approved within a day or two. About twelve days after you know that your forms were received at the lockbox, you can start calling to see if you have received approval. The officers answer the phone, so please don't call multiple times a day and remember, be polite. You will need your SIM number from your lockbox receipt. When the officer answers, say that you want to check the status of your application. The phone number is on your receipt letter. If they say you have been granted approval or provisional approval, that means you're ready for the next step!

Those two weeks you are waiting for your approval is a good time to get your visa for your trip to China. In order to apply for a visa, you must have an "invitation" to enter China. Most consulates now require you to have your travel approval to use as the invitation before you can apply for your visa. However, some people want to leave within a week of getting travel approval and would prefer to apply for the visa sooner. As of the time of writing, the Chicago consulate will process visas for any jurisdiction with a copy of the LOA. Look up Denise Hope's There's Always Hope courier service for detailed instructions and an adoptive family discount. Yes, you will need to send your actual passports in order to get the visa. Don't forget to place the passports in a ziplock bag before mailing to protect them. The good news is that there is now a 10-year multiple entry visa option so you no longer need to get a new visa for each new adoption or homeland tour.

More visa work

After your I800 application is approved, USCIS will send it on to the National Visa Center, where your child will be issued an immigrant visa. It takes a few days for the papers to reach the NVC. When they log you into their system you will be issued a case number that begins with the letters GUZ. This is their system abbreviation for Guangzhou, the US consulate where your child's visa will originate. While the next part of the process happens automatically, there are a few steps you can take to speed things along. Some agencies will give you instructions, but if yours does not, you can check in your online DTC group for updated information. I am including the general instructions here. A week after your I800 approval date, you should begin sending a daily e-mail to the NVC asking if you have been issued a GUZ number. In the e-mail you will need to include your SIM number, the beneficiary's (your child's) name and birthdate, and the petitioner's (your) name and birthdate.

Once you receive the e-mail with your GUZ number, it will include the information you need to complete the DS-260. Yay, another form! This one is the online application for your child's visa. Your agency should provide instructions for completing this form or again, ask around for instructions from someone else's agency if yours does not provide this information. It might take a few hours or a day after you receive the GUZ number before you are able to log in to complete it. Keep trying and eventually it will be activated for you. Your agency will need a copy of the confirmation that you have completed it.

Next you should send another e-mail to the NVC. The NVC has been busy working on getting your case completed, and once they are done, they will send it on to the consulate in Guangzhou. They will send you a letter in the mail informing you this has been done. However, your agency needs the information in this letter for the next step in the process, and it will take a few days to receive it in the mail. If you e-mail the NVC, you can request an e-mail copy of the letter that will greatly speed the process along. Use the same e-mail address as before and include all of the same information, only this time send the GUZ number instead of the USCIS SIM number. In the body of the message say that you would like to know when the visa petition has been forwarded to the consulate, and could they please e-mail you a copy of the letter. You can send this once a day as well. Usually, you will receive the letter within three or four days. Be sure to forward it to your agency.

The final step in the child visa process is called Article 5. Your agency will compile a packet of the paperwork you've collected along the way and it will be submitted to the consulate in Guangzhou. The consulate will finish all of the necessary processing so that when you visit in the second week of your trip to China, your child's visa will be issued. The Article 5 takes ten business days to process and agency representatives can only drop off and pick up the paperwork on Monday, Tuesday, and Thursdays. Not all agency representatives will go to the consulate every available day. The consulate is closed on both American and Chinese national holidays. There is a website where you can track the status of the visa. The status reads "ready" from the time the NVC forwards your case and changes to "administrative processing" within a day or two of your Article 5 being ready for pick-up.

Travel approval and consulate appointment

After your Article 5 paperwork is picked up, your agency representative will send it by express mail to the CCCWA office in Beijing. China needs to know that your child will have a US immigrant visa after the adoption before they will allow you to adopt. Now that you have the visa secured, China will process your travel approval. This can take one to three weeks, but like the faster LOA times TAs have been coming in closer to seven to ten days under the new system. Your agency can see the TA in the system, another 'soft' approval. Agencies can book a consulate appointment with the soft TA. Your agency will need to finalize your adoption dates with the officials in your child's province as well as receive the consulate appointment. Most agencies will need at least a week between TA and your travel date in order to make arrangements and some agencies require families wait two or three weeks between TA and travel.

During your trip to China, you will finalize your child's adoption in their provincial capital. This concludes the China side of the adoption, but you have one more step to finalize things on the American side. You will travel to Guangzhou and must have an appointment at the US consulate there in order to secure your child's visa. The preliminary paperwork for this has already been done, but they will need your adoption certificate and the results of a medical exam before the visa sticker is printed out and stuck into your child's Chinese passport.

The consulate has appointments for adoption visas Monday through Thursday. You might have heard that Mondays are reserved for children under two. That is not technically the case. Usually, the medical appointment is on Saturday. That does not give enough time for the results of the tuberculosis blood test given to children over the age of two to be received for a Monday appointment. This is not the only factor that can affect appointment scheduling. Some provinces do not prepare the child's passport in advance so it must be express mailed to Guangzhou after you leave the province. If your child is in one of these provinces, you may need a Tuesday or Wednesday appointment to give you extra time to receive the passport. Some larger agencies will schedule blocks of appointments on Tuesday and Wednesday because it is easier for them to transport all of their traveling families at once. You will need to discuss your consulate date options with your agency.

After your agency has finalized your consulate appointment, it's time to start making travel plans! I will help you out with all of that in the next chapter. There is one last related bit of information about your consulate appointment. You will not receive your child's visa at the appointment. It will be prepared and should be available in the late afternoon of the following day. It is prudent to allow an extra day when you are planning your flights home. At least a couple times a year the visas will be delayed. Usually, the problem is that the consulate computers are down, or sometimes the printer isn't working, but occasionally there will be a problem that delays the visas for several days. Whatever it is, if you have a flight out and no visa, you will have to change your flight plans. Most people will schedule a flight out for the day after the consulate appointment, which often means beginning to travel to Hong Kong the night before, giving you even more reservations to change. So when you are deciding whether to leave the day after you are supposed to receive your visa, please consider how easily you could reschedule those plans and weigh that against the odds of something causing a visa delay.

Additional Resources

USCIS adoption contact information
http://www.uscis.gov/adoption/uscis-adoption-contact-information

There's Always Hope courier service
http://www.theres-always-hope.com/china_info_visa.htm

NVC contact information
http://travel.state.gov/content/adoptionsabroad/en/us-visa-for-your-child/immigrant-visa-process.html

US consulate in Guangzhou holiday closure calendar
http://guangzhou.usembassy-china.org.cn/holidays2.html

US Department of State visa status tracking site
https://ceac.state.gov/CEACStatTracker/Status.aspx

15

Preparing for the Trip

After a full day of nonstop travel, my family stepped off the plane and into the Beijing airport. My husband immediately set off in search of someone official to ask directions to the nearest bathroom because my ten-year-old son had suffered a bout of motion sickness during the landing. The 10 year old in question was being sponged off by my mother-in-law. My twelve-year-old daughter blearily guarded our stack of carry-on items while I kept reminding my seven year old son that he shouldn't lie down on the floor in the airport to go to sleep. My four-year-old son tugged on my hand to get my attention. "Mama, are we in China now?" When I answered that we were, he replied "Do dey have potties in China? Because I need one right now!"

That's a pretty accurate summary of how most of us feel about traveling to China. We're really excited to be going there but not really sure what we'll find once we arrive. A surprisingly large amount of adoptive parents are already familiar with the trip because they spent time in Asia in college or through business trips. However, for many other families, this might be their first trip outside of the country. Planning for this trip can cause families a lot of anxiety. I'm going to take you through all aspects of your journey to China. We will talk about the itinerary, flights, hotels, food, and I will give you money saving tips throughout it all.

For most people, the trip will be about two weeks long. If you are adopting two children, it could be three weeks long. People begin the trip in many different places but everyone will end up spending the final week in the city of Guangzhou (pronounced GWAN-jo) in the southern province of Guangdong. This is because the American consulate which processes visas for adoptions is located there. A typical schedule looks like this:

Sample itinerary:
Day 1- Thursday, fly to China and land in Beijing in the evening
Day 2- Friday, spend the day touring in Beijing
Day 3- Saturday, spend another day touring in Beijing
Day 4- Sunday, fly to your child's province
Day 5- Monday, meet your child!
Day 6- Tuesday, finalize your child's adoption
Day 7- Wednesday, free day while paperwork is being prepared
Day 8- Thursday, visit orphanage if permitted or another free day
Day 9- Friday, travel to Guangzhou
Day 10- Saturday, child's medical exam for consulate appointment
Day 11- Sunday, free day while waiting for medical results
Day 12- Monday, free day while waiting for medical results
Day 13- Tuesday, Consulate appointment
Day 14- Wednesday, child's visa is ready in the afternoon
Day 15- Thursday, fly home

Deciding who goes with you

While the most common scenario for an adoption trip is for the two parents to travel to adopt their one or two children, in actuality there are as many travel group variations as you can think up. If a couple is adopting their first child after many years of battling infertility, both sets of grandparents might want to go along to meet their new grandchild from the very first moment. Other couples might choose to have only one parent travel because of work obligations, budget constraints, or trouble finding childcare for their children at home. On our first adoption trip we took along our four children and my mother-in-law to help be an extra set of hands on the trip. I was a little concerned that we would be a traveling circus, but our agency travel representative all but shrugged his shoulders over it, saying they've had much larger groups travel. Our guide in-province seemed to verify this when she regaled us with tales of the Mennonite family she had guided the previous year who brought along their eight children and two sets of grandparents! On our second adoption trip we took only our seven-year-old son, so we have had two very different travel experiences.

Many parents ask "Should I bring along my other children or is it better to leave them home?" The best answer to that question really depends on your personal family dynamics. This is a question people really agonize over, but I've got great news for you. When people answer this question, they say "We took/didn't take our children and we wouldn't do it any other way!" so you really can't go wrong here! Most parents who took children said they felt it helped their new child feel more comfortable with them. If you think about it, children from orphanages are used to being around other children and aren't used to the undivided attention of adults. When your child sees that your other children love and trust you, they will be more likely to love and trust you as well.

On the other hand, parents who choose to leave their children at home say they loved having two weeks to bond with their new child and give them their undivided attention. They are glad they didn't have other children to care for or to deal with sibling rivalry issues. Parents who are adopting children with complex medical needs who might need medical care in-country seem particularly happy with their decision to travel without other children.

If you are trying to decide whether or not you want to take your children I think what is most important is to consider the personalities of your children. How easy-going are they? What are they like when they get off their routine? Are they picky eaters? You need to keep in mind that this is not a vacation. This trip is long. There are times where you will spend an entire day waiting around an airport or driving through traffic traveling to a different city to drive around in more traffic to get to your new hotel. The food is unfamiliar, the jet lag is exhausting, and you'll be adding a new family member on top of all that! Age is also an important consideration. If your child or children are very young and need a lot of care, you might want to leave them home with Grandma (or possibly bring her along--more on that in a minute). Bringing a sibling or siblings will work best if your children are fairly flexible, old enough to understand that sometimes they're going to be bored, and tend to be adventurous.

We felt that doing some fun touristy things on the front end of the tour would give us more flexibility after our new son joined our family. Be aware that many children come with medical issues, such as an ear infection. It is not uncommon for them to grieve heavily through this transition time, and our son had his sad moments. We explained to the children that we might end up staying in the hotel all day if it seemed better for him or because of poor weather. I think we would have been more likely to split up and have one of us and my mother-in-law take the older children out or down to swim in the hotel pool if that was the case, but we wanted the children to understand that the trip was not a vacation so they would be prepared and empathetic. Things went very smoothly for us, but these are all things to consider when you are choosing whether or not to take your other children with you on the trip.

One concern for parents of school-aged children is always whether they can or should take them out of school for the trip. Of course, you are the one who best knows your children—their personalities, activities, and academic challenges. As far as the practicality of having children miss school, many school districts will allow children a certain number of days for educational enrichment. My child was allowed to count 10 days as excused absences as long as she kept a journal of her time in China. Other school districts suggest that you withdraw your child from school and re-enroll upon return. You will need to contact your district directly to find what is permissable in your area. The first choice for most families is to travel over summer break or Christmas vacation. However, you will not have very much flexibility in scheduling travel and airfare prices during vacation may rule out your ability to afford to take the children with you.

Parents who have adopted previously might have another concern: will leaving the child home cause them to have fears of abandonment or revisit attachment issues? But considering bringing a previously adopted child with you to China might bring concerns of causing them to revisit trauma. This is a question with no answer that works for everyone. People have done both successfully. Whether you are taking a previously adopted child with you or leaving him with a caregiver at home, it is important to talk through what will be happening. Try to have many conversations to prepare him for his feelings. If you are leaving him at home, practicing overnight visits with the caregiver as well as video chats while you are in China will help reassure him that you will return. If you are bringing him along, be prepared for questions about his own adoption while looking for signs of regression or other indicators that being in China again is triggering fears. Most parents do not recommend using an adoption trip as a heritage trip. Instead, use it as an introductory visit to China, but let your child have his own trip later when you can devote more time to visiting relevant locations and fully focusing on his experience.

There is a lot of time to fill in a two week trip to China, so if you take your children you will need to keep them entertained. Think there's no way China could be boring? One of my children complained of boredom while touring the Forbidden City, complete with "How much longer is this going to take? Can't we just go back to the hotel now?" whining. We usually went out both in the morning and afternoon, but we still had time in the hotel, in the van, and in the airport to kill. Our older two kids took their Nintendo DS and I purchased a new game for each of them to help keep them entertained. For the younger two, we took iPod shuffles filled with audiobooks. Besides these electronic items each bag had items like a coloring book and crayons, word find book, packs of card games, travel play dough, colored pipe cleaners, and other cheap little items that I picked up at a dollar store. My mother-in-law came armed with her own bag of entertainment and she saved us many times by pulling out some new little toy when tempers were running short and people were getting bored.

If you are taking children with you to China, many people choose to take along an extra adult. We decided to see if my mother-in-law would be interested in coming to China with us and were so grateful that she said yes. Because we were taking four children along it was very helpful to have an extra set of hands so that our child to adult ratio was lower. Our kids are old enough that we could have done it by ourselves, but it was much easier with my mother-in-law along. This is something which is also helpful for those who have only one or two children but whose children are young.

If you're thinking of bringing a friend or relative along, regardless of whether or not you are also bringing children, I'd recommend asking the same sorts of questions I suggested you ask yourself when thinking about bringing the children along. Is this person an easy traveler? Do you get along with him or her well? You will be spending two weeks in close quarters, so you want to make sure your companion won't add friction to an already stressful trip. Please do not let yourself be guilt-tripped into letting a relative come along because they don't want to be left out if you know this relative will add stress to your life. **For**

all of these considerations, remember that your primary focus should be on the child you are adopting and establishing a relationship with that child. Also consider whether the extra adult will be respectful of the attachment process. My mother-in-law made sure she let us always carry, feed, and change our son. She primarily cared for the older children and didn't give any extra attention to our new son. Physical health is a final consideration. Some agencies will require a physical for any adult making the trip. The main concerns would be the long flight, the air pollution levels in China, and the large amount of walking involved.

Money saving tips: If you are looking for the absolutely lowest cost trip, be aware that only one parent is required to travel to China. If you choose this option you will need to plan in advance because a power of attorney is required. Additional travelers will add significantly to your cost, especially if you need multiple hotel rooms. While taking other children along can be a positive experience, remember that it is optional if funds are low.

Travel vaccinations and pollution concerns

Some people get no vaccinations while others to the full range of options, including malaria pills. For the most accurate recommendations, you should consult with your doctor and check for travel warnings on the US State Department's China page. Most families choose to get the Hepatitis A and B vaccinations, as well as Tetanus or MMR boosters if needed. Typhoid and malaria outbreaks do occur in China but few families will travel outside of major cities. If you think you will be traveling for a rural area for an orphanage or foster family visit, you might need to see if additional vaccinations are necessary.

Because the pollution in China is well-publicized, people often want to know if they should take face masks to wear. One important thing to keep in mind is that pollution levels can be high even if there is no visible smog, so you cannot rely on reports of traveling parents who say they were fine because the sky was clear. Pollution levels are often higher in winter when coal burning furnaces are in use, although visible smog is uncommon at this time due to cold temperatures. Check pollution levels via the US State Department website. It provides data for Beijing, Chengdu, Shanghai, Guangzhou, and Shenyang. If you do choose to pack a face mask, either a Vogmask or N95 mask are recommended. The sort of loose surgical mask you are asked to wear in a medical setting does NOT provide any protection against pollution. It is intended to protect others from the germs discharged by your nose and mouth if you sneeze or cough. It is not a filter for the air which you inhale. Pollution symptoms typically include coughing and congestion, so pack medications appropriately, especially for those with asthma.

Coming up with cash

Unless you are with one of the few agencies that includes the orphanage donation and other in-country adoption fees in their agency fee, you will need to spend some time at least a month before you travel calculating how much cash you will need for your trip. The required orphanage donation fee is currently around $5,700, with the precise amount dependent on the exchange rate at the time you travel. Some agencies will let you wire this amount to the orphanage while other agencies are not set up to do this. It can also vary by the orphanages, because some only accept cash. Request a list of expenses during the trip from your agency. The exact amount of adoption related fees will be different from province to province. In addition, you need to decide how much spending money you will need. Many people carry under $10,000 for adopting a single child while you will easily double that for the orphanage donations alone if you are adopting two children at once without the ability to wire it in advance.

After you learn from your agency what your exact expenses will be, that will help you know how much additional cash to obtain. Your hotel will let you exchange a certain amount per day, usually around $300. Many hotels also have ATMs in the lobby, so that is another avenue for exchanging money. Credit cards will be accepted at larger locations such as your hotel or the jade/pearl market. You should not depend on credit cards at restaurants or shops you find on the street. Few people find traveler's cheques helpful. It is better to exchange your spending money as you go along rather than exchanging it all at once, because it will be difficult to exchange the Chinese currency back to American dollars. Once you have decided on your total amount you need to contact your bank. It can take several weeks to obtain thousands of dollars in brand new $100 bills. Hotels and banks will not usually change money unless it is in like-new condition.

A final note on transporting the money: while there is no limit on the amount of money you can transport out of the US, you are legally required to declare if you are taking more than $10,000. This counts even if you are splitting the money between members of your party. While what you are supposed to do and what people actually do are often two different things, be aware that if you choose not to declare, the government could seize your money. To declare the funds, you simply fill out a form with US Customs and Border Protection. I have included a link to the information page and form in the Additional Resources section.

Getting there

If you are with a full service agency, they will either make all the arrangements for you or work with a dedicated travel agency. Typically, everyone will be responsible for booking their own international flights to and from China. Some parents will feel comfortable doing this on their own while many choose to work with a travel agent who is familiar with the adoption process. These travel agents are familiar with the problems that can occur on adoption trips, such as consulates which sometimes end up not printing the visa on the expected day because the printer broke. They also know how much time you will need to plan to get through immigration upon landing when you return. The following information was correct as of the time of writing but may change in the future.

Commonly used travel agents:

Todd Galliek
tgallinek@aol.com
(303) 918-9888

Sue Sorrels
sue@suesorrels.com
(817) 784-8219
www.suesorrels.com

Adoption Airfare
www.adoptionairfare.com

Erica Shubin
erica.shubin@gmail.com
(727) 612-0690

When choosing an airline, most people choose the airline offering the cheapest price. People have had good and bad experiences on every airline. Most families will fly United or Delta. Korean Air is generally considered the most luxurious with Cathay Pacific coming in a close second. Because the flight is so long, many people will upgrade to "economy plus" if they can afford it to make the trip more comfortable. Use seatguru.com to check out seating arrangements on potential flights, as well as charging stations and video monitors.

Dress comfortably for the flight. Pick clothing that is non-restrictive, you'd be able to sleep in, and which will clean easily. Comfortable footwear is a must. Most people will do far more walking during this trip than they do in the course of their normal daily lives. Many people recommend buying compression socks for the trip to reduce swelling. If you are carrying money for the orphanage donation, split it up between adults in money belts that you wear around your waist. You may choose to wear a neck style passport holder for your passports and other valuables.

How much the round trip flight will cost is a frequently asked question, but the cost will vary by the time of year and you really don't get any choice in the time of year that you travel. Typically the highest fares are during the summer and around major holidays like Christmas and Chinese New Year. Be aware that lap tickets for children under age two are not free for international flights. Child fares for children over two and under twelve are sometimes available but not offered during peak travel season. Prepare yourself for the shock that the one-way ticket for your child's trip home will cost as much as or more than a round-trip ticket.

Keeping the children entertained for hours on a plane ride to China was one of my biggest fears. If you are traveling with other children, you might have that concern as well. In the end, that was the easiest part of the trip. Before we bought our tickets, we made sure the plane had individual video consoles for every seat. This meant that each child could watch on-demand movies or TV shows for pretty much the entire flight. We tried to get them to sleep, but since we usually have strict media limits, they all kept saying they weren't sleepy because they didn't want the TV time to be over. In the end, this was very helpful in overcoming jet lag. We didn't have to keep awake very long once we arrived in China and we all got a good night's sleep the first night.

Another question for many parents is whether or not they should buy a seat ticket for a child under two or go with the much less expensive lap ticket. Most people suggest buying the extra seat ticket because you will welcome the extra space on the long flight regardless of whether your child uses it or not. Some people do regret having spent the money because their child spent the entire flight on their lap or being walked up and down the aisle of the plane. Toddlers are unpredictable, so you won't know if you will have a child who clings to you the entire trip refusing to sit in their own seat or a child who still hates the sight of you and wants their own space. We chose the lap ticket option on our first trip when we traveled home but we also had our four year old along. They were both small enough that they shared a seat for periods of time on the flight.

Some parents are concerned about the safety aspects of the flight. On a domestic flight in America, people often take along car seats so their children are safely restrained during the flight. This is generally not recommended for the trip to China. The biggest reason is because car seats are not used in China. Many cars do not even have seatbelts, so you will be stuck carrying around a very heavy useless piece of equipment for a long trip. Related to this, your child will be completely unfamiliar with a car seat. While your biological child might settle in for a long flight in a car seat because it is how they are used to traveling, this will not be the case for your new child. Newly adopted children will usually cry when they are first strapped into a car seat, and it can take several weeks for them to get used to a car seat once home. Many parents use a CARES harness as an alternative for the flight. Be aware that the CARES harness is for children who weigh between 22 and 44 pounds so very young children will not meet the weight requirement.

If you book flights through a travel agent, you will probably be asked if you want to purchase travel insurance. It is inexpensive in the grand scheme of adoption costs, but many parents still choose not to purchase it as a small cost-saving measure. Often someone will say "There is no way that I'm NOT getting on that plane!" However, emergency situations can still pop up. One mother who was traveling solo to adopt collapsed in the airport due to a medical issue and the adoption trip had to be rescheduled for the following month. Another couple was in China when they received word that their son at home had to be hospitalized after a car accident, so one of them flew home early while the other finished the adoption trip alone. Instances such as these are very rare but you should purchase travel insurance if you would have difficulty affording to change your travel plans should an emergency occur.

If you are flying into Beijing, you could consider transporting medical supplies for an NGO in China. Typically, the supplies will be sent to your house in a suitcase you can open, so you can honestly answer the airport security questions. A representative from the NGO will either meet you at the airport to pick up the supplies or pick it up from your hotel. If you do not have any extra luggage allowance, many of these charities will reimburse you for your luggage overage fees because it is still cheaper than shipping to China from America.

China Little Flower Project
Contact Serena Johnson or Rebekah Bodden at
info@chunmiaolittleflower.org

New Hope foster home partners with the charity Show Hope for supplies
Contact Rebecca Dorris at suitcasesoflove@gmail.com

Returning home

When you are considering your flight options for returning home, many families will choose to depart from Hong Kong rather than the Guangzhou airport. The main reason is that flights out of Hong Kong tend to be significantly cheaper than those out of Guangzhou. There are also more options for flights to America since Hong Kong has long been connected to the western world because it was a British colony. If you decide to leave from the Guangzhou airport try to get a flight as early in the day as possible to minimize delays. Most will have a domestic flight to either Shanghai or Beijing, where the international flight home will depart. Make sure you have a generous layover in case your flight out of Guangzhou is delayed. Additionally, you will need to pick up your luggage when you depart from the domestic flight, re-check it in for the international flight, and go through security again to enter the international terminal, all of which takes additional time.

A Hong Kong departure brings its own challenges. For starters, Hong Kong is a couple of hours away from Guangzhou. For most families this will mean packing up from the Guangzhou hotel, traveling to Hong Kong by train or private van, checking to another hotel for the night, and finally flying out the following morning. There is no bullet train yet from Guangzhou to Hong Kong, but there is regular train service from the Guangzhou East Railway Station to Hum Hong Station in Hong Kong. The train is a very economical option. Child fares are half price and if your child is young enough to ride on their lap they can ride for free. The trip is about two hours long. The downside to the train is navigating the train station with luggage and/or strollers. Additionally, you will need to arrange for transportation to the train station and from the train station in Hong Kong to your hotel.

Hiring a private van will be more expensive, especially if you are only adoptive parents with one child. The private van option is attractive if you have a larger party, multiple young children, or children with mobility issues. The van will provide you with hotel to hotel service, so you don't have to get taxis or deal with luggage and the train station. While the trip might sound easier riding in a van, I have actually heard far more complaints from families about it. Because of China's horrific traffic the ride to Hong Kong can sometimes take up to four hours. People become anxious as the driver weaves in and out of traffic at high speed. Motion sickness can be a real issue for passengers, especially young children.

Most families stay at either the Regal or the Sky City Marriott because they are closest to the Hong Kong airport and both have a free shuttle. The airport is not near to Hung Hum station, so you should expect a taxi ride to take about forty-five minutes. If you are planning to spend a day in Hong Kong before departing, you might not want to limit yourself to an airport hotel. The Harbour Plaza Metropolis is next to Hong Hum station and easily accessible through a pedestrian walkway which connects the station to a mall adjacent to the hotel. Hong Kong has an excellent train line called the Airport Express. There are five stations throughout Hong Kong. Many hotels including the Harbour Plaza Metropolis provide free shuttle service to the Airport Express. There are check-in desks for the major airlines at the Airport Express stations, so you can check in for your flight and check your luggage. Porter service is free, too. So depending on your departure time, choosing a hotel with a shuttle to the Airport Express could be a better choice than one of the airport hotels.

Money saving tips: Many families reduce airfare costs by purchasing tickets on frequent flier miles or by using points accumulated through a credit card affiliation. The Capital One Venture is the most recommended credit card to reduce travel expenses. You might find cheaper flights booking your round trip flight through a major airport rather than the closest airport to you. Parents travel to the major airport by either driving or booking a separate commuter flight there through an airline such as Southwest.

Important reminders:

- Apply for your passport as soon as you start the process if you don't already have one.

- If you have a passport, check to make sure it will not expire within the next year.

- Because your child is flying home on a Chinese passport, you cannot pass through any countries which would require an entry visa for them. This means you cannot fly through Canada on your return trip unless you meet very specific criteria.

- If you are an expatriate family remember that you must travel back to the US in order to secure your child's citizenship.

Additional Resources

US State Department's China travel page
http://travel.state.gov/content/passports/en/country/china.htm
l

US Customs and Border Protection money declaration
https://help.cbp.gov/app/answers/detail/a_id/195/~/currency-
%2F-monetary-instruments---amount-that-can-be-brought-
into-or-leave-the

US State Department passport application and renewal forms

http://travel.state.gov/content/passports/en/passports/forms.html

US Embassy in Beijing's pollution monitoring website
http://beijing.usembassy-china.org.cn/070109air.html

US State Department website providing pollution data for 5 major Chinese cities.
http://www.stateair.net/web/post/1/1.html

US Smart Traveler Enrollment Program to notify the Embassy of your in country travel
https://step.state.gov/step/

Hong Kong Airport Express guide
http://www.travelchinaguide.com/cityguides/hongkong/transportation/air-express.htm

16

It's Finally Here! Everything you need to know about travel

Public service announcement: squatty potties!

If you haven't already heard, I need to break the news to you that our western porcelain throne style toilets are not the norm in China. I can't say that I ever imagined I would be writing a bathroom instructional at any point in my life, but adoptive moms feel a huge amount of anxiety over facing the "squatty potty" and I'm here to support you. When you enter a stall in a Chinese bathroom, instead of a toilet you will see what looks like a porcelain sink or trench set into the floor tile. There will be an area for you to position your feet and a wastebasket filled with used toilet tissue. What you will not find in the stall is toilet tissue. While I'm giving you the bad news I might as well tell you that there will not be soap by the sinks either.

Be prepared for visits to the bathroom by packing along hand sanitizer and travel tissue packets or your preferred type of travel toilet paper. You can use the tissues as toilet paper if the bathroom is out. If toilet paper is provided, it will be by the door as you enter the bathroom or over by the sinks, not in the stall. Used toilet paper should be tossed into the trash can provided because the antiquated Chinese sewage system can't handle toilet paper.

The key to success when using a squatty potty is to commit completely to the squat. Do not try to hover, squatting just a little lower than 90 degrees as if you are using an invisible toilet. This will only get your pants all wet. Or worse. Instead squat all the way down until your butt is by your ankles. Your pants and underwear should be pushed behind your knees where it will be up out of the way. You might try practicing this position at home before you leave until it is more comfortable for you. What you absolutely don't want to do is attempt it for the first time and end up falling into the squatty potty when you lose your balance.

Or if you don't like that key to success then try this one: look for the handicapped stall. It usually holds a western toilet.

Other Chinese habits to prepare for

I am always saddened when I read adoptive parents making derogatory comments judging the behavior of the Chinese people. If you were a guest at an Asian family's home and neglected to remove your shoes, they would probably assume that you were horribly rude and unsanitary. You are now a guest in China, and while they have different ideas of what is polite you need to remember that you are not in America and should not expect them to behave according to American norms.

First, it is not rude to stare in China. You will be a celebrity. Many people, especially if they are from a rural area but are traveling to Beijing on holiday, may never have seen a Caucasian before. Not only will they stare, but they will point you out to passersby so they won't miss out on the sight. They will take pictures and they won't be shy about asking you to pose for pictures with them. Once, when we were walking along a sidewalk we passed a bench with an elderly woman on it. As we walked in front of her she reached out and grabbed my four-year-old son. She patted him, caressed his blond hair, and cooed over him as we tried to gently extract him from her arms.

Personal hygiene practices are different in China. It is not rude to belch at the table or talk with your mouth full. People can spit on the sidewalk and they do. There is no taboo against public urination, especially for children. Those cute split pants they wear are for easy access. If you are adopting a child who is preschool age, they will probably squat down right on the sidewalk if they can't communicate to you that they need to go. Most people hand wash their own clothing, so you will probably see your guide wearing the same clothes several days in a row. It might even inspire you to pack lighter the next time. Deodorant is not widely used, nor has tooth brushing caught on to widespread use.

Because China is a large country with a huge population, many cultural differences are related to things being just plain crowded. People will not give you as much personal space as you are used to in America. There is less of a conversational personal space as well. They will not hesitate to ask you personal questions, like what is your occupation, what kind of car do you drive, and how much money do you make? All of this is perfectly normal and acceptable in Chinese culture.

Finally, and this is huge for people, there is no concept of "first come, first served" in China. There are too many people and there is never enough of anything. There is not enough space on the sidewalk, there are not enough seats on the train, and there is not always enough food in the grocery store. While it's a common joke that the Chinese will eat anything, the reality is that millions of people died during widespread famine in China in the late 1950's and early 1960's. If you think that sort of thing doesn't have an impact, consider the habits of any Depression era relatives you may have had. That is a lot of people who were hungry for a long time, and it was relatively recently, so keep that in mind when you look at a menu. If you find yourself getting angry because you've been patiently waiting in line at the hotel omelet station and someone elbowed you out of the way, please

236

remember that these habits have been learned because it is ingrained knowledge that waiting in line won't get you anything. Plus, there was never really a line --you just assumed there was.

Touring in China

The majority of adoption trips begin with some sight-seeing, most often in Beijing. The reason for this is to give you time to recover from the jet-lag before you start parenting your new child. It also pads your trip with some extra time so that delays don't cause you to miss adoption day. This part of the trip will be optional, so you could choose to tour only one day or not at all. Some people prefer to travel directly to their child's province and spend a day there doing some shopping and getting settled in. If you are adopting from a southern province like Guangdong, a trip to Hong Kong might be more cost effective. Shanghai and Xian (where the terracotta soldiers are located) are other possible destinations for your adjustment day or days.

What will you do during this time? For the majority of adoptive parents who are Beijing-bound, see the Great Wall of course! If you travel to Beijing, most families will visit the Great Wall and possibly also the Forbidden City, Summer Palace, Temple of Heaven, and maybe a hutong tour by rickshaw. The government wants you to spend some tourism dollars, so you will also probably be treated to a visit to the government run silk, jade, and/or cloisonne factories. These factories will include an educational section on how the product is made and a visit to the store so you can purchase some of the product. A meal is often included. In the evening you might choose to have a meal of Beijing (Peking) duck or see an acrobatics show.

All of these attractions will cost money. If your agency makes the arrangements, you might pay per person and per attraction. If you are comfortable with international travel, you might prefer to get yourself around using the subway system and a guidebook.

You can often pick up an English-speaking guide outside an attraction for very little. If you are on a very tight budget, choose the attractions most important to you and spend the rest of your time wandering the local markets and stores around your hotel. You could also hire one of the private guides, which are recommended by adoptive parents.

Private guides in Beijing:

- Angela from Ladybugs 'n Love
  http://ladybugsnlove.com/

- John Yellowcar
  http://www.beijing-driver.com/
  (verify that he will drive you himself)

- David Wang
  David@chinamissiontrip.com

- John and Mary Ma
  840972269@qq.com

Car safety

If you are being transported by agency group, you will probably be driven in a van. Sometimes people will get around on their own by taxi. Be aware that seat belts are not commonly used in China. In fact, sometimes the vehicle will not have them at all. As I mentioned before, car seats are not used at all in China. It would be difficult for you to find one to buy, but it is possible. Most parents will carry their child on their lap while being driven around.

You will no more have left the airport than you will be amazed in a frightened way by Chinese traffic. There are seemingly a million lanes, people honk their horns in a conversational way, and traffic lights or stop signs seem to be taken as suggestions. Many people will witness a minor traffic accident, but traffic usually isn't traveling at a high enough speed within the urban areas where you will travel for accidents to be serious. It is important for you to keep traffic in mind when you are traveling on foot. Sidewalks are an alternate traffic route for motor scooters and bicycles. Because you cannot count on cars obeying the traffic signal, follow the rule that there is safety in numbers when crossing the street.

In-country travel

After a day or two getting acclimated to China, it will be time to travel to your child's province. This is usually done by taking a domestic flight within China. In most cases your agency will arrange to have a guide take you from your hotel to the airport and help you get checked in for your domestic flight. One major difference between domestic flights in China and those at home, is that in China you will be loaded onto a bus and driven to the runway, where you will climb stairs to board the plane. Check as much baggage as possible to keep your hands free during the trip to the plane. One nice perk of domestic flights in China is that food is provided on most flights, unlike in America. Domestic flights are often delayed in China because the Chinese government controls almost all of the airspace. It is not unusual for adoptive families to find that their flight to Guangzhou is delayed by three to six hours so be sure to pack snacks for your time waiting in the airport.

Many people would like to utilize China's railway system as an alternate method of travel while in country. If you have traveled in Europe, this seems a cheap and easy alternative. Some agencies discourage railway travel in China because of overcrowding and unreliable timetables. If your agency doesn't mind and you are adventurous, this could be a great way to travel. Train fare is much less expensive than flying and the high speed trains make traveling long distances feasible, especially along the eastern coast. Sleeper trains are available for traveling overnight. Because seating on Chinese trains can be a bit "survival of the fittest" it pays to upgrade your seats.

There are several things to keep in mind if you are considering rail travel. First, the train stations are not as foreigner friendly as the airports. English signage will be limited and far fewer people will speak English. Train stations are not very handicapped accessible. You will need to carry luggage and strollers up and down numerous flights of stairs or escalators. Finally, luggage is usually stored at the front or back of the train car on racks. Many people have had a good experience traveling by train but it might not be the best choice for a large party or if you have children with mobility issues. Consult with your agency as you decide which method of in-country travel is best for you.

For more information on booking your own in-country travel:

www.seat61.com/China.htm

http://www.china-diy-travel.com/

http://english.ctrip.com/

In-province

While Beijing and Guangzhou are very westernized, your time in-province will probably be the time when you are most likely to experience "real China". You will be staying in the provincial capital, because that is where foreign adoptions are finalized so the city will still be large. However, there will be fewer English speakers or English language signs. You should have a guide for your time in province and they will be your best resource. A good guide can make all the difference in your trip, so consider that aspect when choosing an agency.

If you are with an agency that does not wire the orphanage donation in advance, one of your first stops with a guide will probably be the bank. My agency travel representative likes to say that banking is more of a contact sport in China, and I've heard many families agree. Allow extra time at the bank for long lines or trouble if some of your bills are rejected. If you do not want or need to exchange all of your money at the bank, you can change it at your hotel. This will be a much easier process, but there is limit on how much you can exchange, often $200-$400. This is usually plenty for your daily spending, so a stop at the desk in the morning to exchange money before you head out for the day will be sufficient for most families.

Your time in-province can be challenging because your child will be going through the grieving process. You may or may not be given the opportunity to visit your child's orphanage or foster family. This will usually involve an extra fee, but it is an opportunity that you should take advantage of if at all possible. Parents almost universally agree that their child experienced closure by having the opportunity to visit one last time. However, you should make the best decision you can based on your individual child and how you feel they are adjusting. If you decide not to visit with your child, you could have one parent make the trip so you will have photos or video to share with your child when they are older. Be prepared that your child might not be the only one emotionally affected by the orphanage visit. Knowing that you are visiting an orphanage that will be full of children is completely different from the reality. Few parents are unaffected by the sight of so many children in care there, even if the orphanage is one which provides loving care for all of the children who live there. The sight of so many children and the realization that this is only one orphanage in one province in

241

China can be overwhelming. You will be haunted by those who are left behind.

Gifts for officials

Your agency will request that you bring along gifts to distribute on adoption day to various officials and orphanage personnel. This causes parents considerable stress, but please don't worry too much about it. Giving small gifts is customary in China for such occasions, much as you might bring along a bottle of wine or food to share if you visit a friend's house. It is considered rude to open the gifts in front of the giver, so more than likely they will be collected on a table. Officials probably won't know which gift came from you! Choose gifts that are easy to pack (consider the melting factor before buying chocolates) and which are American made. Tuck the gifts into red gifts bags. In China, red is the color for good luck while white signifies death as it is the color worn for mourning. For cultural reasons, it is best to avoid gifts which have the number four or clocks, both of which have death associations.

Gift ideas for officials:
- Postcards, specialties from your town/state

- Small lotions, lip balm, hand sanitizers

- Small cosmetics such as lipstick or mascara

- Tea towels or scarves

- Vitamins

- American stamps commemorating Chinese New Year

- Small bottles of liquor

- Chocolates are not considered as tasty to the Chinese palate, but hard candies or jelly beans are a good choice.

- It is better to give a small item with a recognizable American brand name than to give a larger amount of a generic brand which will come across as cheap. This is true of cosmetics and candy.

- If you are choosing a scented item, such as a lotion, flower scents are usually preferred to food scents like vanilla.

Additionally, if you have the opportunity to meet your child's foster parents, you might want to consider giving them a special gift. Many people make a photo book that includes pictures of their child for the foster parents to keep. Lockets or picture necklaces are also a popular choice. Often, parents will include their e-mail address with the gift in case the foster parents want to stay in contact with the child; officially exchanging contact information is discouraged.

You will probably have the opportunity to do some sightseeing in your child's province while you are waiting for their passport to be prepared. Try to remember to record this time and ask questions about the area so you can tell your child about the part of China they are from. Take pictures of the city and especially of the orphanage if you visit. Try to find out what the local specialties are and purchase some souvenirs. In the home province of one of our sons, we purchased a glass bead necklace made in his hometown, as well as some stones and tea native to his province.

Hotel accommodations

When you check in to your hotel in China, you will be staying in 4- or 5-star accommodations meeting the same standards you would expect in America. They will have some English-speaking staff and offer a variety of services, such as a business center, currency exchange, exercise room, and swimming pool. One amusing feature of hotels catering to both eastern and western clients can be found in the elevator. Floors with numbers considered superstitious by either culture are often eliminated, which can add up to quite a few missing floors! Many families utilize hotel point systems or an affiliated credit card to pay for some or all of their stay. Some agencies will require you to stay in particular hotels, so check your agency requirements before signing up for any deals.

One of the most frequent complaints about Chinese hotels is that the beds are hard. Hard mattresses are considered healthier, so those are the norm. Hotels which cater to foreign travelers are more likely to have softer mattresses. China uses a different bed size terminology, which is often confusing when people are choosing their room options. A standard room will have two "twin" beds, but the Chinese twin bed measures closer to an American full size bed at around 47 x 76 inches. Two adults can fit in a Chinese twin bed, although it might be a bit cramped depending on their size. A suite with a king-sized bed will be the same as an American king-size.

Most hotels will limit standard rooms to three adults with two children counting as one adult. This means that if two parents travel with a child to adopt another, they can all fit in one standard room. If Grandma comes too, you might have a problem. Children are considered an adult at age twelve so if you bring two teenagers that would considered four adults. However, there is flexibility in these regulations. Sometimes the hotel will allow an extra person if you pay a small daily fee for a rollaway bed. I've heard of many families who managed to squeeze five or six people into a room either because the hotel didn't care or because they were intentionally vague on the party number when booking the room.

If you are traveling with a large group and need two rooms, many hotels offer adjoining rooms. This might not be available in-province or the hotel may have a limited number of adjoining rooms. Sometimes, the adjoining rooms are two standard rooms with a doorway connecting them. Other times, it is a standard room with a king suite. A suite will sometimes have the living room area as a separate room with walls and other times it will divided from the bedroom by a screen or large television. We traveled with four adults (one was a twelve year old) and three children to adopt a fourth child. In Guangzhou we stayed in a very nice suite which had a standard room, a king suite, and a living room with a half bath bringing us up to two and a half baths total. On our second adoption trip, we choose a king suite to have more room and our seven-year-old slept on the couch with extra blankets we requested from housekeeping.

Many hotels will offer an "executive" option where you may have a more spacious room or access to additional food or drinks. Some people feel it is worth the upgrade to not have to run to a local store to buy drinking water and snacks. If you spend most of your time in the hotel because your child is sick or the weather is poor, this could be a very good investment. You can often upgrade on arrival if you are unsure about it beforehand. We did not do the executive upgrade and were happy with our decision. We enjoyed getting out and exploring every day, found it easy to buy water, and liked to eat at local restaurants. It is certainly far cheaper to eat at local restaurants outside of the hotel.

One feature not offered by hotels in China is on-site laundry facilities. While some families have solved this problem by packing two weeks' worth of outfits for every member of the family, that would make hauling your luggage around quite an ordeal. You can have the hotel launder items, but this is usually an expensive service. Your guide can recommend local laundry facilities. Another option is to hand wash items in the sink. You can bring individual packets of detergent or use a laundry bar of soap. Some hotels will have a retractable clothesline over the bathtub. If you plan to hand wash clothing, plan ahead to items that will air dry easily.

All adoptive families will spend a week in Guangzhou, and some will spend all of their time there if they are adopting from the Guangdong province. Here are four hotels in Guangzhou which are favorites with adoptive families:

<u>The Garden</u>: This hotel has contracts with several large agencies, so many adoptive families will stay here. People love that there is a wide variety of food (especially western food) and shopping options close to the hotel. There is also a lovely garden area with a koi pond inside the hotel and a nice swimming pool. A western medical clinic is located within the hotel. The Garden offers apartments with a washer and dryer, which are a good option for those traveling with a larger party. Be aware that the apartments are in an older part of the building and the condition is not as good as the main part of the hotel. The Guangzhou Pengman Apartment right next door to the Garden offers an additional apartment alternative.

<u>The China Hotel (Marriott)</u>: This is the other hotel with several large agency contracts. People feel that there are fewer Western food options here, although the China Hotel does feature a Starbucks within the hotel and a McDonald's next door. A 7-11 convenience store is also next door to the hotel, making water and snack runs very easy. There is both a playground and outdoor swimming pool. While shopping options are more limited, the China Hotel is located next to two large parks in Guangzhou, which can be accessed through the subway tunnel underpass right next to the hotel. The Marriott credit card point bonus can give you a week's stay for free if you sign up during an 80,000 point promotion, making it a very popular choice for parents. The executive upgrade features food and drinks, including alcoholic beverages, available during certain hours in

the executive lounge in addition to the breakfast buffet. However, these benefits are limited to two people per room. Children under four eat free.

The Holiday Inn Shifu: This hotel does not have large agency contracts, so you might not run into any other adoptive families during your stay there. However, it is a popular choice for families who are looking for a budget friendly hotel option and are with an agency that allows you to choose your own hotel. The Shifu is attached to a mall on one side and an open air market on the other, so you have plenty of food and shopping options. The accommodations are standard Holiday Inn level but the hotel does have a pool and an executive floor option for access to free drinks and snacks. The Shifu is a ten minute walk to Shamian Island. Families report they had no trouble catching a cab for the medical exam and consulate appointment.

The Victory: Back in the heyday of China adoption, all families stayed at the White Swan on Shamian Island. The White Swan has been closed for renovations for a few years and while it has recently reopened, it is geared more to business travel than adoptive families. Because both the US Consulate and the medical exam building have moved off the island, it is no longer the gathering place for adoptive families. Some still like to stay on the island, either out of nostalgia or because they appreciate the quiet atmosphere. The Victory has accommodations similar to the Holiday Inn Shifu. There is a swimming pool and indoor play area but no executive option. Shopping and restaurant options are a little more limited on the island. The West building was more recently renovated.

Money saving tips: Utilize your frequent customer points or a credit card affiliation to earn a few nights free. When deciding how many people to bring on your trip, remember that tipping over into needing two hotel rooms will add significantly to your cost. Skipping room upgrades and executive options is an easy way to keep costs low.

A guide to hotel terms including bed measurements-
http://www.travelchinaguide.com/essential/terms-hotel.htm

Food

Are you concerned about spending two weeks in China because you don't actually like Chinese food? Don't worry! First of all, the hotels you will stay in will feature an extravagant breakfast buffet. My son said it should be called "food fantasy" and ate two or three plates every morning. They have Chinese favorites like congee (a savory rice porridge that will be a comfort food to your new child), steamed buns, and noodles, but also American favorites like bacon and eggs. Most families find they are so stuffed after breakfast that they only need a light afternoon snack instead of lunch. Families who choose the upgraded executive option at a hotel often make use of the free snacks offered in the lounge. Be aware that if you are redeeming points to pay for your hotel stay, breakfast is rarely included and will often cost around $20 per person if you choose to add it.

Western food is readily available in China, with fast food chains such as McDonald's, Pizza Hut, Starbucks, and KFC appearing in all major cities. You might not have as many options available while you are in-province but you should be able to make it through most of the trip just fine. People with food allergies and sensitivities will have a more difficult time finding food that meets their dietary restrictions. Ask your guide to write the characters for Western palate friendly food recommendations or any dietary restrictions on a card that you can carry along when you are eating without your guide. The characters for "take out" will also come in handy.

Avoiding getting sick from what you eat or drink is a major concern for traveling families. It is important to remember that tap water is not safe to drink in China. Use bottled water even when making food or drinks using the hot pot in your room, because the tap water has a high lead content, so even boiling it will not make it safer to drink. In restaurants avoid drinks with ice because it could have been made with tap water. In general you should avoid fruits that cannot be peeled. Food served in your hotel should always be safe to eat. Use your judgment when deciding whether or not to eat from street vendors.

Many families pack extra food. One woman I spoke with said they packed an entire suitcase of food! We packed light, but you will definitely want to pack at least some snacks for times when you are traveling or are too exhausted to go out and get food. Anything you can think of that travels well and can be eaten straight out of the packet or prepared with boiling water will do. An electric kettle will be provided in the room. I also packed some of those disposable plastic red Solo bowls and a ziplock with plastic forks, spoons, and knives. This was really helpful for when we had takeout in the room, and you can take plastic forks along when you eat out for kids who are too young to eat with chopsticks. They're handy for adults who have trouble with chopsticks, too!

Eating the local cuisine will definitely save you a lot of money because it is much cheaper than eating at the western food places like KFC or Pizza Hut. Our meals out for eight people cost between $12 and $20. A good portion of that cost was for soda since we couldn't drink the water and we didn't care for Chinese tea. If you don't like Asian food, you will need to budget more for food each day. Eating at the hotel will obviously be more expensive than wandering out on the streets to find local restaurants. I will leave you with the cardinal rule for trying new foods when you are in a foreign country--if you like what you're eating DON'T ask what it is! In fact, I find that the picture menus are better than the ones with dual Chinese/English. It's just better not to know.

Guangzhou

By the time you reach Guangzhou, the novelty of being in China has worn off and most families are starting to be ready to head back home. If you are staying at one of the hotels which has many other adoptive families, you will probably enjoy socializing with the other families and hearing how their time in-province went. Most agencies will arrange a second round of touring to see the sights in Guangzhou while you are waiting for your consulate appointment and your child's visa. Here are some of the most popular attractions:

Shamian Island used to be the center of the Chinese adoption process for Americans. The consulate and medical exam center were located on the island, so parents all stayed at the White Swan hotel, spending the majority of their time in one location. Now the process has moved off the island, but many parents still like to visit for nostalgic reasons. The island is a quiet retreat from busy urban China and the Spanish colonial architecture brings a European feel. There are many small shops, often operated by Chinese Christians as well as a church offering a Sunday worship service. Taking pictures of your children by the many bronze statues on the island is an adoptive family tradition.

Pearl River Cruise is an evening excursion down the Pearl River where you can admire the lights and unique architecture of the city. Most agencies will arrange this outing and you should be aware that the food provided appeals to the adventurous. One agency orders pizza for their families to take along!

Chimelong Safari Park is usually referred to as the zoo by parents but the Guangzhou zoo is a separate attraction. The safari park is easy to reach by subway. Taking the safari ride and feeding the giraffes are usually family favorites.

Canton Tower is the tallest TV tower in the world. For a fee, you can go to the observation deck at the top. For an additional fee, you can ride in the bubble cars that go around the edge.

Chen Family Academy, or the Chen Clan Ancestral Hall, was built at the end of the 19th century as an academy to prepare members of the Chen clan to take the imperial exams. It is now a folk art museum which is a great place to buy souvenirs like custom calligraphy or handmade traditional instruments.

Traveling home

Returning to the United States is a long, exhausting process. For many families, it will begin with a ride to Hong Kong, but regardless of the route it will be a long trip. Many families find the flight home to be challenging. I wish I could give you some great tips but honestly, you should get through it whatever way you can! Many parents celebrate the moment the airplane touches down on American soil as the moment their child became a US citizen. It's fine if you want to do that, because it's a wonderful moment. However, as this information is passed around so often, I would like to point out that it is not technically true.

Because China is a Hague country, the visa your child receives in Guangzhou is an IH-3 category visa. That means your adoption was finalized in China and your child receives automatic citizenship upon admission to the United States. It will be quite a while after the plane touches down before you are admitted to the United States. First, you will need to be processed through the US Customs and Border Protection. For this reason, even though you are exhausted, it is important to remember to be polite to the officer. You were given a brown envelope at the US Consulate and ordered not to open it or allow it to be damaged in any way. If you succeeded in this quest, you hand that packet over to the officer. The officer will process the documents and then send them on to USCIS so that the Certificate of Citizenship will be issued. When you leave the CBP inspection area there will be lots of signs announcing that you are now entering the United States of America. Until this time, you have been in a no man's land, but once you step past it your child will now truly be an American citizen.

17

Together at Last

After all of these months of hard work, you are finally going to meet your child! There is no moment more exciting or nerve-wracking. You have been dreaming of this moment for a long time, maybe for years. Yet you will be surprised to find how quickly everything you thought you knew flies out of your mind. You are now far from the time that you did all of that reading for your adoption education requirement and in the excitement of the moment you probably won't remember even the things you reminded yourself about right before your child came through the door. This chapter is here to be a reference for you in those early days and weeks when things are crazy.

While a few family day meetings take place at the orphanage or your hotel, most will take place at the civil affairs office of the provincial capital. Take some time to make sure you have everything you need. Your agency will have provided a list of all the paperwork you need to take and your guide will remind you about it. You will probably have some gifts to give the officials. Figure out who will be taking pictures or recording video. Often more than one family will be there and they take turns taking video and photos for each other. Most parents take a small backpack with age appropriate items for the child. In addition, most parents will have the opportunity to ask questions about their child's background, development, and habits. It can be difficult to remember what questions you wanted to ask once you are there, so have a list ready to refer to. Try to remember to not make negative comments about the condition your child is in or change them out of the clothing they until you are in the privacy of your hotel room. Be polite and convey nothing but gratitude for the care your child was given regardless of what your private thoughts on the subject might be.

When your child meets you for the first time, it will be a stark reminder that while you have been dreaming of this moment, the feeling is not mutual. A few children will be well-prepared for the first meeting but for most children, especially young ones, it is nothing but extremely frightening. Expect the child to cry or withdraw. Even if you are adopting an older child, he might ignore you or try to hide as a way of coping with the intense emotions he is feeling. In an ideal China program, you would have spent two days visiting your child at their orphanage rather than visiting tourist sites. As that is not an option, you will have to do the best you can to ease your child's fears.

It is best if you do not rush to grab your child, but rather wait until he is ready to come to you. The Chinese theory seems to be that it is best to get the handover out of the way as soon as possible. You may find that the caregiver all but tosses your child into your arms. Try to put him down and crouch down to his level. Speak to him in a soft, reassuring voice. From your backpack of distractions, get a sucker to offer if you are adopting a small child. The sweetness and sucking will help to calm the distress he is feeling. You might offer gum to an older child because the chewing is relaxing. Bring a water bottle or bottle of formula if you are adopting a very young child, because they could be dehydrated. The anxiety is activating the fight-or-flight response in your child's brain, so you need to use the tools you have to counteract that.

Distract your child by looking through what you have packed in the backpack for her. A favorite for toddlers would be bubbles. The pretty bubbles are mesmerizing, and if she is able to blow the bubbles herself, the blowing action is another calming distraction. A sensory toy like a squishy ball or one that has little plastic nubs all over it can be fun. Roll the ball back and forth or encourage her to squish it. If you sent a photo album to your orphanage, they might have brought it to return to you. You can look through the photos with your child, pointing yourselves out and talking about the other pictures in a soothing voice. Be sure to learn at least a phrase or two in Chinese so you can greet your child in her own language.

Most people do not have a lot of time to play with their child and calm him down on family day. Very soon, your guide will pull you away to complete paperwork. You might be given the opportunity to ask questions and instructed to give the gifts you brought. Your first family picture will be taken to be placed on the adoption decree. Sooner than you thought, you will be whisked back out of the civil affairs office and into the van. Probably you will be surprised to hear that you aren't going back to the hotel but on a shopping trip! This doesn't hold true for all families, but this seems to be the most common schedule. Your guide will help you buy formula (you remembered to ask what kind they use at the orphanage, right?), diapers, and clothing if the child is a different size from what you brought.

Getting to know your child

Finally, you will return to the hotel and have time for all of those bonding activities that I mentioned earlier. Many people choose to change their child into new clothing at this point, using the opportunity to give him a cursory physical exam. Your child might be extremely distressed by this. Remember that his clothing is the only familiar thing he has. It smells like home, while you and the hotel smell strange, very strange. If your child is upset by being changed, let him continue to wear the same clothing for a few days. There is really no harm in it. Or you could only change one item at a time. I have heard of so many children who go to sleep the first few days clutching their shoes.

If you are able to change his clothing be sure to seal it up in a large Ziploc bag to keep, even if it is in poor condition. Your child has very little information or belongings from his early life, so it is important to preserve anything you are able to.

Besides being slow to change clothing, you should also be aware that bathing could be scary for your child. Now, I completely understand the impulse to get them straight in the tub. So many of these kids were carsick on their long trip to the provincial capital. They come dressed in many layers and they're really sweaty underneath. Maybe they weren't wearing a diaper because they're mostly potty trained, but no one took them for a long time and they wet themselves when they were so upset. However, your child is not likely to be used to taking an immersion bath in a tub. Few children in orphanages will be bathed on a daily basis. Bathing is often done on an as-needed basis during cold months because of the poor heating. In orphanages and foster homes alike, bathing is usually a quick wipe down with a cloth while the child stands or sits in a basin. Keep this in mind if your child seems scared of a full bathtub and give her some time to adjust.

Often, children will come with parasites and common orphanage obtained medical conditions like lice, scabies, or giardia. Hepatitis B is also fairly widespread in China and the testing reports in your child's file may not be accurate. It is best to use rubber gloves for diaper changes to avoid spreading parasites and use the universal precautions until your child has been retested at home. Children also frequently have ear infections, bronchitis, or pneumonia especially if you adopt during the winter. Your guide can help you obtain any needed medication or medical care that your child might need. If you used an international adoption clinic for a file review, you probably were provided with prescriptions from them for travel, and they will be available for consultation while you are in-country.

Many parents are shocked and anxious over either their child's behavior or physical condition. It is so important to remember that what you see in your child now is the worst it will ever be! When you take your child home, she will receive plenty of nutritious food. She will get proper medical care and receive needed therapies. Most importantly, she will receive the love and attention that only a family can give. Try not to read too much into your child's behavior during the first few days. Most children are prepared very little for adoption. Each child will react differently to being taken from everything they know and given to strangers. Some will shut down completely, not making eye contact or speaking. Others will act out aggressively or seem almost manic, particularly for older children who are overwhelmed by all the new experiences. A child might try to sooth herself through repetitive behaviors. One of our sons licked his hand and then rubbed his nose with it, repeating the process over and over to the extent that he twice caused a nosebleed. Within two weeks, this self-soothing behavior had stopped. Children will often regress in behaviors—not walking, talking, or toileting although you were told they could do these things. Consider how much you are freaking out inside and multiply that by one hundred for an idea of what your child is feeling. Be patient and give it time.

It is very common for your child to prefer one parent over the other. Most often she will prefer the father over the mother, but no one is really sure why. The most common theory is because the caregivers are primarily women in orphanages. In our first adoption, our son attached quickly to my husband, and it seemed clear he viewed me as a nanny. It took seven weeks before he accepted me and for some children the preference will last for months. Although you may understand this phenomenon intellectually, it doesn't make experiencing it as a reality any easier. Even a baby will give positive feedback to her mother through smiles or showing that she enjoys physical affection.

When I changed my son's diaper, he would look off to the side avoiding eye contact as I smiled at him. When I finish a diaper change, I always stand my child up and give them a hug. During this time, he would stiffen in my arms, not melt into me as my biological children would do. It is the absence of all those little signs of love which can cause such difficulty for the unfavored parent while the favored parent struggles with the burden of never getting a break from the new child.

If you are the unfavored parent, but even if your child does take to you quickly, you might also be struggling with your own feelings of attachment. Mountains of adoption materials have been written about the importance of the child attaching to their parents but parents need to attach to the child as well. When you dreamed of this child for months and spent hours studying her picture, you built up a fantasy child. You are now being confronted with a very real child who is not the child you expected. Probably, you expected an instant connection, an instant realization that she was your baby, as you felt when you saw her photo. Instead, it might feel a lot like you are babysitting a random Chinese kid. This doesn't happen for everyone, but it happens much more frequently than you hear. If you already have biological children, it is more common to have this feeling than if you are a new parent. Try not to compare the post-birth bonding you felt with a biological child to the experience of bonding with your adopted child. What you need to do is fake it until you feel it. The good news is that all of the activities that promote attachment for children will work both ways. As you nurture your child, make eye contact, snuggle, it will help you to begin to develop a bond with your child.

Over the first few days, keep soothing and reassuring your child. Treat him as if he were younger than his age. Hold him to give him a bottle, even if he is three or four. You could also use a sippy cup with a straw for an older child because of the sucking motion involved. Instead of an evening bath at bedtime, give him a massage with lotion to promote touch. Keep things light and playful by playing games such as peek-a-boo to encourage him to make eye contact. Roll a ball back and forth, blow bubbles, squish play dough. If your hotel has a pool, swimming is a great bonding activity because your child will depend on you to hold him while you are in the water.

Food is a big element in bonding. Most children in China are hand fed until they are school-aged so your child will probably be expecting you to feed her. Many children will have experienced malnourishment or food deprivation. You should be prepared for gorging or hoarding food. The hotel breakfast buffet will have both Chinese and American/European food, so you can use that to provide your child with comfort foods, like congee or steamed buns. It's also a great way to introduce her to foods you eat at home. If your child is very distressed by all of the changes, you might want to keep familiar foods like noodles or Chinese snacks in your hotel room. Many American families do not like eating Chinese food in China and eat out at western restaurants every day. Consider that your child is in the same situation, in reverse, and be considerate of how difficult it can be for some of them to be presented with all new food at the same time that so much else is changing in their lives.

Along the same lines, you shouldn't break out the English flashcards on your first evening together. Most children will pick up English very quickly without any special effort on your part, especially if you are adopting a younger child. What you should do is try your best to facilitate communication. You can do this by learning important phrases in Mandarin, or asking your guide to help you if your child speaks a dialect. Sign language is also an excellent tool. Learning even fifteen or twenty signs such as eat, drink, more, etc., will greatly help you and your child to communicate. Many parents like the Signing Time video series for learning signs. For an older child you can use a picture board so that your child can point to a picture to tell you what they need.

It is best to go by your child's cues to decide if you should stay close to the hotel room or if keeping him distracted by going out on sightseeing trips is the better course of action. To promote bonding, many parents use a carrier for children who are still small enough to fit in one. If your child is too heavy, you can rent a stroller at many hotels or ask your guide to help you purchase one. If you have the opportunity to visit your child's orphanage or foster family, you should seriously consider making that trip. Almost all families report that the visit gave their child closure and helped them in their grieving process, not to mention the opportunity to obtain photos to preserve a record of your child's early life.

Early days home

Returning home should feel like the happy ending to your adoption story but the reality is that it brings a whole new set of challenges, not the least of which is jet-lag. It is very difficult to know how to juggle returning to normal life with medical appointments and an unending flow of visitors. Few children will sleep normal hours right away because they have spent their entire life sleeping while you were awake. It is time to really focus on getting your new child attached to you and embedded into your life. This involves a process called "cocooning."

You probably learned about cocooning during your adoption education, but figuring out how to go about implementing it in a realistic way can be daunting. On one extreme, some families do not leave the house except for medical appointments and do not let anyone inside the door, including meal-bearing grandparents! On the other extreme, some families try to push normalcy too soon by dropping their child off at the church nursery, taking trips to visit relatives to introduce their new child, or jumping right back into the 120 activities of their children already home. At the base level, the parents should providing all of the care for the new child. This means you should stay home from work as long as possible so that you are the ones to feed her, change her, bathe her, and put her to bed--preferably in your bed or room.

It is understandable that your friends and relatives want to meet your new child. Try to have them stop by your house and limit their visit time. What is most important here is that you do not allow them to play "pass the baby", as if you have just given birth to a newborn. Limit physical affection and any caring for your child's personal needs by others. Explain that there will be time for that later, but for now she must learn that you are her parents. Optional outside activities should be limited for a time. You might need to take turns going to church or taking part in your children's extracurricular activities for a time. Use your child as a barometer and base your decisions off of how well you think she is doing.

Medical appointments are one thing that should not be delayed. If at all possible, schedule your child's first appointment to be within a week of when you arrive home. If you know that you will need additional specialist appointments because of your child's special need, schedule those as well. Some people are concerned that procedures like blood draws might interfere with bonding, but making sure your child doesn't have undisclosed conditions is more important. If there is an international adoption clinic in your area, that is the place to start. If you will be using your local pediatrician, make sure he or she knows which tests to run. See the additional resources section for a link to the AAP screening guidelines to provide for your doctor. While you are scheduling appointments don't neglect to add in a visit to the dentist. You do not need to schedule a cleaning, but make sure you at least have the opportunity for a dentist to take a peek into your child's mouth while she sits on your lap. Most children will need a lot of dental work. If your child will need work done under sedation, it can sometimes be scheduled in conjunction with other scheduled procedures.

Your pediatrician may want to re-vaccinate your child. You may wonder why this is when you were presented with a copy of his completed vaccination record on adoption day. Orphanages often split doses between children to make them go further. In addition, they are usually not kept at the proper temperature. Between the two factors, it is very likely that, although your child received vaccinations, he is not actually immune to any of the diseases. If you are hesitant to re-vaccinate then you can request the pediatrician check your child's titers. You will need to get a large amount of blood vials drawn after the initial visit anyway, so this will be easy to do. Sometimes, a modified vaccination schedule or a few booster shots are all that are necessary.

Many parents struggle with when to schedule surgeries that have a flexible timetable. Is it better to spend time bonding to build up trust before a surgery? Most parents find that surgery actually promotes bonding. Your child learns that you will always be there. They depend on you as you feed them and care for them during recovery. You will spend a lot of time snuggling in the rocking chair or bed. This is a common question, especially for parents adopting a child with cleft palate. Sometimes the doctor will want to delay the repair for six months or longer. However, this loses valuable time for speech development so if the only concern is the impact surgery might have on bonding, do not let cause you to defer your child's medical needs.

One surgery you might be considering is circumcision. America is one of the few countries where circumcision is still routinely practiced, so your Chinese son will come to you uncircumcised. This is a very controversial topic--you might want to be really sure you would like everyone's opinion before you ask about it online. If you are adopting an older boy, you should give serious consideration to leaving him intact and educating yourself on routine hygiene for the intact penis. If you are bringing home a young son, this more clearly falls under the category of personal decisions made by parents. Your pediatrician will most likely refer you to a urologist for the procedure since your child is not a newborn. The procedure will require sedation, so most parents prefer to schedule the circumcision in conjunction with another procedure if your child has multiple procedures planned. If your son has a urological special need, he might require a circumcision as part of the correction of his medical condition.

Many children struggle with being introduced to household pets. Even if your child was in foster care rather than in an orphanage, keeping dogs or cats as indoor pets is not the norm in China. If your pets are being kept at a kennel during your trip to China, you might want to pick them up your second day home rather than the first to give your child a day to explore the house without pets. You will most likely need to give your child a slow introduction to your pet. This might mean keeping them outdoors for a time if your house can accommodate that, or having the pet spend more time in a crate if the pet is used to that. Many people use baby gates to contain dogs to one area. Some children will warm up to the pets quickly, while others might take months. Our first adopted son fell in the latter camp. Even six months after coming home, he would climb up onto the couch to feel safe if our two dogs were in the room. It was about a year before he felt completely comfortable with them nearby. Our second adopted son, on the other hand, was only hesitant about the dogs for a day or two before he decided they were great fun.

The early weeks home can be intense, and you might be caught off guard by the emotions you are feeling. There is such a thing as post-adoption depression. You have just spent at least the past year of your life focused on the goal of bringing this child home. It might be that your child is having a tough transition or that you are realizing your child doesn't quite match the ideal child you had in your mind. Maybe you are exhausted by your child's medical needs. There does not need to be a catalyst, you can be having the most perfect adoption experience possible and still experience depression. Don't be afraid to seek help if your feelings become overwhelming.

In these early days, please don't forget the resource of your social worker. She is the one who knows your family well, and she will be a wealth of experience on the problems adoptive families can encounter. The one month post placement visit is no longer required by China (although it is required by many placing agencies), but it is a good idea to keep checking in with your social worker on a regular basis in the early weeks. It is easier to head off problems before they become rooted and more difficult to overcome. Online support can be important as well, giving you a community of friends who understand what you are going through better than anyone else. And you don't even have to leave the house to get the support you need from them!

Final paperwork

The first thing you will need to do when you return home is have your child enrolled in your health insurance plan so you can pay for all of the medical visits you have scheduled. The Omnibus Budget Reconciliation Act of 1993 (OBRA93), Public Law 103-66 mandates that your adopted child must receive full health care coverage by all group plan insurers. They cannot decline to cover your child because of pre-existing medical conditions. Your coverage should begin the day your child was placed in your family, even though in China the adoption is typically not finalized until the following day. Your employer will probably need to see the adoption decree (in a red vinyl folder) and your child's Chinese birth certificate, which was given to you on adoption day (in a white paper folder). Your child's coverage should not be delayed until a Social Security number is issued. If you encounter difficulties, consult your placing or home study agency for assistance.

When you returned home, your child's adoption paperwork was processed in the airport. At some point, the **Certificate of Citizenship** will show up in the mail. This often takes eight to twelve weeks so do not be concerned when it takes a while. You can send an inquiry if it has been longer than fifty days since your entry into the US, but it does routinely take longer.

USCIS page with contact information for Certificate of Citizenship
http://www.uscis.gov/adoption/bringing-your-internationally-adopted-child-united-states/certificate-citizenship-your-internationally-adopted-child

Form N-565 to request a replacement Certificate of Citizenship
http://www.uscis.gov/n-565

If you checked the box on your paperwork indicating that you would like to be mailed a **Social Security card** for your child, you might have a similarly long wait. Few people who check the box will ever receive the Social Security card. If you do receive a card, it will probably have your child's Chinese name on it, so you will still need to make a trip down to the Social Security office to request a new one with the correct name. After you receive your child's Certificate of Citizenship, you can apply for the Social Security number. You will need to take the Certificate of Citizenship, adoption decree, and the Chinese birth certificate you received on adoption day down to your local Social Security office. I would suggest printing off the requirements from the Social Security website, because many parents have had trouble with their local office not being knowledgeable about the requirements.

<u>Social Security website</u> on getting a Social Security number for an internationally adopted child
https://www.socialsecurity.gov/people/immigrants/children.html

Many parents chose to apply for a **passport** for their newly adopted child. A passport can serve as secondary proof of citizenship if you have lost the Certificate of Citizenship or do not care to take it somewhere to show as proof. You can apply for a passport before the Certificate of Citizenship arrives. To do so, you will need to provide a certified copy of the adoption decree, the child's Chinese passport with immigrant visa, and proof that the child is residing with you in the US. As with the Social Security office, I suggest you print off the requirements and take them along. The postal employee who took our son's passport application kept trying to give us back documents, saying they weren't necessary for our son's "green card." We insisted he include them anyway and did receive an official passport in return. Yes, you do have to mail your precious original documents. They will be returned separately from the new passport, so do not panic when the passport shows up without the supporting documents.

Information on obtaining a passport is found on this <u>State Department page on the US Child Citizenship Act of 2000</u>.
http://travel.state.gov/content/travel/en/legal-considerations/us-citizenship-laws-policies/child-citizenship-act.html

Tax time brings a new round of questions for adoptive parents. The tax code can be somewhat confusing on the issue of adoption so programs like Turbo Tax and even your local CPA can be unclear. To the best of my knowledge, if your new adopted child resided less than half of the year with you then you cannot claim the child tax credit although you can claim them as a dependent for the year. This is different than if you had given birth to the child, although they are not supposed to be treated differently by law. However, other parents report being advised that as long as no one else in the US is claiming the child as a dependent during that time period, the child can be claimed as a dependent. My advice would be to check with the IRS directly rather than relying on what I tell you or asking other parents what they have done. The adoption tax credit can be claimed in the year in which the adoption is finalized. If you are in the middle of an adoption when you file taxes, you cannot claim the expenses until the following year.

Here is the IRS website on the adoption tax credit
https://www.irs.gov/taxtopics/tc607.html

Finally, many parents choose to **re-adopt** within their state. Although this should not be necessary after the passage of the US Child Citizenship Act of 2000, it does provide an additional validation of the adoption for your child. The requirements for re-adoption vary by state and not all states have a re-adoption process. Re-adoption is sometimes required to receive a state issued birth certificate for your child. Some states issue a Certificate of Foreign Birth instead. Either document would function as a birth certificate for you child for purposes of school enrollment or any other situation that calls for a birth certificate. It is much easier to obtain additional copies of state issued birth certificates than to receive additional copies or replace a lost copy of the Chinese birth certificate. It is best to consult your home study agency on what the process is in your particular state, but the website below gives a state by state summary.

State Recognition of Intercountry Adoptions Finalized Abroad on childwelfare.gov https://www.childwelfare.gov/pubPDFs/intercountry.pdf

Choosing to give back

For many families, once their child is home they find that they have a new interest in helping children who are still in state care. Some parents become active adoption advocates. Others found charities or become active members of charities that have a connection to their child. Sometimes the goal becomes family preservation, which is identifying families in crisis and getting them the help they need before turning to child abandonment out of desperation. If you find yourself asking how your family can do more, here are a few organizations that have family preservation programs in China to get you started.

Love Without Boundaries- Providing medical care, education, and foster care to orphans in China. LWB's Unity Fund provides funding necessary for medical care to families in crisis.
https://www.lovewithoutboundaries.com/programs/

One Sky- Originally founded as Half the Sky, this organization improves institutional care through training nannies and founding nurturing and educational programs within Chinese orphanages. The name was recently changed to One Sky when they began programs focusing on the "left behind" children of migrant workers.
http://halfthesky.org/en

Morning Star Foundation- This charity provides funding for heart surgeries for orphans in China and Uganda. In addition, their Love Project promotes family preservation through funding heart surgeries for families in medical crisis.
http://morningstarproject.org/

Holt International- While Holt is familiar to most as an adoption agency, their primary focus is humanitarian aid. Holt has child sponsorship programs in China enabling you to sponsor a child in a family in crisis—usually a single parent or grandparent-as-parent home. The sponsorship provides the child's educational expenses, allowing the child to stay in school.
https://holtsponsor.org:4443/sponsor/holt.writepage?page=pho tolisting5

Additional Resources

Love Without Boundaries' Realistic Expectations blog series
https://www.lovewithoutboundaries.com/adoption/realistic-expectations/

Purvis, Karyn B. The Connected Child. New York: McGraw-Hill Education, 2007.
The videos on Karyn Purvis' website are another great resource
http://empoweredtoconnect.org/content-types/video/

Gray, Deborah D. Attaching Through Love, Hugs, and Play. Philadelphia: Jessica Kingsley Publishers, 2014.

Quick reference of Chinese words and phrases with audio for adoptive parents
http://people.wku.edu/haiwang.yuan/AudioChinese/parent.htm l

Rowell, Katie. Love Me, Feed Me: The Adoptive Parent's Guide to Ending the Worry About Weight, Picky Eating, Power Struggles and More. Family Feeding Dynamics LLC, 2012.

Creating A Family radio show: Feeding Issues and Nutrition in Adoption
https://creatingafamily.org/adoption-category/feeding-issues-and-nutrition-in-adoption/

American Academy of Pediatrics screening guidelines for internationally adopted children
http://www2.aap.org/sections/adoption/PDF/InternationalAdoption.pdf

Creating A Family's resources on Transitioning Home After Adoption
https://creatingafamily.org/adoption/resources/transitioning-home-adoption/

Post-Adoption Panic, essay by Melissa Fay Greene
https://www.adoptivefamilies.com/adoption-bonding-home/post-adoption-depression/

The Elusive "Happily Ever After": Post Adoption Depression - Creating A Family
https://creatingafamily.org/adoption-category/when-you-cant-find-the-happily-ever-after-in-adoption/

18

Handling Comments About Your Family

One of the more challenging aspects of international adoption is that your family will visibly not match. Sometimes, you might feel a bit like a public spectacle as people turn and look when you walk into a restaurant or down the aisle in the grocery store, especially if you do not live in an area with a lot of racial diversity. When you decided to adopt you probably only thought of adding a child to your family. You might now realize that you aren't prepared for the sheer amount of comments people will direct at you. You are now an ambassador for adoption, whether you intended to become one or not. More importantly, you should be keenly aware that the little ears next to you are listening to your responses. Your child will internalize what you say as well as take their cues from you when they begin to respond to questions directed toward themselves as they grow older.

The most common comment you will receive by far is praise for what a good thing you have done. You will hear "It is so good of you to do that" or "I could never love a child that wasn't my own" or "She's so lucky!" The Chinese you encounter will inevitably say "You must have a good heart to do this." Most parents find it easiest to deflect this praise by commenting "We're lucky to have her" or "We're so happy that she's in our family." This does not bog you down in a long discussion about your motivations for adopting. At the same time, your child will not hear you agreeing that she was lucky (to lose her first family and homeland?) or that she should feel grateful to be in your family. Instead, you are grateful for the opportunity to be her parent.

Most people will make comments out of curiosity, and because they don't know much about adoption they will say things you might find offensive. It can be difficult to be patient if you receive many comments but it is important to remember that it never hurts to be polite. Frequently, it will turn out that the person who asked you a question or made a comment is asking because they are considering adoption. I have a confession to make--I have read so many adoptive parents ranting about stupid comments that I am extremely paranoid about being unintentionally offensive. I'm sorry to say that I never speak to someone I think is probably an adoptive parent. I mean, that woman with an Asian boy in her shopping cart, maybe her husband is Asian. I'm only assuming he's adopted. I once sat for five minutes in a doctor's office waiting room watching my son play with another little Asian boy who had two white parents. He looked Korean and I almost asked if he was, thinking we could chat about the differences between the two programs. But then I was suddenly worried that they might be offended that I thought he looked Korean. Or what if he was adopted domestically? Better to keep my mouth shut. I've missed a lot of opportunities to make more adoptive parent friends due to this problem of mine. So while many parents love to come up with withering sarcastic comments for stupid or offensive questions, that's not my personal style. Remember that you always have a choice as to how to respond to annoying comments. You can choose to be offended, to educate, or to laugh it off. However you respond, remember that your child is the most important audience. How you respond will be formative as to how they handle comments and questions they will have to handle for the rest of their life.

If you are at a loss as to how to respond to comments or questions, remember that you have no obligation to answer. You can say "That's personal" or "I prefer not to share personal information like that." Miss Manner's all purpose "Why do you ask?" is suitable for any occasion. If someone makes a rude comment, you can simply observe "What a rude thing to say!" or remain silent, allowing them to draw their own conclusions about the appropriateness of what they have said. The Center for Adoption Support and Education publishes the W.I.S.E. Up Power Book which is intended to teach adopted children how to respond to comments but their system is equally helpful for parents. Remember that you have the power to choose how to respond to comments. You can choose to Walk away, say It's private, Share information, or Educate others. There are appropriate times for each of those responses; it's up to you to decide which is best for the situation.

If you have adopted a child with a visible special need, you receive additional comments. The W.I.S.E. up options are helpful there too, but really most of your job will be rephrasing what they said using more positive language. "What's wrong with his ear?" "There's nothing wrong with it—it's just shaped differently. He was born that way. Is that what you were trying to ask?" While many adults will ask these questions, children are often more openly curious. You can try to help them to understand that people have limbs that are shaped differently or have ears that need a little extra help or need a cane to help them find their way because their eyes don't see as well. You can add that your child still likes to play just the same as they do. Sometimes, it's best to meet staring on the playground head-on by saying "Hi, her name is Lucy! Were you wanting to ask her to play? She really likes the slide."

Tackling the foster care question

If you adopt internationally, you will get asked why you didn't adopt from foster care. One time I was reading a newspaper article profiling an adoptive family and I noticed a particularly ignorant comment at the bottom (never read the comments!). I have preserved it exactly as it was written, in all its glory for you here:

there are THOUSANDS of children in the US of A that are in need of adoption... Yet this family paid $35k to adopt a child from a foreign country? This is what celebrities have done to America.. make it fashionable to adopt less fortunate children from other countries while drepriving children in the US of role models & a stable family... We need to take care of our OWN first! I dont' have a problem with a family going outside the US to adopt.. IF.. they don't claim the foreign child as a dependent & get a tax break from the govt that I pay my taxes to... When you do claim the foreign child as a dependent & get a tax break for it.. THEN it becomes MY business.. because MY tax dollars are then being used to support a child from another country when there are thousands of children in the US that need families or fostered...

I'm not offended by this, because I know the person who wrote this just has no idea about the realities of adoption. I know I had no idea about adoption before we started! This is a knee-jerk reaction that has no basis in reality. Because I know this is something that families hear all the time, I thought I would take some time to break down the issues involved in a family's choosing whether to adopt from foster care or internationally. Hopefully, you find some information in here that you can use when you respond to people who bring up similar points.

First, while I am no expert, I don't think you can claim a "foreign" child as a dependent. We couldn't claim our son until he was adopted, and after he was adopted he became a US citizen. He is now legally our child, no longer a foreigner but as American as any other citizen, and as such we can claim him as a dependent.

Second, your tax dollars are not being used to support children who are dependents. Getting any tax deduction means that the amount of your income which you pay taxes on is reduced. It means couples with a child pays less in taxes than those without. Why do we allow this sort of blatant discrimination? Because children are investments. They grow up to pay taxes and will support people like the ones who wrote the comment above when they retire. Hear that, buddy? My foreign child will grow up to pay for your retirement.

What about the adoption tax credit? Isn't that paying people to adopt foreign children? Nope. The adoption tax credit is also used to reduce your tax liability. It is not taking money from taxpayers and giving it to people so they adopt. It is used to reduce the amount of tax owed by people who adopt. So this commenter should be aware that his tax dollars are not subsidizing foreign adoptions. It is not a grant, like the Pell Grant, nor does it refund money to people who have no tax liability, like the Earned Income Tax Credit. But the people who adopt internationally do pay taxes, and their tax dollars support children in foster care and other social services supported by taxes. Even if an adoptive couple paid no federal taxes the year of their adoption they would still pay state and local taxes that year and the federal taxes in all the years that they didn't adopt.

So now our irate commenter might be thinking, "Okay, but that's still 20,000 more US kids who could have found families." The people who adopt internationally have made the decision that it was a better fit for their family than adopting from foster care. Perhaps some of them would have switched if they had more information on foster care but many of them had already eliminated adopting from foster care, and were actually deciding whether to adopt internationally or to not adopt at all. The person who wrote the comment was insulted that a couple used $35,000 and somehow deprived US kids. However, they could have spent that money on a car or vacation, and then no child

275

would have a found a family. Don't all children deserve a family, not just American ones?

Here are some common reasons which people give for eliminating adopting from foster care as a choice:

- They aren't eligible to adopt from foster care. The eligibility requirements can vary, but for larger families especially, state regulations regarding square footage or number of children in a bedroom can mean that they are not able to adopt from foster care but can adopt internationally. Military couples might find it too difficult to go through the process to become eligible to become foster parents, get a placement, and complete an adoption before they are moved to another state.

- They might have tried already. Many families try unsuccessfully to adopt through foster care for a few years and then turn to international adoption.

- They have had their hearts broken and they feel international adoption provides a certain outcome. Particularly for couples who come to adoption from infertility, they have endured the loss of control over their fertility and often have had many pregnancy losses. Some states require you foster children to be eligible to adopt, and they don't want to chance falling in love with a child and then having the child be reunited with their family of origin. Because the goal of foster care is family reunification.

- They don't want their children's hearts to be broken. Some couples feel that they couldn't bear the heartbreak of parenting a child for months or years and then lose the child to family reunification. For families who already have children in the home, not only do they want to spare themselves the pain of losing a child, they also want to shield their children from that loss and uncertainty.

- The age of children in foster care. Most people who adopt would prefer a young child. The median age of a child in foster care is eight and a half. I could not find the median age of children who are legally free to be adopted but when I searched waiting children at http://www.adoptuskids.org/ there were only twenty-two children under the age of four listed, and almost all had major medical needs. For comparison, there were over 2200 children listed between the ages of fourteen and eighteen, many of them in sibling groups. Although there is a great need for families for older children, few couples will wake up one day and decide to adopt teenage siblings.

- The perception that children from foster care are emotionally damaged. According to the American Academy of Child & Adolescent Psychology about 30% of children in foster care have severe emotional or behavioral problems. However, that means two-thirds of them do not. Many adoptive parents feel that they avoid a child with emotional problems by adopting internationally, although the reality is that children adopted from other countries can also have endured abuse, neglect, and trauma. Parents are becoming more educated about this, but this perception will play a part in many people rejecting foster care as an option.

- Couples with children might have fears that children from foster care would pose a danger to the children they already have. They might also have concerns that their own children could be removed from their home if a foster child's biological parents report them to CPS as a form of payback.

- The idea that things are worse there than here. Yes, some children in foster care need a family (but not the majority, as we will see in a moment). However, children in US foster care receive food, medical care, education, and the majority are in family homes rather than institutional care or group homes. Some families will choose to adopt internationally because they know that in some countries, children will grow up never leaving their crib in the orphanage. Many live on very little food. Few are given an education. Children die from lack of medical care or malnutrition. Some families will chose international adoptive over foster care adoption because the situation seems more dire to them.

Looking at numbers

There is certainly the perception that people are racing to adopt foreign children while American kids languish in foster care. This is not the reality. We keep statistics on this sort of thing, it's easy to find.

- In 2014, there were approximately 415,000 children in foster care. **Only about 25% were targeted as eligible to be adopted**. The goal of foster care is family reunification.

- In 2014, there were about 108,000 children waiting to be adopted, and 51,000 who were adopted.

Did you see that? 51,000 were adopted from the US. Know how many international adoptions there were in 2014? About 6400. The number of international adoptions decreased by 9% from 2013 to 2014. The number of adoptions from foster care are increasing, while the number of international adoptions is declining. Even when international adoption was at its peak, it topped out at around 20,000 foreign adoptions, well under the amount of children adopted from foster care.

The facts to note here are that there are more children adopted from foster care than there are adopted internationally in the US. Most children in the foster system are not eligible for adoption. International adoption is not in competition with adoption from foster care.

How to respond

It is so difficult to find a short way to convey all of this information when someone you know or often a perfect stranger says to you "There are kids here in America who need homes too, you know!" You may feel hurt or angry. That is perfectly justified in that situation. The person making the comment is being rude and you have no obligation to justify your decision. It is helpful to have a response prepared. Here are some responses commonly given by families who have chosen to adopt internationally.

- You're right, all kids deserve a family regardless of where they were born!

- International adoption was the best fit for our family.

- Our child was in China.

- Have you considered becoming a foster parent or adopting from foster care, yourself? It sounds very important to you.

Additional Resources

Center for Adoption Support and Education (CASE)
http://adoptionsupport.org/

IRS website on the adoption tax credit
https://www.irs.gov/taxtopics/tc607.html

The AFCARS report on children in foster care
http://www.acf.hhs.gov/sites/default/files/cb/afcarsreport22.pd
f

US State Department statistics on intercountry adoption
http://travel.state.gov/content/adoptionsabroad/en/about-us/statistics.html

Children's Bureau foster care fact sheet
https://www.childwelfare.gov/pubPDFs/foster.pdf

American Academy of Child and Adolescent Psychiatry foster care fact sheet
https://www.childwelfare.gov/pubPDFs/foster.pdf

New York Times article on the decline of international adoption
http://www.nytimes.com/2013/01/25/world/us-adoptions-from-abroad-decline-sharply.html?_r=0

W.I.S.E Up! Powerbook by Marilyn Schoettle

19

Preparing for Big Children with Big Questions

One day about a year after our first adoption, my son Gregory (age 8) was playing with his little brother from China in the living room while I sat nearby. Gregory said rather randomly, "I like to think that Leo's parents were poor." Gregory is the talker in our family, so he went on to give a very long but touching explanation. He said, "I like to think that they were poor and they gave him up because they couldn't pay for a doctor for him but they wanted him to get better. I don't like to think that they just didn't want him because that makes me sad. Sometimes I think that when he's older he'll wish that he got to meet his parents. I mean, I know that he was with them for a little while but he doesn't remember. I think he'll wish that he knew what they looked like and could remember being with them like when we visit Grandma and Grandpa."

I am often surprised at how much my children think about adoption and all of the implications of it. We talked about it a little and then we went on with the day, but I kept thinking about what he said. I have no idea what Leo's thoughts will be about his adoption as he grows older, but I imagine he will think all of the things Gregory mentioned. He will want to know why he was abandoned. I can tell him reasons why children are usually abandoned in China, but I won't be able to tell him with certainty why he was abandoned. I can assure him that he was wanted by our family but I don't know if anything I say can eliminate the fear that he was unwanted by his parents in China that he is sure to have.

It occurred to me that the way adoptive parents approach this issue tells you a lot about their feelings on adoption. A frequent criticism from adoptees is that adoption is all about the adoptive parents feelings, and this is true to a certain extent. Some adoptees object to the term "Gotcha Day" because it places the emphasis on the adoptive parents "getting" their child. Many parents will choose to celebrate Gotcha Day every year. Often, it is treated as a second birthday, with with cake or ice cream and the child receiving a gift (some parents pick up enough gifts in China to have something to give every year). Some adult adoptees felt that they were only allowed to celebrate their adoption on this day, although inwardly they felt sadness or loss because it reminded them that they were not with their first family in their country of origin. We prefer the term "family day" at our house and keep things low key. We like to get out the photo album of our trip to China or Leo's baby photo album and talk about how he came to our family. Leo is still young and our son August has barely been home a few weeks, but we will follow their cues as they grow older so they know we will support their feelings about their individual adoptions whether those feelings are positive or negative.

Besides celebrating Gotcha Day, in recent years it has become popular for adoptive parents to celebrate Birthmother's Day, which is designated as the day before Mother's Day. It is laudable to take a day to remember your child's first mother, but there is a certain aspect of Birthmother's Day which implies wanting to get that taken care of and out of the way so it won't take any time away from "real" Mother's Day. Currently Birthmother's Day seems to be linked more to domestic adoptions than to international ones, probably because the birth mother is more likely to be a part of your child's life in a domestic adoption.

When it comes to birth mothers in China, it seems that most adoptive parents take one of two extremes–either they make the birth parents into saints or they demonize them. Let's look at the "saints" line first because that is what I find myself naturally falling into. Like Gregory, it is difficult for me to even consider that our sons' parents might not have wanted them. I can only imagine giving up a child as being a huge sacrifice. Both of our sons had birth defects, were not abandoned immediately after birth, and were left in a very public place where they would be found quickly, so it easy for me to think that both sets of parents spent days agonizing over whether to keep their son or abandon him.

However, I really have no way of knowing that. I will never be able to tell either child what his parents' specific reason for choosing not to parent him was. Perhaps one set of parents spent the time arguing and one day, when the parent who wanted to keep him was away, the other parent took him out of the apartment and left him. That is the story behind one girl's abandonment in the documentary *Somewhere Between*. Or perhaps one mother was a single college student who knew she could never keep her baby but managed to hide her pregnancy. When she went into labor, she found a safe friend to stay with, but after ten days when she was fully recovered from birth, she dropped him off on her way back to school and told everyone she had been sick with the flu.

In a way, one of the attractions of adoption from China is that you can make up any story you like. There is no legal way to make an adoption plan or relinquish a child, so they are all abandoned. If you adopt domestically, from foster care, or from other counties, in most cases you will know the reason why they ended up needing a family. It can be difficult for parents to choose to adopt from a country where you meet your child's family of origin and see for yourself that the reason their child is coming home to your family is poverty. Poverty is the root of most of the abandonments in China but it's easier to pretend when you don't know that for sure. That reality stares you in the face when you're hanging out with the birth mother at the orphanage day after day while waiting for the court date to approach, as is the case when you adopt from many African countries.

Perhaps it makes you feel guilty that you are benefiting from the hard circumstances that the birth parents have. That is probably why some adoptive families swing the other direction. Now don't get me wrong, there are many children who end up being adopted because their birth parents made bad choices or were just not nice people. Sometimes, when you see that your child was left in a pile of trash on the side of the road, it's pretty easy to conclude that at least one of their parents didn't want them. I'm not really talking about those circumstances. I'm talking about adoptive parents who make statements such as:

"It makes me so angry to think that they didn't want her just because she was a girl."

"They throw their babies away like trash in China"

"They didn't want him because he wasn't perfect."

In most cases, the adoptive parents have no way of knowing this with certainty. I've seen many adoptive parents who are certain that their daughter was abandoned for being a girl even though their daughters had serious medical conditions, which to me seemed like a likelier cause for abandonment (in order to try and obtain medical care for them). As I've written before, the situation in China is much more complex than "want boys, hate girls." But I'll bet it must be so much easier to live with the happiness you feel with your child in your life when you can say to yourself that the birth parents didn't want her anyway, so they don't deserve her. She is better off with you.

This can even lead to the sentiment that I frequently see, that "God planned/created her for your family." I try to be respectful of everyone's religious beliefs, but this one is hardest for me to understand. I do truly understand why you would want to believe that God chose your child for your family, just as He would any biological child, only they were somehow born in a different country. But this really glosses over all of the hard aspects of adoption. Make sure you are open to negative feelings relating to adoption that your child might have in the future. Many adoptees are comforted that God placed them in the family where they were meant to be, but for others this view means that if they have any desire for it to have been best if they had been able to stay with their birth family, they are put in the place of opposing God's will.

I sometimes wonder why God would intend for my sons to be abandoned, spend two or three of the most developmentally important years in their lives in an institution, and then leave behind everything they know to go live with strangers? Yes, we are a family now, but surely God's plan would have been for him to grow up with the family he was born to? And if you think too much about this idea, you start to wonder about all the other children who didn't get the great plan. The number of children who achieve the "happily-ever-after" ending is only a fraction of those in state care. Some die before they are adopted, some are never chosen, many never even have the chance to be adopted because they aren't deemed "adoptable." They will grow up in state care and maybe spend their entire life in the same orphanage because they can't live independently. When we visited my son's orphanage, there was an entire building for the children who were over fourteen and no longer eligible to be adopted by Chinese law. The children under age two took up just a few rooms out of the whole complex. None of them are any less loved by God than those who do end up in a family. And I think that some children will one day begin to ask hard questions such as "Why did God choose a family for me but not them, if he loves everyone?"

The stories that you tell yourself about the circumstances of your child's adoption and how you view her birth parents are important, because it will color your child's view. If you are negative about her country and parents, she might inwardly feel ashamed because this reflects on her sense of self. But at the same time, painting too rosy of a picture can set her up for disappointment. There are children who eventually meet their birth family, even when they were adopted from China. In the end, it's best to be honest about what you know and what you don't. Never assume you know why your child's parent or parents made the choices they did. You can speculate about the maybes, but really, this is your child's story, not yours. What is most important is to listen to her feelings about her story. Her hopes and fears. Try to make sure you aren't writing the narrative for her.

This is the point where I'm supposed to wrap everything up with a little lesson and a happy ending. However I think the whole idea I'm grappling with, and which every adoptive parents should grapple with, is that there aren't any easy answers here. The stories we tell ourselves are ultimately about helping us come to terms with our feelings about adoption, when, as the adoptees point out, it should be about helping our children come to terms with their feelings about their adoption. We have to do our best to answer our children's questions as they come up, to be honest with them and with ourselves that we will probably never know how or why.

Now that you are home with your child, you might think you have achieved the happy ending. Or maybe you are too busy dealing with medical or attachment issues to really think about it. But as your child grows older, one day he will have questions about adoption. He will want to talk about race. I've noticed that if you read any adoption blog of adoptive parents who have young children, you'd think that interracial adoption is a fairly recent phenomenon. They know what they have learned during their home study from their social worker about the importance of instilling a sense cultural heritage, but very few seem aware that there are generations of adult adoptees who have experiences they can learn from. Or if they are aware, they are dismissive of the "angry adoptees." They are certain their child will never feel that way. Those adoptees just didn't get a good family or aren't grateful for how fortunate they were to be adopted rather than being left to grow up in an orphanage.

Did you know that international adoption began after the Korean War? Anyone remember when that took place? Let me give you a hint, long enough ago that there are people who are adopting through my agency who are themselves Korean adoptees. Adult adoptees grew up to share their experiences and they have highly influenced the required education that today's adoptive parents receive. I watched two documentaries produced by adult Korean adoptees and wanted to share my thoughts about them with you. I hope you will find it thought-provoking and perhaps you will decide to look into the perspectives of adult adoptees further.

Barb Lee directed the documentary *Adopted* which she co-produced with another adult adoptee. It was a very uncomfortable documentary for me to watch, and I assume that is why most adoptive parents prefer to pretend that adult adoptees don't exist. We don't like to feel uncomfortable and we don't want to think that our children could grow up with any negative, or even conflicted, feelings about their adoption. *Adopted* follows 30-something year old Jennifer Fero, who was adopted from Korea. When she learned that her (adoptive) mother has terminal brain cancer it spurs her to seek the relationship with her parents that she has been tip-toeing around for years. Jen falls into the stereotype of an "angry adoptee."

Jen's feelings are common for some adoptees. Other adoptees will go through life never struggling with these issues.

On Jen's visits back home she repeatedly pushes her parents beyond their comfort zone. When Jen asks her mother why she thinks Jen's birth mother left her at the police station, her mother immediately answers "Some people just aren't meant to be mothers." Jen challenges her to think about more possibilities—what if she wanted to keep Jen but couldn't because of poverty. Jen's mom plays along for a minute or two but then abruptly shuts down the conversation with "I don't think about her at all. I don't want to think about her. You're my daughter now, not hers."

Jen's father tells the story of how they decided to adopt her. He says that after having a son, they tried for a few years to have another child. When that didn't work out, "I said we should go get a baby girl from Holt, the adoption agency here in Oregon." Just like ordering up a product. Later in the documentary, Jen goes on a trip to New York with her father and uncle because her father is very interested in genealogy. Jen proudly explains to her father that because of his research, she has discovered that he is eligible to join the Sons of the Revolution because he is a direct descendent of a man who fought in the Revolutionary War. Moments later in the film, the man at the Sons of the Revolution museum explains that only Jen's father's "linear children" are eligible to join. As Jen's father clearly isn't catching his meaning, he is forced to explicitly state "only your biological children are eligible, not adopted children." Jen politely smiles and follows along on the tour but later ducks out to wipe away her tears.

Jen's parents are older working-class folks who live in a double-wide and are struggling to cope with her mother's terminal diagnosis. They try really hard to understand Jen's feelings, but clearly none of it makes sense to them. Jen's older brother, who seemed to be the hero of the film to me, lives with his parents to take care of them. He is eternally patient with Jen, always validating her feelings while trying to gently suggest that she be a little easier on their parents because of their age. Frankly, while I could understand all of Jen's feelings, I didn't like her much. It was extremely painful to watch her railing about her feelings to her mother knowing this was her last few months of life. While I wouldn't have chosen that moment to suddenly spring an adoptive parent educational course on them, I think today's adoptive parents would benefit from listening to Jen and other adoptees.

During the New York trip, Jen drags her father and uncle to eat at a Korean restaurant. They are clearly unhappy about being there and the meal is awkward. At another point in the movie, we see Jen telling her father that it isn't fair that she has to make all of the accommodations. She has to be white. Despite the fact that he has chosen to have an interracial family, there is no acknowledgement that she is Asian. She must always adapt to them, they won't do any adapting to her. The fact that his family his interracial is clearly news to Jen's dad. Throughout the film, both he and his wife make statements typical for people of their age. "I never see Jen as Asian—she's just my daughter" or "I was taught to never see race."

As I watched Jen's dad and uncle sit sullenly picking at their Korean food, I was reminded of a fairly recent conversation I had with another adoptive parent. When we moved to a larger city, my husband learned from a Chinese-American coworker about a Chinese school in the area. Founded by Chinese immigrants for their children, it offers a variety of classes in Chinese language, dance, martial arts, and music. When I met another parent of a Chinese adoptee, I asked if she had heard about the school. She responded that all of the adoptive parents in the area put their kids in language class with a white guy who has a college degree in Chinese. She felt it was really great because their daughters were able to be friends with other adoptees and the parents can all talk while their children are in class.

I think it's wonderful for adoptees to have friends who are also adoptees, but I reflected that the Chinese school was a great opportunity for a Chinese adoptee to become a part of the Chinese community in our city. After all, when our children are adults, they will be perceived as Chinese, not as adoptees. Having friends or adults who can help them to understand the Chinese-American experience will be valuable. We ended up signing our biological son up for Chinese language classes. At the Chinese New Year celebration, our family one of a handful of non-Chinese. The building was full of Chinese people, everyone speaking Mandarin and eating Chinese food. My daughter commented that it was like being back in China again. I wondered if the adoptive parents avoided the school for just this reason. I had a sudden flash of sympathy for the one black kid who attended school with me in the rural area where I grew up. This is what so many of us ask of our adopted children–to be the only non-white person in the area while trying to avoid being in that situation ourselves. I always appreciate the opportunity to connect with other adoptive parents, but there is something to be said for the opportunity to connect with Chinese-Americans as well.

Right after watching *Adopted* I watched *Approved For Adoption*, a film by Jung, a Belgian-Korean adoptee. *Approved For Adoption* is Jung's memoir, mostly in cartoon format, although there are home movies and video footage from his trip to Korea interspersed. It is in French with English subtitles and it is a little European-earthy with some PG-13 moments.

Jung is much more personable than Jennifer, and I think the cartoon format makes this film more approachable for the adoptive parent than the documentary format of *Adopted*. Yet Jung's story has many of the same themes. He talks about how he shunned the other Korean adoptees in the village and resented his Korean sister because he didn't want to face being Korean. In one humorous episode, he becomes obsessed with

Japanese culture and starts to pretend he is Japanese. Because he was older when he was adopted and had lived on the streets for a time, he acts out in many ways common to children from that scenario. This causes friction with his adoptive family. Towards the end, he discusses the depression and self-destructive behavior common among adoptees.

I think many adoptive parents avoid listening anything by the "angry adoptees" because we don't want to deal with the uncomfortable feelings that come from listening to their point of view. Adoptive parents love "Gotcha Day" because that was the day that WE got our child. But some adoptees think of it as the day they lost their culture. They don't want to be told that they should be grateful they didn't grow up in an orphanage. Surely you can love your family while still feeling that it's unfair you couldn't grow up with your first family in your country of birth. Humans are complicated—we can feel all sorts of conflicting emotions. We need to be prepared to support our children throughout their lives, and even when their feelings make us uncomfortable. Parenting through adoption is a lifelong journey, not one that ends once the initial attachment has been achieved. I would like to encourage you to listen to a variety of experiences so you are prepared for the full range of feelings that your child might one day experience.

Additional Resources

Adoption documentaries: *Somewhere Between* (2011), *Approved For Adoption* (2013), and *Adopted* (2008)

Ballard, Robert L., editor. Pieces of Me: Who do I want to be? Warren, NJ: EMK Press, 2009.

Eldridge, Sherrie. Twenty Things Adopted Kids Wish Their Adoptive Parents Knew. Delta, 1999.

Keck, Gregory. Parenting the Hurt Child: Helping Adoptive Families Heal and Grow. Colorado Springs, CO: NavPress, 2009.

20

Travel Journal: Our first adoption trip to China

I first began my blog as a travel journal to keep our friends and family back home updated on our trip. Many people love to read adoption blogs to try and prepare for travel, so I thought I would include my entries as the close to this book. This is just one experience but it's all here: the excitement, the boredom, the grieving, and the smiles. It was truly the experience of a lifetime and we are so fortunate to have been able to have this experience.

August 21, 2013, The Itinerary

Our trip to China will be approximately two weeks long and take place in three different stages, each in its own city. Although personally I think that we might consider that taking our non-stop action 4.5 year old through air transit for 18 hours will be a trip all by itself!

We will depart from the US on Wednesday morning and arrive in China on Thursday afternoon. Matt's mother is going with us and I know we will really appreciate having an extra set of hands along to help with the children. We will begin in Beijing for two days of sightseeing. Beijing is in the northern part of China about the same latitude as Philadelphia, PA. It has a population similar to Chicago. This is mostly to let us all adjust to the time zone because it's not a good idea to hand a kid over to very jet-lagged parents. We will keep awake during the day by visiting the Great Wall and the Forbidden City. Someone in our party was very excited to hear that our hotel is very near to Snack Street, which is a street where you can buy fun Chinese street food such as starfish or scorpion on a stick. Only we won't actually eat any of the snacks because we don't want to get food poisoning.

On Sunday we will fly to Nanjing, which is the capital of Leo's province. It's about the same latitude as Montgomery, AL. It is best known for being the capital of China during the Ming dynasty. Leo is not currently residing there but will be transported to Nanjing to meet us because adoptions must be finalized at the Provincial capital. We don't have much planned for Sunday except traveling and getting settled into a new hotel. No snack street at this place but I hear there's a mall with a Starbucks. We will meet Leo on Monday morning, known as "Gotcha Day" in adoption lingo. He will come back to the hotel with us and we will return on Tuesday to officially adopt him. We will stay around Nanjing until Friday because his passport will need to be prepared. He will fly home on a red Chinese passport which will become void once he reaches US soil. We will pass the time getting to know Leo's home province. I hope to visit Leo's orphanage and possibly meet his foster parents during this time. My agency says "Orphanage and foster family visits are prohibited but sometimes allowed." Leo's orphanage welcomes visitors and families are usually given permission to visit if they request to do so, which makes me optimistic that we will be able to travel there.

On Friday, after we receive Leo's passport we will travel to the southern part of China to Guangzhou, where the American consulate is located. It's hard to find an East Coast city on the same latitude, but Key West, FL is closest. We expect warm weather! It is the 3rd largest city in China. Friday is just a transportation day but on Saturday Leo must have a medical visit. Then we have another break on Sunday and Monday.

Tuesday is our appointment at the US Consulate where we will receive his US adoption paperwork. We will receive his visa to enter the US on Wednesday and we are free to leave after that. For various transportation related reasons we will be flying home on Friday morning.

We will fly from Guangzhou to Shanghai where we will catch the long flight home. From there we will enter the US in Seattle, where we will be detained for a few hours as Leo journeys through customs to become an official US citizen. At that point we will travel to our "home" airport of Cincinnati, arriving home on the same day that we left thanks to the time difference. I'm expecting it to be twenty hours of cozy bonding on the uneventful flight home. Just let me live in my dreamland, okay?

Internet access in China can be unpredictable. I will try to post once a day while we are in China and I have a friend who can post an update for me as long as I have e-mail access. I hope to post additional pictures to Flickr so you can click through to the right if you want to see more than I put in the posts. Squatty potties, Nanjing duck blood soup, and crazy Chinese traffic with no seat belts–here we come!

August 28, 2013

You know you have small town kids when they're impressed by the airport parking lot! It just got more exciting when we got to the escalators and train. We made it through security and finally secured seats together for the flight to Beijing. The next time you hear from us we'll be on the other side of the world!

August 29, 2013

It was a very long flight, but we made it to Beijing. I don't think anyone but Linda slept more than 5 minutes the entire flight! The bad news is Max threw up during the landing. The good news is we didn't get quarantined when Max threw up again right in front of the customs officer processing our passports. We are trying to stay awake a little longer and going out to buy some water. Tomorrow will be a long day with a lot of scheduled activities.

August 29, 2013 (the blog repeated one date because of the time issue)

We're getting ready for our trip out to the Great Wall and it sounds like the jade factory, too. Our guide Nancy said she was going to keep us very busy today to help us get over our jet-lag. We're all feeling much better after getting 12 hours of sleep last night. I guess the bright side of not sleeping on the flight over is that you get adjusted to the new time quickly. Max is feeling much better this morning. I think I forgot to say yesterday that he gets motion sickness sometimes and our landing was a little rough. I was able to get the two pictures to load on the post yesterday so you can see them there or by clicking through to Flickr on the right. One of the view from our room and the other is our lack of success at keeping Vincent and Gregory awake. They kept trying to lay down on the marble floor in the hotel lobby while Nancy was getting us checked in.

Our first impression of Beijing is that it was not nearly so urban as we were expecting. I could see farmland outside of town as we landed and the entire drive to the hotel there were lots of trees to be seen along the roads. I was expecting the buildings to be crammed together like New York City (not that I've been there either) but there is a lot of landscaping, and even the traffic isn't as nonstop as I thought it would be. It is not noisy in our hotel. Okay, time to go now!

August 30, 2013

Before I start talking about the Great Wall, Gregory would like me to tell you about the breakfast buffet at our hotel. He says that buffet isn't the right word, it should be called something like "Food Fantasy." I didn't take any pictures but there was a

European/American section with pancakes, waffles, pastries, cereal, fruit, and yogurt. There was a Japanese section with sushi. There was a Chinese section with dumplings and grilled fish. Oh, and an omelet bar. Sadly for Gregory, he did not have enough time to finish his third plate because we were just out of time and had to meet our guide.

We are the only people who signed up for tours this time so it was just us, Nancy, and the driver. There are several sections of the Great Wall where people usually tour and we went to the closest section which is about an hour outside of Beijing, depending on the traffic. Nancy told us that Beijing is mostly a new city because the government has systematically bulldozed down the older housing sections and replaced them with large apartment buildings so most of the city looked like wall to wall tall buildings driving through.

As we drove out of the city you could see the mountains ahead, and then we could see some of the Great Wall going up the mountain! Nancy told us repeatedly that we were extremely lucky because she has never seen such good weather. There is absolutely no smog, a beautiful blue sky, and a nice breeze. It was the perfect day to climb the Great Wall. Or at least a tiny section of it.

Everyone was very excited, so there was a festive atmosphere. People were smiling at each other and giving encouragement to those who took a little longer. The steps are uneven, with some being close together and other far apart. They all had grooves or missing chunks. Nancy told us that most of the Great Wall is crumbling and too dangerous to climb except for these few preserved areas around Beijing. Linda recently had knee-replacement surgery because she said she wanted to be able to climb the Great Wall and it was a great motivator for her physical therapy. She was able to make it to the 3rd tower.

It was so beautiful there that we all could have stayed for much longer. But Nancy has lots of plans, so we kept going. She has a great schedule too, because there were lots of busses pulling in as we left but it didn't seem crowded while we were there. Next we went to the government jade factory. We were able to see someone carving a jade family ball and many samples of exquisite jade carving craftsmanship. We had lunch at the restaurant upstairs and then headed back into Beijing.

The next stop was the hutong tour. Hutongs are the old city dwellings which were small houses with courtyards which grew into a maze of dwellings. We were driven in rickshaws in the small alleys. It was nice to see people sitting around and chatting. There were many people playing majong, having a drink, hanging laundry, or reading a kindle. It definitely had more of a community feel than the giant apartment buildings. We had the opportunity to tour the inside of one and when we talked with the owner we found that she was born in the same month and year as Linda. The hutong tour was the last stop on our schedule for the day. We spent some time resting when we got back and now the kids are downstairs swimming in the hotel pool with Matt and Grandma.

After swimming yesterday it was time for our first trip out to an actual restaurant. We just wanted to sleep when we got in on Thursday. Several of the adoptive families had talked about this great dumpling restaurant that is behind our hotel The Novatel Peace. The problem was that it was hard to find more specific directions other than "behind the hotel" and it doesn't have an English sign so we couldn't google the name. We finally decided to just ask the concierge. He said "Dumpling shop? Yes! Follow me!" and he led us through a door the left marked Employees Only. We went through several back hallways and out a back door into the employee parking lot which was full of bicycles and had a guard stationed.

The dumpling shop was in a hutong, and the owner said we could eat outside or in one of the little rooms. We choose outside and were seated in one of the little courtyards. There was a beautiful tree growing up to shade the table. We ordered a pork rib soup which came in a huge tureen and several different kinds of dumplings. While we were waiting for the food, Vincent fell asleep at the table. The other children watched a mother cat and kitten walking across the roof above the courtyard. We managed to wake Vincent up and eat by enticing him with Sprite. We were all completely stuffed, and the bill came to $20!

A few odds and ends stories. When we first got off the plane, everything was kind of crazy. Matt was asking an attendant where the nearest bathroom was for Max, who was puking again while Linda sponged him off. Gregory was trying to lay down on the floor to sleep while Mary Evelyn was guarding the stack of backpacks and luggage. I was keeping an eye on Vincent who looked up at me and said "Mama? Do dey have potties in China? Because I need one!"

Also, at the Great Wall yesterday we had our first taste of our Caucasian celebrity status. We had been warned that many Chinese have not seen Caucasians before and it is not considered rude to stare in China. The boys were very popular and we were stopped several times by people wanting to have their picture taken with Gregory and Vincent or Max. Even at the jade factory where their main business is tourists, we were the only people eating (I told you Nancy had a great schedule!) and the waitresses gathered around to gaze at the boys adoringly while we ate. Nancy said it will be even worse at the Forbidden City.

August 31, 2013

This morning Nancy came bearing a gift—a red folder with an update on Leo. It had some new pictures, Chinese phrases, advice on getting around in China and things along those lines.

We went out this morning to Tiananmen Square and the Forbidden City. As we approached Tiananmen Square, we got to urban Beijing that I was expecting when we got here. There were people everywhere and 12 lanes of traffic. I was very glad to see an underpass so we didn't have to cross the street. As large as the Square was, the crowd was never shoulder to shoulder crowded, just state fair on a Saturday crowded. There were lots of tour groups and sellers with Chinese army hats and things like that.

Chinese ladies here certainly take their sun protection seriously. I've only seen face masks on commuters. Most women were wearing large sun hats or carrying umbrellas. I saw quite a few Muslim Chinese women wearing hijab. Our guide Nancy was wearing a full array including a light jacket, gloves for her hands, a sun hat, and an umbrella. When her umbrella broke, she immediately purchased a new one from a street vendor. Again, we attracted a lot of attention. One man counted the number of children in English and then gave Matt a thumb's up. For the first time someone wanted a picture of Mary Evelyn with her daughters and as I thought, Mary Evelyn was less enthusiastic than the boys to have her picture made with strangers.

The children got tired of the Forbidden City pretty quickly. I think we were expecting to walk from room to room, but instead it was open area to open area. It was another clear day but hot and sunny since most of the areas didn't have any shade. Like our visit to the Great Wall, it was very impressive to walk on something that is older than our country. Some parts in the outer area had been well preserved but I was surprised at the poor condition of the inner areas where the Emperor and his concubines lived. There were windows where you could look in and see the furniture and everything was covered in dust. The wood in the ceiling above was rotting away. I hope they eventually restore those areas.

When we finished at the Forbidden City we stopped for lunch where we met Sue, a staff person from Holt. We shared several dishes of food. We were so hot from the Forbidden City that we paid to buy an extra liter of Coke to share because there are no free refills. Nancy keeps marveling at how independent Vincent is. She tells us that since most people have only one child, they

301

are usually spoiled and it is normal to see parents hand feeding children until they are 6 or older.

We were pretty wiped out after the food but we still had to go to the silk factory for another sales pitch. It was very fascinating to hear about the two types of cocoons, to see how the threads were spun, and we all got to help stretch silk batting out for a quilt. Once we were done there we finally got to come back to the hotel for a rest. We are planning to go out again for our last night in Beijing. Tomorrow morning we will pack up and fly to Nanjing in the early afternoon.

September 1, 2013

Last night (Saturday evening) was our last night in Beijing so we wanted to go out and see a few more sights after we spend some time in the hotel recovering from the morning of walking. I got in touch with an adoptive friend Jennifer, that I knew through an online group and we decided to meet downstairs in the lobby. Our two families walked down the street a few blocks to Snack Street, which is also called the night market, because it is only open for a few hours in the evening. The children and I had looked at pictures online and they were excited to see the starfish, squid, and other gross things in person. What the internet doesn't convey is the nauseating smell! Some areas were okay but others we just kept walking quickly because the smell was so terrible.

Not all of the food was gross. Quite a lot of it looked great. There were bowls of noodles, some baked goods, and every person who was selling fruit on a stick would gesture to our children and wave their fruit sticks enticingly at them. One stall had little pots and I was curious what they contained but we didn't see an english sign for them. A few stalls were selling food that met Muslim standards. The most popular stall by far was one selling a large haunch of roasted lamb on a stick.

After we finished the line of stalls we stopped for a bit to decide what to do next. Our original plan had been to eat Beijing (Peking) duck tonight. But we were still really full from our huge lunch and Nancy had warned us that on a Saturday night it might be difficult to get seating for a party as large as ours without a reservation. We decided not to worry about the Beijing duck and we would get something light if we got hungrier later. We then headed over to a different street to visit St. Joseph Cathedral, which was built on the site of one of the original Jesuit missionary houses from the 1600's. It had a nice public gathering area in front but the church was closed with locked gates. We had hoped to be able to go to Mass here on one of our days since the Beijing bishop is recognized by the Vatican but the only Mass time is 6:15 am, so we never made it.

From St. Joseph's we walked back to the area before the night market, which was a large shopping area that had a Times Square feel with large glowing billboards. There was a multistory mall, which we entered through the Apple store. It was like any mall in America, with many of the same stores like Forever 21 only the signs were in Chinese. The mall had escalators for each floor but since it had so many stories it also had "express" escalators that take up two stories at a time. We ended up eating some noodles at a shop there before heading back home.

We stopped by the restroom before going back to the hotel because the kids had all had a full can of Coke. I'm not sure how they work these things out but based on my experience in Beijing it seems like Coke has an exclusive contract for all of China. Not that I'm complaining! Anyway, I haven't mentioned the restrooms yet. First, most places have what are called "squatty potties." I'll try to get a picture later if you don't know what one looks like. Sometimes they will have one Western style toilet at the end. I actually don't mind the squatty potty. It's nice and sanitary because you don't touch anything. Bathrooms may or may not supply toilet paper and if they do it's by the door and not in the stall. I brought travel kleenex packs to pass out as needed. You toss the used tissue in a trash can by the door because the sewage system here can't handle toilet paper so most of the stalls do not smell nice. But I am not bothered by any of that. The thing that I find most difficult is that there is no soap provided, only sinks. I carry hand sanitizer for us, but when we are at a restaurant I really try not to think about how the people preparing our food do not have soap available to wash their hands with after using the bathroom!

September 2, 2013

I have to tell you that I'm a little envious of you, my few readers. I'm sitting here in the hotel on Monday morning with 7 hours to wait until we meet Leo. But you can wake up on Monday morning and sit there and read all about our meeting while you drink your coffee!

Sunday was just a travel day. I had no idea a one hour flight would take nearly all day. We didn't have any delays, it was just going from one thing to another. We packed up, checked out of the hotel, and drove 45 minutes to the Beijing airport.

I have no memory of the Beijing airport from our arrival, but it is absolutely amazing. I couldn't get a picture to do it justice, but it is a huge ceiling which stretches on forever. Nancy said it is the largest air terminal in the world. We went through security there, got a snack and waited for our flight. For the flights there, you all crowd onto a bus and they drive you out onto the runway and then you walk up steps into the plane. A friend had warned me, so we checked our carry-on bag and just brought the backpacks.

So there was the normal waiting in the airport, then the flight, and we landed in Nanjing. As an aside, while I know the phoenix is an important mythological creature, I don't think anything that dies a fiery death is a good symbol to choose for your airline. We met our new guide, Denise, and she told us a bit about the history of Nanjing and what the city is known for as we had another 45 minute drive to the hotel. Nanjing has huge city walls, the longest in China according to Denise and we drove by as the sun was setting.

We were completely exhausted by the time we got to our rooms at around 6:30 pm. We unpacked a little and then went to the mall that is attached to the hotel to buy food and get supper. It was very crowded. The mall was having their 5th anniversary celebration so there was special entertainment. We got some noodles for supper and then came back for bed.

Leo's orphanage is not in Nanjing but he will be transported here because it is the provincial capital. It is a four hour drive from his orphanage so that is why it will be late afternoon before we meet him at the Civil Affairs building. I will try to at least post a picture by the time people will be getting up in the morning but it might be bedtime here before I sit down to write out all the details. It will be a long and scary day for Leo, so please keep in him your prayers.

Later--

As you probably knew, today really dragged by. This morning we ate another big breakfast and then Matt and Linda took the kids swimming while I did laundry. Lots of laundry. After that we just sat around played cards or things like that until 2:30 finally rolled around. Denise came with the van and we drove to the Civil Affairs building. Leo was already there and Denise was actually trying to drag us in because Matt was trying to show Linda how to use our camera to take a video.

Then we went in and there he was!

We spoke to him and gave him a sucker. Matt tried holding him first and he started to cry. Then I took a ball out of the backpack and distracted him with that so he ended up in my lap. We passed him back and forth as we filled out guardianship papers and the children talked to him and rolled the ball with him. It really wasn't long at all until we were out of the Civil

Affairs office. We will come back tomorrow to finalize the adoption. Today we are his guardians for a 24 hour "harmonious period."

Denise then took us to a local store so we could buy any baby supplies we needed. I brought some of the clothing that I had packed and it seemed to fit fine so we mostly bought some snacks for him. Then we headed back to the hotel. Leo was mostly withdrawn in the van and at the store, looking around with a hesitant look on his face and not saying anything. Once we got back to the hotel he looked around at the tv and beds and burst into tears. He just cried and cried for probably 10 minutes. Matt left with Denise to get some food. I changed his diaper and then offered him a box of milk. He was very thirsty and gulped down the milk. After that, he seemed to really settle in well. He started playing with some of the toys that we brought.

After he had some food and more milk, he was having a lot of fun. He loved the giant green balloon and chased his brothers around whacking them with it. He was giggling and laughing. He liked Mary Evelyn too, and she got the only hug and kiss from him. He had a 10 year old foster sister in his foster home, so I wonder that helped. When it got close to his bedtime he started yawning and rubbing his eyes. We got him changed and he sat on my lap while I read Frog and Toad to Vincent. I stood rocking him and patting his back for a bit and then put him in the crib. He was asleep about one minute later. We definitely had a good first day together.

September 3, 2013

Today Leo woke up and was disappointed to see that he wasn't back home with his foster family. He is very stoic though and has only had a few periods of crying today. Mostly he looks forlorn, sad, or confused. We got him down to breakfast and he ate a bowl of congee (the Chinese version of oatmeal, made of rice cooked down to a porridge consistency), some steamed buns, and fruit. We tried him on two different kinds of fruit that he made a face at before I remembered the picture we had of him with the watermelon. Mary Evelyn handed over one of her pieces and he ate it right away.

After breakfast, Matt and I met Denise in the lobby to go back to Civil Affairs to finalize the adoption. Leo is still very curious, and looks around at everything as we are driving. Finalizing the adoption took a surprisingly short amount of time. We left the other children back at the hotel with Linda thinking we would spare them an hour of tedious paperwork but apparently international adoption involves fewer signatures than buying a house. Leo loved getting his red fingerprint stamped on the paperwork. We got him an extra piece of paper and let him stamp all over it.

He was very excited to see the orphanage director and her associate again. It was great to see his real personality as he laughed and played with them, giving them hugs and kisses. He even gave Matt and I a kiss when they told him to. But it was hard on him when they left again.

We had worked out a schedule for the week with Denise. We would like to visit his orphanage in Lianyungang which is a 4 hour drive. Denise has now gotten us permission from both the civil authorities and the orphanage director. We had another optional trip, which Denise said she doubted we would want to do if we visited the orphanage. For the visit, we have to pay a fee which will cover a van rental, driver, and having Denise for the day. The other trip is basically the same. She said "You see lake, there water and trees. I think you see these at home before, right? I think you not want to pay if you go to the orphanage." We agreed, but I asked if there were other things we could see within walking distance of the hotel. She said that she would return to drop off the adoption decree and we could walk to see the city walls at that time. Then tomorrow morning we will walk to the Confucius Temple area, which is a kind of touristy pedestrian park area.

We came home and let Leo take a nap, then met Denise again at 3 pm. Denise warned us that it would be a 15 minute walk and worried that Vincent might get tired. We tried not to laugh at her too much. Which reminds me of a story I didn't tell you about Sunday. When we were in the Beijing airport we stopped next to one of those moving sidewalks to use the restroom. While we were piling our stuff on the floor, Vincent reached up and grabbed onto the moving handrail, tucked up his feet, and let it carry him a few feet down from us while giggling his head off. He did not appreciate Matt plucking him off the conveyor belt and stopping his fun.

Anyway, we put Leo in the ergo carrier, which he loves, and walked to the city walls. If we had any idea how many intersections we needed to cross we would have just gone to walk in the nice sedate mall some more. But no one died. The city wall was very impressive. Denise said that it was built about 600 years ago by the Ming emperor who eventually moved the capital to Beijing. She said he required the craftsmen to sign their name on each brick to insure the highest quality of the bricks. There was even a large ramp so that they could bring horses to the top of the wall.

We then walked to a riverside park and followed the wall along the river for a while. We saw many people relaxing. If we were a spectacle before as the crazy white family with four kids, we are even more of one now that we're the crazy white family with four kids and a Chinese baby. People would call out to each other to turn around and look so no one would miss us. Several people asked Denise questions. But everyone is very friendly and good-natured, so we haven't been bothered by the attention. We met a grandfather walking his 18 month old granddaughter who had a bird perched on her stroller.

When we reached the end of the river walkway, Denise said that we should go back a different way since we had gone so far. We followed her along through the backstreets of Nanjing. It was similar to our hutong tour in Beijing. We saw so many little shops where the owners had children playing out front next to where their laundry was hanging. People gathered to smoke and play cards. People were walking dogs or riding bikes or talking to neighbors. It was really a lot of fun at first but the walk went on and on. Denise let us through one street after another. There weren't really any crazy street crossings taking this back way but often she preferred to walk in the street when a perfectly good sidewalk was available, so there were always motorbikes and the occasional taxi zooming pack. Finally, a good two hours after we started off on our walk, we made it back to the hotel. Denise even took us to a restaurant across the street which was cafeteria style (tonight's total was $10) and helped Matt to order before she headed home.

After supper we came back to the hotel and gave Leo his first bath. He finally perked up a bit and started to play with the children again. He's been clinging to either me or Matt all day and not as interested in playing with them. As bedtime approached, he started to sag and make this little grunting noise he makes when he's trying not to cry. He lost his battle and started to have another good cry. I just patted him and said soothing things to him. We know he misses his foster family. It is great that he likes me and Matt and lets us hold him, feed him, and care for him. That means that he will build a strong attachment to us. But it will take time. The children are doing well with understanding why he is sad. Vincent came over to pat his back and tried to comfort him by saying "You know, I was about your age when Mama and Papa came to get me, too." The orphanage visit on Thursday might be hard for him but I hope it will also help him to have some closure, too. Being able to see everyone one last time and say goodbye can be important, even for a little guy.

September 4, 2013

Today was one of our days off because we didn't have anything adoption related to do. We were still pretty footsore from our walk around the city yesterday but we still met Denise at 9 am. Fortunately this time the Confucius Temple area really was a short walk and there weren't even any major streets to cross to get there. We didn't actually enter the Confucius Temple but we saw it, along with the river and all of the nice shops. It was interesting to see signs that Denise said were from the Ming dynasty era. One was mentioning Nanjing as a center of education because it used to be where scholars would take their exams to enter the imperial service and the other said "Black coats only" which Denise said referred to the imperial guard.

We were able to do a little shopping. Matt pointed out that the mall prices seem like normal prices to us, but when you get out and see what regular prices are in the rest of China, it's easy to see why Denise says the mall is so overpriced. I'm doing most of my shopping in Guangzhou so I don't have to carry things around through our in China flights. But I want to make sure I buy some items from Leo's home province. One of Nanjing's local things are "rain flower stones" which are pretty agate stones from the river. They are usually shown in water because they make pretty patterns when the sun shines in. We bought a few of those along with some local tea which is also named rain flower. Many adoptive parents buy a "chop" for their child which is a decorative stamp that has their child's name carved on it. We bought one for Leo made from rain flower stone and had his Chinese name carved on it.

While the chop was being carved, Denise pointed to some glass beads and remarked that they came from Leo's home city. I decided to buy one and have it made into a necklace. It was a large glass bead which had been hand painted with a design on the inside of the bead. When I chose one, the seller asked if I'd like to have it personalized, so I had Leo's name painted on the inside as well. The man took out the tiniest paint brush I've ever seen and sat down in front of a magnifying glass and painted the characters for YuQiang on the inside of the bead. I then chose a red thread for the necklace because Leo's foster mother gave him a bracelet made of red thread, which also has significance in the adoption community. It's a very beautiful necklace but I forgot to take a picture so you'll just have to squint at the other pictures to try and see it.

We asked Denise to take our picture next to a statue of what she calls "the city's animal." I'm not sure there is an English name for this mythical creature (how would you translate something like manticore to another language, right?) He is one of the nine sons of the dragon. Anyway, this creature is known for eating a lot but never going to the bathroom. She says "Always in, never out." So he guards the city gate to keep the luck going in, but never out and many shops have him guard the door to keep the money coming in, but never going out.

After we did our shopping we made sure to ask Denise to take us by a place to buy Nanjing salted duck to take back to the hotel. She said she wasn't sure we would like it, so we bought half a salted duck and half a roasted duck. Later, Matt made a trip to the mall and bought some rice and side dishes and we ate it all for supper in the hotel. Contrary to Denise's predictions, we all loved the salted duck and found the roasted duck to be bland.

We've been in China for a full week now, and I would say we're still in the honeymoon period. So far every morning we all choose Chinese foods for breakfast along with our normal American ones. Usually we have steamed buns and dumplings with our bacon and eggs. Other than getting ice cream cones at the McDonald's at the mall, we have eaten Chinese food for every meal. Chinese Chinese food is much better than American style

Chinese food. I hear things get more rough the second week and I'm sure we'll be craving a hamburger and fries soon.

Tomorrow we will travel to visit Leo's orphanage. We will be gone basically all day, about 12 hours. I may or may not update tomorrow night before bed, so don't be concerned if you don't hear from me until Friday morning. Which would be Thursday night in America. Leo had his sad moments again today but he spend a lot more time playing with the other children. He walked around more, exploring the 2nd room in our suite. He gave me a spontaneous hug and kiss and called me Mama once! He also had hugs for Matt and the other children and called Linda Nai-Nai, which is Chinese for your grandmother on your father's side.

September 5, 2013

We got up at 5 am this morning so we could be on the road by 7 am. Our plan was always that I would go with Leo and one or two of the older children. But then Gregory really wanted to go and Mary Evelyn sounded interested and Linda was dropping hints that she would kind of like to go too. The deciding factor was when Denise reported that she had confirmed with the orphanage director "and she say you bring your whole big family with you, okay?" While we were having lunch today the director told us that when she told the nannies that we would be visiting, they all begged for her to tell us to bring the whole family because they really wanted to see all of his siblings.

So we got in the big van and headed out of town. Leo slept the first two hours but he was increasingly apprehensive and scared after that. I'm sure he was thinking of the long van ride that brought him to us and wondering where this ride would end. The older two both played on their DS and the younger two listened to audiobooks and we all watched the Chinese countryside roll by. It looks a lot like any American countryside. There are a lot of rivers in the area. Denise told us that this town is a lobster town and that town cultures pearls in the river. We passed over one waterway that Denise said brought water from the Yangtze to Beijing. Matt was surprised that such a huge city could be in an area without a natural water source and asked Denise how that came to be. She said that Beijing was attractive to the emperor who moved the capital because of the Great Wall, so it had natural defenses, and also because of the people in the area. She said there is a minority group there who are not Han Chinese who are known for being industrious and energetic, and so it was though that they would be good administrators.

Four hours later, we arrived in Lianyungang. Lianyungang is a coastal city, right across the bay from South Korea. Denise said that it is a vacation city because people travel to see the famous Monkey King Mountain and visit the beach. It is also common to travel from there to vacation in South Korea but that requires an $8000 deposit at the police station to make sure you return!

We arrived at the orphanage and were given a very warm welcome. The nannies were just leaving for lunch and they all swarmed Leo, smiling, laughing, and take pictures of him and us. It was wonderful to see how excited they were to see him and how happy he was to see them. It shows that he had a good bond with them. I met the woman who was his primary nanny until he was moved to foster care, the "grandmother" he was assigned through the Half the Sky program, and a woman who was introduced as his "recovery" nanny. I'm not sure what that was but I got the impression she worked with him on activities to help him meet his developmental milestones.

After the nannies left we took a small tour of the orphanage. We were only shown the areas where Leo had been. We visited the baby room where the older babies were all getting ready for naps. Many of them sleep two to a crib because space is short. This set of buildings is about 20 years old but they are going to be moving to a new facility before the end of the year. We were able to see the plans but it was frankly very sad to see that they needed so much space. The director asked if we were planning to adopt again and tried to entice us with a very adorable little girl saying she could tell we were short of girls. I made sure to move Matt along before he could get too attached. We saw the room where the toddlers play as well as a sort of preschool that they had downstairs. I noticed they had bookcases in the hallway where children placed their shoes and they had put the child's picture in each place so they know where their shoes go. Although the building is older, it was bright and cheerful. Just like a school, they had children's artwork hanging everywhere in the classroom areas. In the stairwells they had pictures of children who had been adopted out of the orphanage.

After the tour we went to the staff lunchroom to eat. The other blogs I had read where people visited the orphanage usually had the family eating out at a restaurant with the director. I wondered if that was too expensive because of our group size but I didn't have any regrets. We were served a mountain of food and the director told us that some of the dishes were the same as the children were served for lunch that day. I loved that I was eating fish stew made from locally caught fish and it was the same that the children ate. How wonderful that they get fresh cooked food every day. I guess I had thought they were getting the sort of factory made frozen foods that they serve in schools here in America!

The director told me at lunch that about 100 babies are abandoned in the area each year and come into their care but only about 30 are adopted out, most internationally. I have heard many adoptive parents say that when children in China "age out" meaning they can no longer be adopted at age 14, they are then turned out into the street. I read on the Love Without Boundaries website that they actually remain in care until age 18. The director told me that the kids receive some education at the orphanage and those who are able to work, they try and train for some job. She said they try to help them get a job in town, or maybe they can work cleaning at the orphanage. For those who are disabled to the extent that they can't work, the state will continue to care for them, and they will be moved to the home for the aged which is located in the same facility.

After we finished lunch we said goodbye to the director. She said we must come back to visit when Leo was older, maybe ten years from now. She said that would give us enough time to save up enough money to bring the rest of the family to visit with him! Then she said that she would be retired by that time but not to worry because her apartment is very close to the orphanage so she can still come by when we visit to see us all again. She was such a great person, you can tell she really has a heart for the children.

For such a long drive we really weren't there very long. We were able to stop by Leo's finding place on the way out and take a picture for him. Leo napped the first two hours home again. When he woke up he actually seemed much happier than before. I guess he decided he wanted to stay with us because he wasn't at all upset that we didn't leave him at the orphanage. However, he has decided that Matt is his favorite parent and now he doesn't want to have anything to do with me. If Matt sets him down for an instant he will immediately start to cry. I'm not insulted because I know this is a normal behavior and it doesn't last forever.

We are exhausted from the long day so we just had a quick supper at the hotel with food that we had packed. Now we're getting ready for bed.

September 7, 2013

Yesterday (Friday) was our day to check out of our hotel in Nanjing and fly to Guangzhou where we will stay for our last week in China. While in Nanjing we were staying in a suite at the Holiday Inn. The attached mall was nice, because we could go out and walk around easily if we wanted. The suite had one room with a king size bed where Matt and I slept with Vincent and Leo slept in a crib. The other room had two beds that were about the size of a double bed. Linda and Mary Evelyn slept in one and Max and Gregory in the other. The Holiday Inn wasn't quite as fancy as the Novatel Peace in Beijing but it was quite comfortable for us.

As we were taking the elevator down with our luggage, we shared the elevator with a Chinese gentleman who spoke excellent English. He looked around the elevator and asked "These all your family?" When I said yes, he smiled and nodded and then gestured toward Leo. "This is your youngest?" I said yes again, and he said politely but in a slightly confused way "He look . . . Chinese?" So I explained that we had just adopted him and then he nodded in understanding.

We went back to the Nanjing airport with Denise and the same driver we have had all week. Denise mused on the food in Guangzhou, remarking that the Cantonese "are very adventurous eaters. They eat cat, snake, monkey brains . . ." Many people warned us to avoid domestic flights in China but really we haven't had any trouble with the flights. The airport bathrooms have a good supply of soap and Western toilets. We haven't had any trouble communicating with the security personnel and the signs are in dual Chinese and English. One thing that I have noticed is that the female security guards and all the stewardesses are gorgeous. There is not an old or homely one to be found. Another interesting custom is having the person you should address questions to being indicated by the person wearing a beauty pageant style sash. It looks perfectly natural on the lovely baggage claim girl but the male security guard in his black police uniform looks a little silly in the red sash with a bow at the waist.

Many domestic flights are delayed but so far we have been lucky enough to avoid that. As we waited in the terminal for it to be time to climb onto the bus to take us to our plane we heard two other flights to Guangzhou announced as delayed. We chuckled as the English announcement apologized for the delay and suggested delayed passengers should relax and rest in the waiting area. It was swelteringly hot and the waiting area was standing room only. Not relaxing at all! We have been fed on both our domestic flights even though they were short and the food is much better than on US domestic flights. We arrived in Guangzhou at about 6:30 and then had another long drive to the China Hotel.

Guangzhou will be our home for the next week. The adoption has been completed as far as China is concerned, but now we have some things to do for the American side. This morning (Saturday) Matt took Leo for a medical exam. This afternoon we will complete paperwork for Leo's visa. He will travel home on his Chinese passport so he needs a visa to enter the US. We don't have any plans on Sunday or Monday, but Tuesday is our appointment at the US Consulate. We will receive the paperwork that we need to make Leo a citizen once he is processed through customs on entering the US. His visa should be ready on Tuesday afternoon and then we are free to leave. As I mentioned before, we will not be flying home until Friday morning for various travel related reasons. But our suite here at the China Hotel will be a luxurious home for us for the next week. It is larger than the apartment Matt and I had for four years during his time in graduate school! It is a similar layout to the last suite only we have an extra half bath which is always a nice perk when you have 7 people living here (plus one in diapers).

I don't expect us to do a lot of touring here but there is a lot that is walking distance from the China Hotel. There are two different large parks adjacent to the hotel. We won't even have to make a crazy Chinese street crossing because there are underpasses leading to the parks. There is also the tomb of an ancient Chinese king next door to the hotel, so there is plenty to keep us busy on our free days.

Since I don't have a lot more to say today, I thought I'd tell you about laundry. The hotels here don't have washers and dryers for our use and the hotel laundry service has dry-cleaning prices. There are local options for us to send our laundry out but even at a more reasonable dollar an item price it really adds up for a family our size. I wanted to pack light so I did not pack 16 outfits per person. We were lucky as to our travel time, because those who travel during cool weather need to pack for two different seasons because when it's snowing in Beijing, it is warm and sunny in Guangzhou. We packed a reasonable amount of mix and match clothing and I wash the laundry in the bathtub.

Washing is actually the easy part, it's the drying that's a challenge. It is difficult to get the water wrung out so the clothing can dry sooner. I mostly hang the clothing in the closet to dry but there is a surprising amount of places in the suite to hang laundry to dry. The Holiday Inn suite had a retractable clothesline over the bathtub. After seeing all the Chinese laundry hanging out on balconies and in the street, I don't even think that the maids think we're weird. It does take some planning because we have to have enough time for the clothing to dry before we can pack it. The iron provided by the hotel helps with the last bit of dampness. I packed the clothing in large packing ziploc bags, and I try to keep putting the outfits for one day back in a bag as the clean laundry dries to try and keep things organized better. That's it for today, hopefully I will have more Guangzhou pictures for you tomorrow.

Later--

Matt went out bright and early today for the medical exam. He didn't take any pictures since he was on his own but he said everything went well for the exam. After he got back we had a few hours before I needed to go downstairs to fill out paperwork so we decided to go out to lunch. Matt was finally started to crave some American food, so he wanted to go across the street to eat at the Coffee Cafe, which the guide had suggested. I guess everyone else thought it sounded like a good idea because there were two other families with our group there. Our table had a combination of pancakes, sandwiches, and hamburgers and it was good, but we had some Western food sticker shock at the bill. One of the perks of liking Asian food is that it really saves you a lot of money when you're traveling.

After we ate, we went back to the hotel so Leo could take a nap. He is still doing well and turning into a very happy boy, just as the orphanage director said. He still prefers Matt to anyone else, but unless he's very tired or something he will let me hold him in small amounts. He is a surprisingly picky eater for someone who loves to eat. Matt says he's the equivalent to an American kid who only eats fries and chicken nuggets. He will eat congee, steamed buns, and watermelon for breakfast, but no other fruit. Oatmeal is the only American food we have tried him on that he will eat. He also loves rice. Matt was asking our guide for the correct way to order rice while we were in the van once and Leo perked right up at all the talk about "mi fan."

Although the orphanage personnel were quite adamant that he doesn't take a bottle anymore he has no idea how to drink from a cup and he found drinking from a sippy cup (the kind without a valve because he can't form a suction) frustrating. He is very comfortable drinking from a bottle though so that is what we're sticking with until we get back home.

I spent about an hour downstairs filling out paperwork for our consulate appointment. Once I got back then we decided to go walk around and find a place to eat. It is very warm and humid in Guangzhou. You see a lot of Spanish moss on trees, and palm trees as well. Again, we felt very safe walking around and had no problem finding lots of little shops and places to eat. We found one where they spoke no English but had a picture menu so we pointed at a few things and waited for the food. They first brought out three pots of what seemed to be duck broth. It was

319

so delicious! Leo just ate and ate it, refusing even to take a bite of his beloved rice until Matt had the idea to pour some of the broth over the rice. Then the main dishes came out and we all shared them. They were all very tasty. We are teaching the children the cardinal rule of being a good traveler–if you like what you eat, then don't ask what it is! And the total for tonight's meal was $12 for the eight of us. I think we'll stick with Asian food!

On the way back to the hotel, Matt stopped in a local bakery to buy some moon cakes for us to sample. The mid-autumn festival is approaching and moon cakes are a special food associated with the festival. In the airport we saw many people with gift bags of moon cakes with them. Our hotel has a large area near the door where people walk in off the street and buy moon cakes. I've walked by there four times and each time it has been packed with people. They have a giant moon cake for sale in a shop off the lobby. We only bought three to sample because Chinese desserts aren't usually what Americans consider good in a dessert. We really like sweet desserts. The moon cakes weren't bad (unlike the green gelatinous bean curd covered with raw garlic sauce that we had at the orphanage) but we decided the next time we go by the bakery we'll get a cake instead of the 12 pack of moon cakes.

September 8, 2013

We had today free and we enjoyed being able to sleep in and have a leisurely breakfast. After breakfast we decided to go to one of the two large parks that are nearby the hotel. It isn't oppressively hot out but it is very humid. It feels like a steamy bathroom after a shower out there. As we walked the short distance to the park, we saw several people who had set out wares on blankets to try and interest the tourists from the two large hotels.

Liuhua park was beautiful. On the map it looked like a park with a series of lakes. On the ground it looked like one huge lake with many walkways across and around it. There was a huge marble building right in the center but somehow we never made it to that building. I think you can tell from this picture that we're all starting to get tired of smiling for pictures in front of interesting landmarks.

We saw all kinds of interesting things. There were many people fishing from the banks, and one guy who set up an elaborate net and pulled fish into a boat. There was an exercise area that was packed with people young to old using the equipment. People were playing instruments or badminton. There was a ladies fan-dancing class and rental paddle boats. We found one building that we could enter and it was had a display of local artists' work.

We enjoyed the walk but we were hot and tired when we got back to the hotel. We had a light lunch and put Leo down for his nap. After he woke up, we decided to go swimming at the hotel pool. It is outdoors on the fourth floor and it was perfect weather for a swim. I didn't take the camera because I assumed that Leo would just cry and cling to Matt but I was completely wrong so I'll take the camera next time. He was a little hesitant at first, but then the he had a lot of fun. He was splashing and laughing. He even let me hold him a little at the end. We swam for close to two hours, and then decided to just order Papa Johns for supper. The Chinese don't eat much dairy and they usually think American melted cheese food is gross, so I was also surprised when Leo loved the pizza and ate a slice and a half.

Other than still being suspicious of me, he's still doing very well. He hasn't had any more grieving times since we visited his orphanage. He sleeps well at night and takes a long nap. He spends time playing with the other children every day. He still thinks Mary Evelyn is special. He laughs and runs over to Matt when he sees him put on the Ergo carrier. He's a happy little guy, just like the director said. We think we're pretty lucky to have him!

September 9, 2013

Monday was another free day for us but we will be busy tomorrow. We basically did the same thing today as we did yesterday. We had made plans to go to the Guangzhou Safari Park with another family but decided to stay close to the hotel after all. Leo does not like the heat and the Safari Park is more of an all-day event. After breakfast we decided to visit the other park near the hotel, Yuexiu Park. Yuexiu Park is so huge that I printed off an extra page from google maps to be able to get most of it on a page. I think it's Guangzhou's version of Central Park. Yuexiu Park is home to Guangzhou's famous five goat statue.

Legend has it that five deities came to Guangzhou riding on five goats and they blessed Guangdong Province with a wonderful climate that insured plentiful harvests for the people who live here. You see the five goats statue everywhere as a symbol of the city. This park was different from yesterday's park but we enjoyed it as well. Yuexiu is very much like walking through the zoo's rainforest climate biosphere, only you never get to leave the biosphere.

We came back to the hotel for a light lunch and nap for Leo. We headed out to walk in the neighborhood we had eaten at on Sunday to look for an early supper. We found a large restaurant this time and they had a menu that was written in English for us but no pictures. I decided that the picture menu is better because I'd rather not know what all my options are. There were regular exotic fare such as snails or eel along with pretty much all of the pig—feet, ears, offal. I was just thinking that pig offal was a mistranslation of intestines until I turned the page and saw cow intestines offered as well. We picked some items that were safe to eat and had a good supper.

I don't think I've mentioned before, but the tap water in China is not drinkable. Apparently their pipes are old and sometimes sewage seeps in. So when we eat out we can't order water because you don't know if they will be serving tap water or not. You can request bottled water but restaurants offer name brand

Evian instead of Chinese bottled water so it is about three times the cost of soda. We order soda and usually it is served European style, that is warm with no free refills. It's nice when they keep the cans or bottles in a refrigerator and we can drink it cold. Occasionally it is served with ice, which we really shouldn't have because we don't know if they've made it from tap water or not. So far the time or two we've had ice, we just tried to drink the Coke quickly enough that the ice doesn't melt. Restaurants do not keep western style utensils around so it's chopsticks or large soup spoons. I try to pack along a couple of plastic forks for the younger two who haven't quite mastered chopsticks yet. Finally, while it isn't as annoying as the national habit of hand-washing without soap, one thing that I dislike about Chinese restaurants is that half the time they don't provide any napkins. If they do, the Chinese style napkins are basically a box of tissues. If someone happens to spill a drink then you have to use up half a box!

After we finished eating we stopped into a large Chinese bakery. They had lots of western desserts and many interesting cakes. We bought some bread and a few samples of desserts to try back at the hotel. Then we went swimming in the evening. Leo loved the water again. It turned to be a sort of boy adoption pool party as we were joined by three other couples adopting boys. Two Spanish speaking couples were adopting boys who were under 18 months and then there was another American couple with a son about Leo's age.

We have just three days left in China and we are starting to be ready to get back home. We have really loved our time here but we are getting very tired of living in a hotel! Earlier today Matt wanted something to eat but he was tired of the granola bars and other easy to pack food that we had in the room. He remembered that the hotel convenience store had some cans of Campbell's soup so he decided to go buy one of those. He got down to the store and saw that his choices were oxtail soup and borscht. He bought the oxtail soup, but saw then that it wasn't a pull-top lid. He stopped by the front desk to ask if the hotel had a can-opener that he could use. They told him to call the help line from his room and housekeeping could bring one up. He went upstairs and called the help line. The nice lady didn't understand the world "can-opener." Matt googled the Chinese word for can-opener. She said she would send someone right up. A few minutes later a uniformed staff person knocked on the door. He requested the can, and then said he would be back in a few minutes, and left with the can. Five minutes later, Matt finally had an open can of oxtail soup. It was tasty but I'm not sure anything would be worth all that trouble!

September 10, 2013

Today was our appointment at the US Consulate. The medical exam results from Saturday were in and it was time to go apply for a visa for Leo. I don't have any pictures for this portion of the post because the consulate doesn't allow: cameras, cell phones, backpacks, wristwatches, ink pens, or strollers. The consulate just moved to this new location recently, and it is a complex with a few buildings. The back part had a high privacy fence and as we came around the front there was a blue plastic barricade. There were a lot of Chinese people waiting around the barricade area, I assume because they came with people who were inside. We went through the barricade and then to a separate security building. We had to show our passports and when our name was matched to the appointment list we were let into the inner courtyard.

Once we entered the main building we were sent to a separate area upstairs. We could see the main area down below where Chinese citizens waited in a long line that snaked around like the wait for a popular amusement park ride. Our room was specifically for adoptions and there was a playhouse and several toys for children. We sat with our paperwork and waited with the other families who had this appointment time. After a few minutes an American man began to give us instructions by using a microphone on the other side of bulletproof glass. Apparently, they don't take any chances even though we all went through security. Unfortunately because of the tile floor, lots of of shiny wall surfaces, and a large amount of loud children, it was difficult for all of us to understand him. Eventually we rose to take "the oath." I've read several accounts of people who said they teared up taking the oath so I assumed it was like the promises we made to China to care for Leo—to not abuse him, to love him, and provide him with an education. What really happened was that we swore we hadn't falsified any documents. A little anti-climactic, but okay. Then we were called to the window one by one while a consulate employee went over our paperwork. We left Leo's passport and it will be returned tomorrow with a US entry visa sticker in it.

After we got home, we decided to go back to the street where we found three bakeries and buy a cake to celebrate. While the consulate employee stressed that Leo is not a citizen and won't be until his paperwork is processed when we return to the US, we don't anticipate having a lot of time to celebrate before we have to run and catch our connecting flight. We choose one cake but the employee talked us out of it, making faces to indicate that she didn't think we would like it. We chose the one she recommended and then headed back. Mary Evelyn wanted to stop in a tea shop to buy a teapot so we made another stop.

The owner went through a little ritual to give us samples of tea. There was a machine that cleaned and sterilized the little cups, so she removed some cups from that. There was one of the great instant tea pots they have here that boil water in 30 seconds. She put loose tea leaves in a small pot and poured the water over it after covering it with a lid. She then poured out a sample of tea over an area that had a decorative drain to catch any tea that spilled out. She also filtered out the tea leaves for us. The Chinese usually drink their tea with the leaves still in it. On the street you see many people with water bottles that have tea leaves floating around on the bottom slung over the handlebars of their bikes. After we bought some tea we made a quick stop at the McDonald's that is right next to our hotel. Leo decided he also likes fries.

After naptime (and more laundry), we were ready to get out of the hotel room again. We decided to go back to Yuexiu Park since it seemed like we had just scratched the surface there. We rented a stroller from the hotel to see if Leo liked that any more than the ergo carrier. He really gets unhappy in the heat and being strapped to someone's back can heat you up fast. We had another really great walk in the park. We found the old Guangzhou city walls that were built during the Ming dynasty. We found Zhenhai Tower and watched a team practicing on the soccer field. We walked to the Sun Yat-sen memorial and found a wonderful view of the city close to sunset.

Then we walked back to the hotel. Matt picked up some carry-out and decided what to order by asking the guy at the stand what was most popular. We all ate noodles and mystery meat and then had the cake for dessert. The bakery lady had given us a birthday party in a box, including little paper plates that said happy birthday, a cake server, forks, and a pack of candles. I saved the candles for Leo's real birthday next week. It was the perfect end to a great day.

September 11, 2013

This morning Matt was left at the hotel with the four boys to wait for paperwork to arrive while Linda, Mary Evelyn, and I had a girls' morning out shopping. I hired a local woman who offers a guided shopping service. She used to work at a touristy store and now she takes adoptive families to the wholesale shops where the touristy shops buy their wares to sell. We were completely amazed to walk into a huge multi-level mall which had nothing

326

but jewelry stores. Linda and I really had a lot of fun looking at everything and making our purchases but I think Mary Evelyn was regretting agreeing to come along.

Our guide asked us what sort of items we wanted to buy and then took us to a variety of stores. She took us to all of these little back alley places. We didn't see anyone who wasn't Chinese so I know we were hitting the local spots. We stopped at a store that sold traditional Chinese clothing. I was trying on a dress when the guide said that I would need to get a XXL. I said to Linda that shopping in Chinese sizes sure kept you humble. The guide asked what size I wore in America and I said that I was usually considered a small in American sizes. She said something to the store owner and they both chuckled. But I liked my dress just fine despite the XXL on the tag. The boys liked their outfits, too.

While I was gone shopping Matt was finishing up some odds and ends with our agency. We got Leo's visa in and the "magical" brown envelope which will turn him into a citizen once the immigration officer opens it so long as we can complete the quest of traveling home without losing it or damaging the envelope. While Matt was down in our agency's office I had him take a red couch photo of Leo. Back when China adoption was in full swing, pretty much everyone stayed at the same hotel on Shamian Island. The hotel had red couches in the lobby, and it became a tradition to take a picture of your child on the couch. Now the consulate and medical exam building are no longer on Shamian Island and the White Swan Hotel is closed for renovation but our agency bought one of the red couches so that parents can keep up the tradition.

It was almost supper time by the time we were able to get Leo's passport with visa so we didn't have time to go out and do anything this afternoon. We decided to get takeout from one of the many restaurants in the hotel, finish off the last half of the cake (delicious, by the way!), and go swimming one last time.

Tomorrow is our last full day in China so we need to make sure our suits are dry in time for tomorrow's major packing party.

September 12, 2013

I thought 16 days in China would be a really long trip, but I'm sad that it's time to leave. We have truly enjoyed our days here and I wish that China were closer so visiting regularly would be an option.

This morning we visited the tomb of the Nanyue king. This was an ancient king who ruled over a small kingdom here in the south of China before an Emperor began to rule most of the country. The tomb museum is on the same block as our hotel and I have heard from many people that the tomb was found when they were building the hotel, so they had to move the hotel site.

The museum was large, modern, and air-conditioned which is something that we really appreciate in this sweltering city. They had a large collection of ceramic pillows. They looked quite beautiful but not especially comfortable. We saw many artifacts which were uncovered in the tomb as well as the king's jade burial suit. The suit was made of many small tiles of jade which were sewn together with red silk thread. There were also many jade discs buried on and under the body.

The best part of the museum was that they had preserved the burial site. There are no artifacts remaining but we could walk down into the tomb and through the rooms. You could even see traces of painting on some of the walls. Mary Evelyn said the museum was well worth the $2 admission charge.

We spent nap time packing up our suitcases then we went for one last walk in Yuexiu Park. After supper, Linda and I walked down my favorite traditional street one last time while she looked for a few more souvenirs to buy. It's an early bedtime for everyone tonight since we have to be in the van on the way to the airport at 5 am.

September 14, 2013

Boy, was that a long trip home! We got up at 4 pm EST on Thursday and didn't walk in the door at Don and Linda's house until 9 pm EST on Friday. For the most part, the flights went smoothly. We continually had a problem with our tickets so for two of the three flights home we spent about 45 minutes at the check-in counter. This made gave us very little time to make it to the flight and each time we had to go through security twice. It seemed like we had to show our boarding passes and passports about four times each trip. It seems redundant to have to show our passports to get the boarding pass, the boarding passes and passports to be able to get on the plane, and then have the stewardess standing by the door to the plane request to see it all again! They actually held our flight for us in Shanghai, and we spent so much time getting processed through security and running from the domestic to international terminal with suitcases and a 30 pound toddler on my back that we didn't even have time to use the restroom or get a drink of water. It was such a relief to step out into the cool weather at home after a week of being constantly sweaty in tropical Guangzhou.

Since Leo is barely under 2 we decided to purchase a lap ticket for the flights home. We figured he would be clingy and not want to sit in his own seat, anyway. He slept most of the flight from Guangzhou to Shanghai on my lap and during the flight from Shanghai to Seattle he often shared Vincent's seat. That flight was the worst trip we had because Leo spent a few hours in the middle crying. Fortunately, he wasn't very loud and the noise of the plane drowned out most of the sound. Vincent and Leo slept several hours of the long flight and Gregory took a half-hour nap. None of the adults did more than doze off for 5 minutes here and there. We finally arrived at Seattle and while we were processed through customs Leo's magic brown envelope was opened and he became the newest US citizen. He looks pretty happy at the thought but really he was just happy to be off that plane!

I was dreading the flight from Seattle to Cincinnati but because we were all so exhausted that everyone but Linda slept pretty much the entire four hour flight. Gregory was asleep before take-off and I woke him up as we were landing. Even Mary Evelyn fell asleep for the first time on the trip. Matt's dad met us at the airport along with his sister and her family. It was great to see some familiar faces and to be back home in America. Sometimes it's the simplest things that make the biggest impression. Mary Evelyn remarked "You know, I was never homesick for America when we were in China, but it is *really* nice to use a restroom with lots of toilet paper and soap and not a single squatty potty!"

One thing that I had wondered about was how the Chinese people would react to seeing Leo be a part of our family. While the Chinese adoption program is common knowledge here in America, most people in China don't seem to be aware of it. It is common for someone to approach a family's guide and ask why the American couple has a Chinese baby. Of course, it is similar here in America. Most people are unaware that some American children are adopted out of the country each year (most are private infant adoptions, but a few foster kids will find a permanent family in Canada). I know Americans feel both angry and ashamed that we do not have homes for all of our children, and I expected the Chinese to feel the same way.

It really didn't seem that way, though. The only remotely negative reaction I came across was when we were flying from Nanjing to Guangzhou. As we exited the plane there were two Chinese women waiting to clean the plane and I heard one say to the other "orphanage baby" in English. For the most part, people have made very positive remarks. At the end of our long flight home a Chinese stewardess came by to coo over Leo and said "You have changed his future. He had no future in China without a family, and now his future is bright. He is fortunate to have these brothers and sister, and now he will have many opportunities in American."

330

That's it for today. We need to get back home to our real house where I am actually looking forward washing laundry using my labor saving washing and drying machines! I do anticipate writing a few more posts over the next week or two letting you know how Leo is adjusting, how his doctor's appointments went, and things along those lines. Thanks again to all of you who followed along on our journey!

21

Travel Journal: Our second adoption

About two years after we adopted Leo, we decided to adopt from China again. In many ways, we had a very different experience. My husband wanted us to wait to be matched by our agency this time, so our time from match to travel was much shorter. I wrote the majority of this book during that time period. Leo was from a wonderful Half the Sky (now OneSky) orphanage, while August was from a very large, closed orphanage which we were not allowed to tour. We did not receive much information at all about him. Leo had spent some time in foster care, while August had only been at the orphanage. It's a good thing we decided to take our whole family on the first trip because the weather was perfect. The second time around, we took only our seven-year-old Vincent, and it was freezing cold in Beijing in January. Even our travel experience was quite different. For the first trip, we traveled to three cities and flew out of Guangzhou. Because August was from Beijing, we only traveled to there and Guangzhou for the adoption portion of the trip but returned home through Hong Kong. Their grieving process, adjustment to our family, and personalities are quite different as well, as was only to be expected.

January 3, 2016 - The Itinerary

It's less than a week until we leave for China! I will try to blog every day that we are in China. I usually only put 3-5 photos in a blog post for ease of reading. However, if you click through the Flickr thingy on the right then you can see additional photos. Yes, I know everyone else switched to Instagram 5 years ago. I had a Flickr account um, 10 years ago, so I find it easier to post pictures there.

There will be a few differences between our first adoption trip to China in 2013 and this one. The biggest is that we will not be taking our whole big family to China with us. Our older children have school commitments that they cannot easily miss and mostly we can't afford to take everyone again. It was the trip of a lifetime, no regrets there, but this time it will be only ourselves and one child traveling. Our son Vincent will be coming along with us while the other children stay at home with their grandmother. He is wonderful with small children, he doesn't remember our first trip to China, and he even speaks a little Chinese. A few of you might remember that Vincent used to think that he was also adopted from China. He asked us to sign him up at the local Chinese school while he was still a little confused about that so we will see how helpful that will be for us.

We leave on January 8th for China and will arrive in Beijing on the 9th in the late afternoon. Our son August is from the Beijing CWI so we will spend a full week in Beijing this time. Beijing is in the northern part of China, about the same latitude as Philadelphia, PA. Which means it will be cold! Beijing has a population similar to Chicago. We will be touring the Summer Palace and Temple of Heaven on Sunday, hopefully with Nancy who was our guide previously.

Leo's orphanage was located about 4 hours away from the provincial capital so we did not meet him until late Monday afternoon. For this adoption we will be meeting August early Monday morning in a reception room at his orphanage. Although we will be at his orphanage we will not be allowed to tour it the way we did Leo's orphanage. We have various adoption related appointments throughout the week. Vincent expressed a desire to see the Great Wall (again) so as long as August is doing well we will probably fit that in.

On Friday the 15th we will fly to Guangzhou in southern China. All adoption trips end in Guangzhou because that is where the American consulate is located. It's hard to find an East Coast city on the same latitude but Key West, FL is closest. Packing for two seasons means we will be taking almost the same amount of luggage as we did on our first trip with twice the amount of travelers! Guangzhou is the 3rd largest city in China. Our consulate appointment will be on Wednesday the 20th because the Beijing municipality doesn't prepare the child's passport in advance so we will wait to receive that by mail. As long as all goes well we should receive our visa on Thursday. While we are in Guangzhou Vincent will turn 7 and August will turn 3 just two days later.

This time we will be flying out of Hong Kong instead of Guangzhou. We plan to check out of our hotel early Friday morning and take a train to Hong Kong. Hopefully we will have time to see a little of Hong Kong in the afternoon. On Saturday morning we begin our journey home. We land in our home city around 8 pm on the 23rd. I can't think of a better way to spend most of January!

January 10, 2016 - Sunday in Beijing

We made it to China! As expected the trip was long and exhausting. I think people in our family have an immunity to sleeping on airplanes. We had been awake for about 26 hours by the time we could finally collapse into our beds at the hotel. Vincent did well on the plane. I think he watched the first half of every movie on the kid's menu of the in-flight entertainment system. He also requested Sprite at every opportunity. Once we landed in Beijing we still had to go through customs, be cleared to enter the country (we appreciated that families with children were moved to the express lane), and claim our baggage. At that point we were finally able to meet our guide Nancy. She told us that she now works in the office rather than as a tour guide but she had agreed to be our guide again because she likes to see previous families. We had transported a suitcase of medical supplies for New Hope Foundation in Beijing and she helped us to meet up with their representative to hand over the suitcase.

Nancy got checked in at our hotel, then told us what time she would meet us on Sunday morning. We are staying at the same hotel as our last trip but we will be in Beijing for a week this time. The hotel is a French chain so the staff at the front desk speak excellent French but only moderately good English. Busloads of Air France employees are dropped off at regular intervals from the airport. The hotel has a European feel. The pastry selection at the breakfast buffet is amazing and I appreciate the cold meat and cheese area. We could live without the European style shower though, which is a handheld model attached to the wall at waist height.

That's pretty much our Friday and Saturday. This morning we were up bright and early due to jet lag. We decided to attend the 6:15 Mass at St. Joseph's Cathedral which is very close to our hotel. Then we ate breakfast on our way back in. We still had an hour to video chat with the children back home before meeting Nancy. Then we headed to the Summer Palace. We did pack masks to wear because the pollution index is so much higher than on our previous trip. You can feel the pollution as a burning in your nose, sinuses, and the back of your throat.

Although it's cold, it was a great day to walk around there. The lake was frozen and people were ice skating, ice biking, pretty much ice-anythinging. The architecture is beautiful and the mountain view picturesque. We liked it better than the Forbidden City which was more austere. We spent probably two hours there, walking around. As always, Nancy did a great job telling us about the history. Nancy was so tickled that Vincent has been learning Chinese. She would quiz him on characters. We came to one place where a man was writing characters on the pavement with water using a giant sponge paintbrush. When he asked if anyone wanted to try, Nancy immediately volunteered Vincent. The whole crowd was delighted when he wrote the characters for China and the number one.

From the Summer Palace we went for the obligatory sales visit to the silk factory, then got to eat lunch. Nancy took us to a place which specialized in "old Beijing food." We had a sour beef and egg dish as well as hand pulled noodles with soy bean sauce which are native Beijing dishes. Another dish was a breaded and fried chicken cut into pieces but arranged on the plate with the head in front. Nancy teased me, asking if I could eat the chicken while it looked at me but I replied that I was raised on a farm so it didn't bother me at all. I don't think she had met an American before who had eaten rabbit, pig tongue, and frog legs as a child. She asked hopefully if I had tried donkey too but I told her that isn't a common farm animal where I'm from.

After lunch we went to the Temple of Heaven. Like the Summer Palace, it seems to be visited by locals more for the public park than for the historical site. I really wish our public parks had the same sense of community and camaraderie that you feel in parks in China. We passed older women dancing to music, a men's group singing old Red party songs, a line of people playing cards or chess, and individuals singing or playing the traditional Chinese erhu. Where the playground would be in an American park there was an area full of exercise and agility/massage equipment filled with older Chinese citizens earnestly getting in their daily activity. We eventually made it up to the Temple of Heaven, then headed back to the hotel where we said goodbye to Nancy. We will have a different guide for our adoption trips the rest of the week. We will leave at 6:30 am tomorrow to meet August.

January 11, 2016 - Adoption Day

Its late afternoon on Monday so it seems early to write a post for the day but I know everyone is looking forward to hearing how things went. We got up very early this morning. We met our guide in the lobby at 6:30 am. She said that the orphanage is in another part of Beijing and with rush hour traffic she expected it to be an hour long drive. We arrived at the orphanage as the sun was coming up. The lobby lights didn't even seem to be on but the door was open.

We were shown into an empty waiting room. With adoptions from China the policy is that you have a 24 hour "harmonious period" while you have custody of the child but the adoption is not yet finalized. This is to give you a chance to decide if you want to proceed. I had been warned that this orphanage does not practice the harmonious period. I had joked with a friend that we would have a harmonious 20 minutes. What actually happened is that we filled out the adoption paperwork before they even brought August in to meet us!

August was brought in by the orphanage director. In all of the photos and over seven minutes of video we received he is always very serious. He never says a word and we've only seen one brief smile. We actually asked in an update request if he could talk but the response was not clear so we had no expectations there. The director set him down with a bag of snacks. She told him to share the crackers with us and he replied back to her! We didn't hear what he said but it was a two word response. As we spoke to him and gradually moved him from the director's arms to ours he remained solemn. The orphanage director and other employee kept talking to encourage him. They took lots of photos of us together.

After we finished at the orphanage we had to drive to the civil affairs bureau which was another long drive. Several of us including August took a nap. He seems very stoic. He has only cried a little but tries to avoid eye contact. We continued to wait at the civil affairs bureau. There were two more couples who arrived at the orphanage to adopt as we were finishing. Apparently we were waiting for them to arrive at civil affairs along with an orphanage employee. One of the other couples arrived first and we began to chat while we waited for the orphanage employee. In an incredible occurrence, we realized that they were the Spanish couple which was adopting with us in Nanjing in 2013! The wife said "Our destinies are surely entwined together!"

They remembered that we had brought our other children with us last time. They have four boys and are adopting their first daughter. The husband told us that they had applied to adopt from China through the standard process in 2006. They had three biological children and one domestic adoption before they were matched from China, all boys. This was their first adoption through the special needs program. The husband is an architect

338

who designs hospitals so he and Matt had a long discussion about the special requirements for radiation departments.

Eventually we got to the paperwork part of the visit. When it was time for August to put his handprint on the forms he was very uncooperative. He clinched his little hand into a fist. Our guide kept trying to get him to spread it out. Even after she got the red ink on it it took several tries to get the handprint onto the paperwork. Everyone chuckled at him. He was happier after we wiped his hand off but he kept frowning at the red ink residue.

From the civil affairs bureau we visited August's finding spot. We then came back to the hotel. Matt went out to get lunch. August had ignored the little bag of toys we brought previously but in the hotel room he was very curious about them. He packed and unpacked the bag, stacked the items, and poked at the carrot nose on Vincent's small stuffed Olaf. When Matt returned he ate a good lunch. We hadn't been able to get him to drink anything all day. After trying two different containers we decided to switch to plain water in case he didn't like the juice. Matt pulled up a website to find out to say "drink water" in Chinese. When August heard the voice from the computer, he looked up and said "drink water" very clearly! He repeated it for Matt when he tried. He actually drank the water too. He handed the bottle back to Matt and made a thank you gesture, kind of bowing with his hands together. This was all very exciting although he hasn't spoken since then. It's good to know that he can communicate. I'm sure he will open up more over the next few days as he begins to feel comfortable with us.

August came to us in a very nice outfit. Two outfits if you count the under layer. We've peeled off an item or two but when we took off his hat he put it back on again. He smells like soap so he must have had an early bath this morning. When I took his hat off I saw that the back of his head is beautifully round. My adoption friends will appreciate the rarity of that. Now he has taken a long nap and is up and playing again. He is very seriously trying to crack the code of the stacking cups and taking peeks at us when he thinks we aren't looking. He's such a brave little guy!

January 11, 2016 - Night Life

We are here in China between Christmas and Chinese New Year. In America we are rather Chinese-centric by using that name because many Asian countries celebrate the lunar new year. Here in China they call it the Spring Festival. The national holiday lasts two weeks but just as Christmas isn't really one day in America so the Spring Festival goes on for about a month. In the evenings the street outside our hotel is full of decorative lights. When I asked our guide what they were for she sort of shrugged and indicated they were good for either Christmas or Spring Festival. There are lots of lights, but also some which are definitely Christmas and others which are definitely Spring Festival.

On Monday night we walked down to the Wangfujing area which is close to our hotel. In the evenings there is a night market which is also called Snack Street. It is a long area of vendors which sell anything you can eat on a stick. Fruit, candies, ducks, squid, starfish . . . We came on our last trip but didn't buy anything. This time we decided to try a favorite Beijing street food called candy haws. They are Hawthorn apples, which are about the size of an apricot with a candy apple coating. They had a slight tart flavor which was great with the candy coating. I can see why they're so popular.

We did have to cross the street to get to snack street. Crossing the street in China is not for the faint-hearted. All of the traffic signals and signs are more like traffic suggestions. People do whatever they can get away with. To cross the street you may or may not wait for the crosswalk light. What you really must wait for is a large group of people to cross with. You want about six people minimum to dissuade a standard car. Sometimes there aren't enough people waiting to cross. At that point it becomes necessary to debate a little about which 1 or 2 people you want to cross with. You don't want to be crossing when the other person goes and jumps in front of a car, which you obviously don't want to do, so then you're stuck standing in the middle of traffic without a shield. Monday evening we were standing on the street corner trying to decide which individuals looked crazy and which looked safe to cross with when one of them decided to let us know they knew English by replying "Cross with us!" We did, and we're still alive.

Today we once again headed out to the shopping district in the evening. August has a lower limb difference which means he can't walk any great distance. He's a big kid, so a stroller would be very helpful when we are out and about. We started out at the mall. As we were coming in a young couple who spoke excellent English engaged us in conversation. Sometimes people do that. Usually they are being friendly but sometimes they're trying to scam you. When we had talked for a few minutes without any sort of invitation or sales pitch, I asked if they knew a store in the mall where we might find a stroller. They said yes and offered to show us the way but the way was headed out of the mall. We hesitated but they pointed to a store a few doors down in the same shopping district. We followed them to a large department store. Every few feet an employee was stationed to make a sales pitch but the entire place was empty except for us. They did have a selection of about six strollers. The first one we were shown was more than we wanted to pay, though probably what we would have paid in the mall. We said we didn't want to spend that much and turned around as if we were heading back to the mall. Lo and behold, it turned out that the stroller next to it was just that day marked down for the Spring Festival sale. It was basically the same stroller in pink (guess we won't get a lot of use out of it back home) only now half price. Matt went to pay and reported later that the cashier chewed out the salesman for the markdown. As we headed out our new friends then started pushing us to go see their stall where they sold something or other. We thanked them for their help but firmly insisted we needed to get the little guys back out of the cold and ditched them as quickly as possible.

Tomorrow is a free day. We're headed to see a different section of the Great Wall. The stroller will be no use to us there. But perhaps we'll take another night stroll once we're back.

January 12, 2016 - Great Wall Visit

Tuesday we had nothing adoption related scheduled so we decided to plan an outing. It's tricky to know what to do before you have your child because you don't know how they will be grieving. Vincent wanted to see the Great Wall because he doesn't remember his first trip. Since that's mostly a long van ride and Matt could carry August in the backpack on the wall we thought it would be a good activity. Happily, today is his 7th birthday so this seemed like a great way to celebrate. I hired John "Yellow Car" on the recommendation of a friend. John is a Beijing native who has worked as a driver for his entire professional life. He speaks excellent English and loved to chat with us on the trip. He isn't a tour guide but he does help you purchase the entrance tickets. He even had a spare cell phone to loan to customers so we could call him when we were ready to be picked up.

It was a beautiful sunny day—the sky was clear and blue. Yes, it was freezing but it was much warmer up on the wall than down at the bottom. There was hardly anyone there. We went to the Mutianyu section of the wall which is further away from Beijing from the section we visited last time. It is higher up on a mountain too. The nice thing about it for us is that you take a shuttle halfway up the mountain. Then you walk along a little street with restaurants and run the gauntlet of vendors. They were particularly aggressive since there were few customers available. At the end of the street you can take cable car up and down the mountain. At the top you can walk along the wall in two directions. If you walk to the right there is a toboggan ride down the mountain. Or you can take a ski lift from the cable car to the toboggan and skip the wall altogether. We walked to the left which John recommended as having the better view.

We stayed up on the wall quite a while. If it were warmer I think we could have packed a lunch and stayed all day. It's so incredibly beautiful. We had a few China moments, too. We found a handicapped accessible ramp which was added. It was essentially a smooth path that you could use to roll Grandma straight down the side of the mountain. At another point Matt heard a noise he was trying to identify. "Is that someone raking leaves??" he finally guessed. We looked around a bit. Eventually we noticed a park employee at the foot of the wall diligently raking leaves next to the wall. A complete exercise in futility considering the miles of wall situated in the middle of the forest! There was no footpath or anything.

When we were finished we summoned John to pick us up. We were hungry so he took us to a local place to eat. I know quite a lot of it was due to a long walk in the cold fresh air but it was one of the best meals we've eaten in China. There was soup with little pebble sized dumplings, the doughy American kind, not the filled Chinese kind. We also had a pork dish with peppers and onions. It was heavy on garlic and chili sauce but wasn't spicy. The pork tasted like cured country ham. Vincent had sweet and sour pork, and we also had a vegetable dish.

Although August was silent and solemn most of the day, he began to perk up after his nap on the ride home. Vincent was playing his DS. August decided to try and grab it. I heard him call Vincent older brother in Chinese but Vincent was soon shouting no at him in Chinese. Brothers already! A few people have asked me how Vincent and August are getting along. Vincent usually gets along well with toddlers because he's nonstop action. However, August likes to do things like set out all the stacking cups in a pattern then carefully put a toy car in each. He does not like Vincent interrupting his precision concentration by tossing a balloon into the middle of it to try and entice him into a game. I wouldn't say he dislikes Vincent but he definitely isn't entertained by him the way I thought he would.

Since we got back to the hotel this afternoon August has seemed much more comfortable. Instead of sitting in one spot he has been walking around the room. He has been smiling at us as he does things like dump everything out of the suitcases. We were very shocked when he started talking after all that silence. We don't know enough Mandarin to understand everything he's saying but at one point when Vincent got out a water bottle, August said "Older brother drink water?" very clearly. Early this morning when we were video chatting with our children back home he ran over when he heard them on the iPad. He waved and said "Hi!" in English. So far today he has said hi, no, and more in English. A few minutes ago he was dancing around singing "I'm little brother! I'm little brother!" in Chinese (I'm pretty sure that's what he was saying). We're so excited to see more of his personality coming out.

January 13, 2016 - Paperwork Day

Today was kind of the opposite of hugely exciting. We drove in the van with our guide to an official building. We waited around. We signed papers. We drove to another building and repeated the process. We did this a couple of times. I think we've determined that it takes exactly an hour to drive to any building in Beijing. Our adoption process in Nanjing was easier because they prepared the passport in advance as well as had a notary within the Civil Affairs building, eliminating an extra trip. In the end, we spent over 6 hours of our day getting all of the paperwork in order. Which means I don't have much interesting to blog for you.

How about some more China cultural differences? It's winter here, so bundle up. Heating in China is unpredictable. In our hotel, we're running the air conditioning because the hotel's heat seems to be set on 73. Any vehicles we ride in are the same way, swelteringly hot. It's enough to make you decide to dress lightly excerpt that other buildings aren't heated at all. The Beijing Civil Affairs office was in a very shiny new building. All digital everything. But the employees were bundled up for work in their winter coats because it was in the upper 50's within the building.

You know how in the US people carry around insulated coffee mugs all the time? Sometimes they'll go empty their drinks in the bathroom sink then rinse out the mug to go get a refill. In China what everyone carries around in their thermos is green tea with the leaves still in it. I guess that can cause a real mess in the bathroom sink because I found one restroom with a trash can which had a sieve sitting on top of it. It's specifically for people to dump their tea into.

While we were at the notary office waiting for our paperwork to be completed our guide took us to the restaurant in the building to get lunch. They usually serve everyone hot tea automatically at restaurants, the way you get ice weather in the US. Iced drinks are considered unhealthy in China. At this restaurant we ordered a Sprite for Vincent, because he won't drink hot tea and nothing for August because we had a bottle with water for him. When the waitress realized we didn't order a drink for August, she came over and poured him a mug of boiling water. Boiling water is a common drink if you don't care for tea, and it's even served in the summer when you are hot and thirsty. Living in a country where every disposable cup of coffee comes with a warning label, it seems very strange to have a 2 year old served an open mug of visibly steaming water straight from the pot.

We ordered some chicken noodle soup thinking it might be a nice change for Vincent who mostly eats sweet and sour pork. We asked if it was a large bowl because bowls of soup here seem to only come in half gallon sizes. The guide told us only a small bowl was available. Sure enough, a gigantic bowl of soup came to the table. Don't tell Vincent about the chicken's feet that were in it. We ladled around them.

Finally, as strange as it sounds, my little post about the dumpling shop behind our hotel in Beijing is one of the most read posts on my blog. I know I have a lot of readers who will be traveling in the future on adoption trips so I wanted to help you out. We finally figured out how to get to the dumpling shop without having the concierge take us through the employee bike parking lot. You walk down Jinyu hutong street which the hotel is located on and turn into the alley next to the Waldorf Astoria. This is taking a right out of the Novotel Peace or crossing the street if you're staying at the Peninsula. It's not far at all off Wangfujing if you are at another hotel in that area. According to google maps the alley is probably Xitangzi Hutong. Look for the restaurant with red lanterns and yellow sign.

I'm having trouble keeping an Internet connection for more than a few minutes and I wasn't able to upload any photos to the blog at all. I did get the pictures on Flickr so you can see the illustrations for this post there. I will edit the post to add the pictures later when I can get it to work.

January 14, 2016 - China National Museum

Today is our last full day in Beijing. We leave tomorrow morning for Guangzhou. We did not have any adoption related business to take care of so we enjoyed another free day. Yesterday we met the Spanish couple again at the adoption offices and they had suggested we go to the China National Museum. They also joked that they would see us again in China in another two years. After breakfast we headed out. The past two days the pollution levels have been low but they were high again today so we wore our masks. We walked down through the pedestrian shopping area of Wangfujing. There are a lot of red and gold decorations out for the Spring Festival. This will be the year of the monkey so there are a lot of monkeys as well.

Once past the shopping district we walked toward Tiananmen Square. We picked up another helpful English speaking companion who made conversation, eventually inviting us to her painting shop. We shook her off, then came to the Tiananmen intersection.

You will surely die if you try to cross the road. Fear not, we remembered from our last trip that you can cross underneath using the subway tunnel. Crossing under required a security screening but that was quick. On the other side we made our way into the museum. Admission is free, though you have to show your passport. Coming inside the museum you are immediately faced with a wall of a dozen black suited security guards. The screening here was more intensive. We had to send our stroller through an X-ray machine, walk through a metal detector, then get wanded. But finally we were free to explore the museum. It was a beautiful building with a large interesting collection. We viewed porcelains, jade, ancient coins, and a few other areas. No matter where we walked the docent would immediately walk over to follow us around because of August. One spent quite a bit of time looking from August to Vincent, kind of squinting at Vincent trying to see a resemblance. None of them asked any questions although they clearly wanted to. When people do ask us about him, they always say "He look a little Chinese?" No one ever comes out and says "He's Chinese."

August fell asleep in the stroller after a while. I guess appreciating all that cultural heritage is hard work. We walked back to the hotel for lunch and nap. Afterwards we packed up for tomorrow's trip. August was apprehensive as we packed. He has been coming out of his shell in the hotel room but his main defense is still to withdraw. Yesterday he sat solemn and motionless on our lap for hours as we traveled around the city for our appointments. Our guide asked how he was doing. When we said he was running around and talking in the hotel room she said "He talking?" politely skeptical. She did hear him say "all done" in English after lunch.

These early days are hard. It's hard to see him flinch when I sit down next to him. To see him upset and not be able to comfort him. He sits stiffly if you try to cuddle him. There is nothing which will help but time to build trust. The first two days he refused to drink anything. Yesterday and today he refused to eat much. Both days he accepted soup so we were able to get both a good meal and liquid in that way. However, when he is happy we can see that he's going to be quite a troublemaker. He and Vincent are getting into arguments over toys. August will yell at Vincent in Chinese and Vincent yells no back in Chinese. Once when Matt told August no, August told him no back in Chinese. At one point when Vincent called him August I heard him correct Vincent by saying his Chinese name. He is very curious about things. He's constantly digging through the luggage or grabbing things from our hands. He likes to show you that he knows what to do. He helps me get himself dressed. If he thinks we are going out he will run to get his shoes and coat. He might bring you his hat and point to his head or pull the stroller out. He collects dishes from around the room to put up on a shelf. He gives you a mischievous grin right before he does something he shouldn't. I think he's going to fit in just fine with our family!

January 15, 2016 - Travel Day

Yesterday was a long day. It seems like taking a single domestic flight shouldn't be that much effort but every time it takes an entire day. We had breakfast, checked out of the hotel, and headed to the van. Another hour long ride to the airport. The pollution index was high but we skipped the masks since we were going to be in the van or airport the whole time. I could still feel slight symptoms, though.

At the airport our guide got us checked in but had to send us into the security checkpoint alone. Our security person seemed unfamiliar with the process of using an adoption certificate rather than a passport. The female guards on either side of him alternated between making faces and cooing over August and teasing him about not knowing how to process us. He kept counting the four plane tickets and three passports and scratching his head over what to do. I kept glancing back at our guide who seemed increasingly worried at how long it was taking. Eventually the female guards had pity on our guy and walked him through the process. I waved at our guide and we headed to the security screening station.

Security screening turned into another ordeal. Our guide had been concerned that the bottle of milk for August would be a problem but they only shrugged at us over that. They wanted August to walk through the metal detector by himself. I set him down and he took a tentative step. Once the guards saw that he had trouble walking they came over and carried him through. A female guard held him, speaking to him soothingly while the male guard gave him a tiny pat down. We got through the pat down and wand part okay but then got called over to the metal detector for our bags. Every country has different requirements. They didn't care about our liquids but we didn't take as many electronic devices out as we were supposed to. We tried to put out everything that was on the sign but the language barrier still makes it difficult. Anyway, I had forgotten to take out Vincent's DS. I took that out and they ran it through again but it was still beeping. The guards started pulling everything out. It was all kid stuff—plastic slinky, stuffed animal, blanket, etc. They were rolling their eyes at how much trouble they were having over a bag that was clearly not a real security threat. They ran it through the metal detector at least three times. I'm not sure if they ever figured out what was causing the trouble or if they gave up because they were tired of dealing with us.

We grabbed some food at McDonald's (mm, tastes like America!) before our flight. They were advertising a red bean paste pie for the new year with cute little fuzzy monkeys. If we eat at the McDs in Guangzhou then I'll try to get a picture. I don't take pictures in the airport because of all the security. I did try to get a picture of the airport for you from the plane. They have the skylights arranged on the roof so that the airport looks like a long dragon with spikes on top. Unfortunately, as you can see, the pollution is so bad that you can't see it at all in the picture.

Once we landed in Guangzhou it was another 2 hours before we finally made it to our new hotel because of the traffic. We were so exhausted that we went straight to bed rather than updating anything. We did all sleep very well. Vincent was looking forward to the breakfast buffet this morning. I had told him about a doughnut tree they had last time where doughnuts were hanging from the branches. It wasn't there this home but they had a Christmas tree made of colorful macarons in its place. Vincent lost no time in plucking one for his plate. It wasn't until I went by to get myself food later that I saw the "For display only" sign. Oops. When a waitress came by to ask if we wanted coffee I noticed her give the macaroon and Vincent a side eye glance. I'm sure that's not the only time a child has made off with part of the Christmas tree, right?

January 16, 2016 - Settling Into Guangzhou

It's nice to be back in Guangzhou. We spent a week at the same hotel last trip, so everything here feels very familiar. This morning we went down to the breakfast buffet. No more crepes or pan au chocolat but otherwise this buffet has about four times as many choices as that of our Beijing hotel.

After breakfast Matt took August to the medical exam required for his visa. Vincent and I stayed at the hotel where he asked me 572 times if we could go swimming. Guangzhou may be semi-tropical but it's about 50 degrees and rainy. I had told him that the pool wouldn't be open but he had immediately noticed that people were swimming in it. All day long there were a few people swimming laps, always Asian men. Sometimes their wives and children stood on the sidelines bundled in winter coats to watch them. Cast your bets now as to whether Vincent will wear Matt down by the end of the week. I mean, I'd certainly be happy to take him but August didn't like swimming in Beijing so I feel it's really best for him if I keep him company.

After nap time we headed out to find a place to eat. I had heard from other adoptive parents that there is a great noodle place a short walk from our hotel. It was surprising to us how much had changed from our trip two years ago. Many of the little local shops where now different little local shops. The noodle place turned out to be run by Chinese Muslims, presumably from Xinjiang because a few of the dishes said Xinjiang style. I find the Xinjiang province to be a fascinating place so I was very excited by this. The food was excellent. My favorite was a roasted mutton noodle dish which was heavy on curry and allspice, so it had a very middle eastern flavor. Vincent liked his dish better than anything else he's eaten in China so far. It was spaghetti noodles (all the noodles served were hand pulled) with beef and tomato paste. The flavor reminded me a lot of spaghetti-os.

When we finished eating we walked down the block a little further. We wanted to get a birthday cake for Vincent and August to share. We hadn't seen any western style bakeries in Beijing but last time there were two on this block. We did find one and placed an order to pick up tomorrow. Then we headed back to the hotel where Vincent watched Frozen while August ran amok in the room. August found the travel yesterday very scary and upsetting. He seemed to really appreciate our low key day spent mostly at the hotel. I think we're going to try to venture out more tomorrow. He should enjoy the cake at least!

January 17, 2016 - Sunday in Guangzhou

Today the jet lag seemed to hit us pretty hard. You'd think we'd be really settled into China time but instead we were all ready for bed at noon. It seemed much more like midnight. Vincent was not his usual self and he joined us in nap time. Although we made plans a few different times, in the end we didn't venture much past the hotel.

After breakfast we visited the park next door in an effort to stay awake until nap time. Yes, I know we took the picture on the wrong side of the goat statue. There was a long line on the right side of the goat statue. Anyway, it has finally stopped raining. It was a gorgeous day, like April back home. Sunny and a nice cool breeze. After a nice walk we headed back to the hotel for the middle part of the day.

We then went out for a late lunch/early supper at the same noodle shop where we ate yesterday. It was close and tasty. At that point we decided that we just weren't feeling up to the trip we had planned. Instead we headed down the street to pick up the birthday cake we had ordered for Vincent and August yesterday. On our way back in to the hotel we picked up the train tickets to Hong Kong for Friday. In the afternoon we spent some time watching Netflix. We also visited the garden within the hotel. There is a small play area, plus a waterfall leading to a small stream. Vincent really liked it, telling me we needed to take some pictures there. He ran a few laps around. Even August asked to get out of his stroller. Holding my hand he lead me all around the garden a few times.

Then it was back to the room for cake time. Although August's orphanage doesn't allow parents to send cakes he did seem familiar with cake. That is the most sincere smile I've seen from him! He kept saying little brother, I guess because he was afraid only big brother would get the cake. He ate almost all the apple slices off the top although we haven't been able to get him to eat any fruit before now. He really enjoyed the cake. We all enjoyed the cake, except we wished we could be all sharing it as a family. Sorry Mary Evelyn, Max, Gregory, and Leo that you only get to see the picture!

August had a harder day in some respects. He has been yelling at us more and throwing tantrums. It's a positive development compared to his default of withdrawal. Three is a challenging age, but he's more than entitled to feel angry about the situation. He wasn't given any choice in the matter nor does he understand what is happening. It's good that he feels safe enough to let his feelings out. On the other hand, he wanted to snuggle with me after his bath tonight. I think the cake created a lot of goodwill. I chatted with him, saying I love you in Chinese. He parroted it back to me in the tiniest whisper possible! I got him to say that he loved Papa and older brother the same way. I don't know if he understands that either, but it was still a wonderful moment for us.

January 18, 2016 - Safari Park

The Chimelong Safari Park is probably the favorite destination of adoptive parents in Guangzhou. We didn't go last time because Leo started getting unhappy after about an hour outside and everyone told us it is an all day trip. After our malaise yesterday we decided to sign up for the organized tour offered by our agency so that we would be motivated to leave the hotel. August does well enough on outings. Plus, the weather is gorgeous. We left the hotel at 9:30 am and didn't return until 5 pm, so it is quite a trip. It took us about an hour to get to the Chimelong complex. Besides the safari park they had a circus, water park, and a couple of other amusement park options.

We started off on the safari ride, where you ride in a train/car kind of thing that drives you through for a safari. The animals were all contained in different areas, but you did get to see them fairly close. There were park employees feeding the animals as you went by. I don't know if we got there at feeding time or if they feed them all day. It was pretty fun regardless.

After the train ride we walked through a Jurassic Park kind of area. There were huge animatronic dinosaurs. One spat water at you as you walked by. There was a cave to walk through where a huge T-Rex loomed over you. It was Vincent's favorite part. He wanted to know if we could look at more dinosaurs. As we were heading to the parking lot at the end of the day he asked if we could go through the dinosaur part one more time.

Then we toured the normal zoo part the rest of the day. It was similar to a zoo in America but kind of on steroids. For example they didn't have koalas, they had 50 koalas. You got to walk through and see so many of the best animals rather than maybe 6 at most in one or two exhibits. One of their specialties is white tigers. If our tour guide is to be believed a quarter of all the white tigers in the world reside in this park. We watched a white tiger feeding session. They put raw meat on a cord and enticed the Tigers to climb poles, jump off rocks, and jump into water to get the meat. At another point you could feed the giraffes.

What the biggest attraction is at the park is the pandas. About a year ago this zoo had the only known surviving panda triplets in the world. They have panda triplet signs everywhere! The panda area went on and on. The Kung Fu Panda movie tie-in signs were everywhere. The amount of panda merch you could buy was endless. When our guide finally let us stop for lunch it was at a restaurant which had a panda exhibit on one side so you could watch a mother panda with baby while you ate. Super adorable!

August started out well enough. He seemed to enjoy the animals, especially the pandas. However, his hunger strike at breakfast paired with lack of nap meant the afternoon was challenging. He started throwing tantrums toward the end. He fell asleep in the van on the way back, but raged for a while when he woke up back at the room. I eventually got him to let me snuggle him on my lap while I sang to him. Then he ate a huge supper. The happy kicked in shortly thereafter. He has been looking at the safari park map and telling me all about it in excited Chinese while I write this.

One of our guides in Beijing commented that he thought August looked like he was from the south, particularly his round eyes. Looking around in Guangzhou, I can kind of see what he means although August is very fair completed compared to the Cantonese. I decided to ask our (very talkative) guide for the safari park what he thought. He said that he didn't feel there was really in difference in how northern and southern Chinese people look. Which I thought was a little humorous because he looks very typically Cantonese to me. Even more humorously, he went on to comment several times throughout the day that he found the resemblance between Matt and August to be uncanny excepting the hair and eye color, of course.

January 19, 2016 - I Don't Even Know What Day We're On

After our very long excursion yesterday we all slept in this morning. We went down to breakfast where August again would only eat yogurt and broth. We went back to the room for about half an hour. August wasn't happy so we decided to go out for a walk. We went to Yuexiu Park again. Over the weekend they had put up a big spring festival decorative entrance. Decorations aren't quite everywhere but people are definitely getting ready for the year of the monkey.

We walked around the park for a bit but were caught by a pop up shower as we were approaching the Ming dynasty era city wall. I remembered that there was supposed to be a museum in the Zhenhai tower just a little way up the hill. We walked up and saw that the entrance fee was only going to run us $2.50. Sounded like a great way to get out of the rain!

The tower is a 5 story structure. According to the museum it is one of the four most famous such towers in China but I can't say that we've heard of any of them. This one dates back to the 1600s but was remodeled to become the Guangzhou museum in recent decades. It was used as a military stronghold at several points in the past so there were cannons displayed in the front lawn.

The first floor of the museum contained displays about the origin myth of Guangzhou, a story involving 5 deities/fairies who landed in this area on goats to bless Canton with a good climate and plentiful harvest. As you went up each story you traveled forward through the eras. The top floor involved the modern era with Guangzhou's involvement in western culture. You could also walk out onto the balcony to admire the view. The two points which stuck out most strongly from the museum are that the Cantonese are very proud of their long history of involvement with the West and the Chinese are still very sore about the Opium wars.

August was starting to get unhappy by the end of the trip so we headed back to the hotel. The afternoon has been pretty low key. I attended an exit meeting with our agency representatives and Matt took the boys to the hotel garden/playground. This evening we will be going on the Pearl River cruise to admire the lights and architecture in downtown Guangzhou. It will be late when we return and we leave for the American consulate tomorrow morning so I decided to write this entry early.

When I last left off we were going to the Pearl River cruise. In the end, we decided that Matt should stay home with August because we weren't sure how well he would do in the evening. Vincent and I went with the other families in our group. Guangzhou is home to the Canton tower which I think was the tallest TV tower in the world for a short time. The night River cruise is a popular attraction because so many of the bridges and buildings along the river are covered with decorative lights. The food on the cruise is notoriously um, adventurous so our agency has the tradition of ordering Papa John's to be delivered to the boat right before launch. Vincent and I shared the pizza. It was the first American food we've had on the trip besides the McDonald's at the airport. The weather was great for the trip and the scenery was beautiful. The cruise also included a woman playing a traditional Chinese instrument.

We had to be up early today for our appointment at the US consulate which is the entire reason for our weeklong stay in Guangzhou. The consulate in Guangzhou is the only consulate in China which processes the immigrant visas for children adopted by US families which will bestow citizenship upon entry to the US. Our visit with Leo was uneventful but this trip was more high stress. First, we were the only family with our agency who had a Wednesday appointment. Our agency was able to arrange for us to ride with some families with a different agency who were staying at the same hotel. I had been talking to a friend with that agency who told me that the meeting time in the lobby was earlier than my agency facilitator had told us. We showed up at the earlier time but no one from our agency was there with our paperwork. Matt went to try and track down our paperwork while I talked to the big agency group. Their agency facilitator said she wasn't aware of any of this then promptly loaded up the van and left without us! Fortunately Matt showed up at this point with our agency person and the paperwork. The group which had left was NOT the one we were supposed to ride with so all was well.

I have no pictures from the consulate because cameras and cell phones are on the long list of items you aren't allowed to take. When you come to the front of the consulate there is a huge crowd of people. A long line of them are waiting to try and enter while others are there waiting for friends or family trying to enter. As a US citizen you get to walk right in past everyone waiting. It makes you keenly aware of the privilege you have. After we got inside there was another long wait as everyone's paperwork was processed. We took an oath that nothing in our paperwork was falsified then the details of immigration at the port of entry were gone over. Finally it was time for individual interviews. When it was almost our turn a woman came in who had apparently had a paperwork issue. She thought she had corrected it but she was told it was not corrected. She burst into tears and left. Then the people immediately in front of us had their adoption certificate scrutinized. The consulate officer was holding it up to the light and frowning. Apparently he decided it was legit but I was biting my nails over our outcome by this point. We had an uneventful interview so we should have August's visa tomorrow. The woman who had such a problem was able to get it resolved and she rode back to the hotel with us. Happy endings all around!

It was well after noon when we returned to the hotel. We fed August and got him down for a nap. Matt got takeout from the noodle place. I think I will have eaten my weight in cumin mutton noodles by the end of the week. We were so worn out by the long morning that we didn't do much in the evening. It's rainy here too, so not the best weather for walking in the park. We met the other families in our travel group up in the lobby for a group photo. Afterwards we walked across the street to buy a roasted duck. Well, half of a roasted duck. We kept seeing the happy roasted duck restaurant sign on our walks and couldn't resist trying it. They didn't have an English menu but the guy at the counter spoke English. We were happily surprised that August loved the duck. He kept yelling for more every time he thought we were going to stop feeding him.

August was talking up a storm after our visit to the safari park. I recorded about a minute of video of him pointing to the park map and talking nonstop. I asked one of our guides to watch it so he could translate. He said that other than "push the stroller" he couldn't understand any of it. He said it was just baby talk. He does use some Mandarin phrases regularly. His favorite is "Yao bu yao" which means literally "want? not want?" Sometimes he will use it in context such as by grabbing something out of the suitcase and asking us if we want it or not. Other times it's more of a rallying cry. We kind of wonder if he thinks it's the only intelligible thing we can say.

Since I don't have any more interesting things to write I will close out with a picture of the infamous macaron Christmas tree from the breakfast buffet. Now missing one pink macaron from the bottom row.

January 20, 2016 - Travel Update

Due to the impending snow disaster on the East coast we are in the process of changing our flights. We will be leaving on Friday instead of Saturday. We are frantically trying to pack while rebooking hotel and train reservations. I feel sad that we lost the day to do all of our "one last time" things but will be so glad to be home with our family one day sooner. I will not have time to blog further until we're home but didn't want anyone to worry about the radio silence for the next 2 or 3 days. Hopefully I will be able to update you on the craziness from the comfort of my home on Sunday.

Thursday morning we woke up to a message from the airline in our inbox warning us that our travel was likely to be disrupted due to the massive snow storm pending on the east coast. They were offering people the chance to change their flights at no fee and keeping the same fare you had paid for the original tickets. We were able to get in touch with our travel agent (the amazing Sue Sorrels) who worked after hours to get us rebooked. Initially it looked as if we would have to delay our return until Sunday because the flights were completely full with everyone else switching flights, too. She was eventually able to get us tickets to fly to San Francisco on Friday although we would have two connecting flights to get home. Beggars can't be choosers, so we took the tickets and quickly got moving on returning home a day earlier. We began packing up and going over what other travel arrangements needed to be changed. Thursday was the day I had planned to do all of my shopping but in the end I only had time to run out for a little over an hour to get some souvenirs for the kids.

This is what a shop selling decorations for the spring festival looks like. Apologies for the quality of photos in this post. I think they were all taken in a hurry with my cell phone. Almost as soon as I returned to the hotel, we shoved the gifts into the suitcase and went down to the lobby to check out. Originally we were going to travel to Hong Kong on Friday morning, spend the day there, then travel out Saturday morning. We lost the cost of the hotel room in Hong Kong Friday night because we had booked nonrefundable thinking there was no way we would travel home earlier, only later. Of course, we were happy to be out a little bit of money to be home a full day earlier. The bonus of not having to spend 24 hours camping out in an airport somewhere was nice too.

Our agency helped us to rebook our train tickets to Hong Kong as well as a van to take us to the train station because we didn't want to split up into two taxis. We waited in the lobby for a few minutes for our agency people to arrive with the new train tickets and August's visa. While we were waiting Vincent lived out every kid's dream by riding the escalator in the lobby up and down about 20 times. You can see that the last dregs of Christmas decorations are still up at our hotel.

We got to the train station and on our train uneventfully. The train station is definitely more of the authentic Chinese experience than the airport. Few people speak English and only the most important signage is in English. Our agency people had given us instructions on where to go and how to get on the train. There were crowds of people everywhere so we shameless shoved like everyone else to stay together going through security or on escalators in the Chinese manner. Did I mention that the elevators were well hidden so we had to haul luggage and the stroller up and down about six escalators? Once on the train, it was a better experience than a flight. Very comfortable and smooth. We missed the scenery since it was already dark but nothing we could do about that. We knew we had really arrived in Hong Kong when the train station people directed us to the "lift" rather than the elevator.

When we arrived in Hong Kong we then had to get to our hotel near the airport. The train station is not close to the airport. We had planned to take public transportation there but we were tired with a lot of luggage and one of the very persistent taxi drivers following us around wore us down. He assured us that we would all fit in the taxi with luggage and he offered us a very cheap fare for which he would accept Chinese cash. This would save us the headache of changing money, plus get us to the bed at the hotel faster so we agreed. He got our luggage in the trunk using a system of bungee cords to hold the lid down, stowing the last few bits in the back seat. Matt rode up front with him. On the left, because the driver is on the right, British style.

In the end, I think we would have gladly paid the driver more in exchange for silence. Our trip over to the airport island was like something out of a movie. Weaving in and out of traffic at breakneck speed, the taxi driver kept up a monologue. Bizarrely, he kept throwing in phrases in Spanish, which he said he was learning because he knew all the young people in America are mad to learn Spanish right now. Mostly he was railing against China and "the f*cking stupid Chinese." He said he was Chinese himself, so it was fine that he had these opinions. He also occasionally added that he was sure our son was smart, of course, not like the rest of them. We were spared the last 10 minutes of his ranting when August threw a well-timed tantrum which was too loud for him to talk over. We were so glad to see our hotel!

Since we were only in Hong Kong about 12 hours we didn't get a chance to see much of other than the view from our hotel lobby. We took the hotel shuttle next door to the airport the next morning. When we checked in, the woman at the airline desk said that she could not get any seats for us together, only four seats in random locations. That clearly wasn't going to work, so she wanted to reroute us. She asked why we wanted to go to San Francisco when our ultimate destination was in the midwest? We explained about avoiding the path of the snowstorm. She wanted to put us on a flight to Newark which was leaving in an hour. She said she could seat us 2 and 2 right together, plus it would cut out our 2nd connecting flight. This was highly tempting, but we didn't want to get stranded in Newark. We asked if the connecting flight was likely to be delayed but she did not give us the impression that she really understood this "snow" stuff we were talking about or how it could cause flight delays. Our understanding of the storm is that it wasn't supposed to hit Newark until Saturday so we decided to take our chances and book the flight.

Matt was at the desk with her for almost an hour working on changing the flights and getting checked in. This gave us little time to catch the flight to Newark. We had to really rush through security but we did make it in time. The plane had already started boarding but it was still 20 minutes left to takeoff. While Matt was still at the check in desk, Vincent and I found this great Chinese dragon display in the airport when we were walking August around to keep him happy.

The flight to Newark was long at almost 15 hours, but went relatively smoothly. August slept for probably 3 hours total during the flight. He didn't cry much and was fairly happy playing with the small bag of toys which I brought. There was a teenage Asian girl on the other side of him who smiled so big when I strapped him in that I thought she surely hadn't flown before. No one is happy to have a toddler next to them on a flight! On my other side was an American expat living in Hong Kong who had adopted herself twenty years ago. She and I enjoyed talking to each other. The biggest challenge with August was that he was still on hunger strike on the plane. I think he ate 2 dinner rolls, 3 cookies, and drank about 3 oz of water the entire trip. One of the cookies was donated by the Asian teenager when she saw it was the only thing he was eating out of the breakfast provided.

We arrived in Newark and were processed by immigration in only 5 minutes. It took closer to 45 minutes our last trip. We sat down to wait for our connecting flight. Three of us ate supper but August spat out the yogurt we tried to feed him because it had granola in it. He finally broke down into a huge screaming fit from exhaustion and I assume hunger, too. He eventually fell asleep in his stroller. Vincent finished his food, said "I'm going to go to sleep now" then curled up into a tiny ball in his seat, instantly asleep. The snow was hitting DC really hard the hour we were waiting in Newark but it was only light flurries there. No delays.

August was not happy to be on another plane but he cried less than 5 minutes before falling asleep again. All four of us slept from takeoff to landing on our 2 hour connecting flight. The only other touchy moment came when we were waiting for our baggage. I went over to sit down in some chairs while Matt kept an eye out for the luggage. I guess August assumed the chairs meant we were waiting for another flight because he screamed bloody murder for the 10 minutes it took for the baggage to all show up. Occasionally he would point down the corridor as if to say that we needed to leave NOW. He was perfectly happy sitting in his stroller in the freezing cold while we waited for the parking lot shuttle. He even seemed to feel that the car ride home was progress. He did very well meeting the other children at home and ate a full bowl of oatmeal mixed with yogurt before bed. He slept pretty much the full night, waking a few times with bad dreams.

We've been having a slow day today but things have gone well with August. He was quickly following the other children around playing. He doesn't like the dogs but I think he will come around to them sooner than Leo did. He even tried 4 bites of chili at supper before eating a reasonable portion of macaroni and cheese mixed with some scrambled eggs. Hopefully as he continues to settle in his appetite will improve. Currently the only thing in his life he can control is what he eats or drinks so it's not surprising that he's exerting control there.

Thank you to everyone who read along on our journey! We appreciate all of the prayers, comments, and messages we've received.

Appendices Index

Appendix 1

Master List of Questions for Potential Agencies

General:

- How long has your China program been running?

- About how many adoptions did you finalize last year in the China program?

- What support to do you offer in compiling the dossier?

- If the agency compiles the dossier is there an extra fee for this service? Is a discount available if you do it yourself?

- How long does the dossier review typically take?

- If you have all of the dossier except the I800a sent to the agency, will they review it in advance to save time?

- Are dossiers sent immediately or in weekly batches?

- What method does the agency use to submit the dossier to the CCCWA?

- How will the agency notify you of your log in date?

- Will you be notified of things like "out of translation" or "in review" while you are waiting for your LOA?

- If your LOA wait is long, at what point will the agency check on it?

- Can the agency tell you of a time when a client had a problem and how they handled it?

- How will you be notified of LOA?

- Does the agency have any in-country staff or offices?

- What does the agency do for vacation time or other absences by personnel to ensure families in process will continue without interruption?

- Are there any holidays where the agency is closed longer than the federal holiday schedule?

Matching:

- How does your agency decide which family will be matched with a file if multiple families are interested in a waiting child?

- How long is your average wait for a match for a child that matches our profile of gender/age/needs?

- How many families do you currently have waiting to be matched?

- How many families do you usually match per month?

- What is the current wait time for a child with the profile that we are looking for?

- Will we be updated on changes in wait times, or told how many couples are ahead of us in the process?

- Do you have any partnerships? If so, how many?

- What can you tell me about the care the children receive in your agency partnership orphanages? Are any of them affiliated with Half the Sky?

- Does anyone from the agency visit the partnership orphanages and meet children who will be placed by the agency? How often?

- Do you also match from the shared list?

- Do you match strictly from the MCC or will you sometimes give a referral that is outside of what we marked on our MCC?

Post-matching policy questions:
- When can I share my child's photo on my blog or social media?
- How often can I get an update?
- Is there any cost for an update?
- Can I send my child a care package?
- Can I use a third party vendor to send my child a cake or gift package?

Special situations:
- Ask questions you might have regarding your marital status— single parent, cohabitating, divorce history, etc.
- Do you require a signed statement of [protestant Christian] faith?
- If you have a large family how comfortable is the agency with your family size?
- What is your policy if we should become pregnant during the process?
- If you are in process for a domestic adoption or stalled in another international program, what is the agency's policy on concurrent adoption?
- What is your policy on disrupting birth order?
- What is your policy on artificial twinning?
- Will you allow us to adopt two unrelated children at once through the China program?

- If the agency allows adopting two at once, is there any agency fee reduction?

- How soon after an adoption is finalized can we begin the process again?

- How much experience does your agency have with expedited adoptions for an aging out child or for a life-threatening medical condition?

- What happens if we meet our child in country and his or her condition is completely different from the information in the file?

- What sort of post placement support do you offer?

- Can you tell me about a recent instance when you had a family struggling with the placement once they were home? How did you help them to find the resources they needed?

Travel questions:

- Do you require we travel with a group?

- How often do you schedule the groups?

- Can I book my own in country travel arrangements?

- Will I be able to receive an itemized receipt for the travel costs?

- If you don't have parents travel in groups, will we be responsible for getting ourselves to and from the airport and various adoption related appointments?

- Will I be able to travel during a trade fair or Chinese holiday if I don't mind paying the additional travel expenses?

- If I am adopting an aging out child or a child with a medical expedite, will I still be required to wait for a travel group?

- What is the typical length of time between TA and travel for your clients?

- Am I required to stay at a particular hotel or work with a particular travel agency?

- Are the guides used by your agency employees of a guide service or of the adoption agency? For either answer, ask why they choose to do it that way.

- Are guide fees separate, and if so how much are they? Can we choose to forgo the guide on days when there are no adoption related appointments to save on guide fees?

- Does your agency have an office in the hotel at Guangzhou?

- Can I stay at a hotel other than the one you use?

- Can I use frequent flier miles or hotel points to save money on my travel expenses?

- Do you plan any outing for parents or are we on our own between adoption-related appointments?

- Are group trips to destinations like the Great Wall or the Guangzhou safari park optional or required? If I don't attend, will I still need to pay for it?

- Do you allow one parent to travel alone?

- Can we bring along our whole family (children or extended family)?

- Does your agency allow us to send the orphanage donation by electronic funds transfer?

Financial questions:
- Do you have an annual financial report available which shows your operating budget?

- Do you have an independent financial audit conducted? If so, is that report available?

- What sort of aid programs does your agency sponsor in China?

- Do you offer grants for waiting children?

- Do you offer a returning client discount? Military discount?

- If you know you would like to adopt two children at the same time, ask if there is an agency fee reduction for this.

- Are the grants automatic or is there an application process?

- Do you partner with any organizations such as Brittany's Hope?

- If I have funds available through an organization such as Reece's Rainbow or Adopt Together, will you count those towards our bill? Do you charge a processing fee for the transfer of these funds?

- Do you have a way for people to contribute directly toward our adoption costs? Is there a fee associated with this?

- If people contribute funds that are more than the amount owed to you, will you keep the extra funds or are those returned to us?

- If I receive notice of a grant after my child is home which is paid directly to the agency, will that amount be refunded to us (since you're already paid off the bill), or does the agency keep the grant money?

- Does the agency require a post-placement report deposit or that all the costs be paid upfront?

- If it is a deposit, what will happen to the money if you move or the agency closes? I can't stress this point enough because many parents have lost their deposit money for these two reasons.

- Does the placing agency charge one post-placement fee that covers all of the reports or a fee per visit for translation and submission of the reports?

- How much does the home study agency charge per post-placement visit?

- Does your agency require that all post-placement reports be written by a social worker or will you be able to self-report the ones allowable by China? Now that China allows some reports to be completed by the parents you can save the cost of the social worker's visit if your agency allows this, which almost all do.

Choosing an agency:

- Did this agency respond to my phone call or e-mail in a timely manner?

- How well did I connect with the contact person?

- Was the agency evasive in answering any of my questions?

- How many of my priority issues did the agency meet?

- Did the agency have any of my deal breaker practices?

- When I really think about it, which agency just feels like the best fit?

Appendix 2

Update Questions

- What name is he called? Does he have a nickname?
- Who chose his name? What does it mean?
- Has there been any change in his living arrangement?
- Who is he closest to, another child or caregiver?
- What are the names of some of his friends?
- Where does he sleep?
- Does he drink from a bottle or cup?
- What is his daily diet?
- What are his favorite foods?
- Is he potty trained? If so, what does he say if he needs to go to the bathroom?
- What are his favorite toys?
- What are his favorite TV characters?
- How is his health? Have there been any recent changes in his health?
- Has he had any recent medical procedures or surgeries?
- What makes him upset?
- How does he like to be comforted when upset?

- What is his most challenging behavior and how do you handle it?

- Does he take a nap? What is his usual nap time?

- What is his daily routine?

- What songs do the caregivers sing or does he hear in the playroom?

- How does he play with other children his age?

- What is his verbal development? How many words can he say?

- How is his verbal development compared to other children his age?

- Can he sit up or stand independently? Is he crawling or walking?

- How is his development compared to other children his age?

- What are his current measurements?

Questions for older children:

- Can she dress herself?

- Can she care for her own needs?

- What are her favorite pastimes?

- Does she attend school outside of the orphanage?

- Can she read? How many characters?

- Can high can she count in numbers?

- How is her academic development compared to her same aged peers?

- What is her favorite subject?

- Does she study English?
- Who is she closest to?

Questions for children in foster care:

- What are the names of the foster parents? What does she call the foster parents?
- Are there any other children in the home? What are their names?
- Where does she sleep? Does she sleep alone?
- Can we receive a picture of her with her foster family?

Appendix 3

Things to Do Before Travel

- Figure out your system for keeping track of everything you need to do: voice memos, an app such as Evernote, or good ol' fashioned pen and paper.

- Decide which vaccinations, if any, you want to receive before travel. Be aware that some require multiple doses spaced out over time so plan ahead.

- Check with http://www.redthreadsessions.com/details to see if there is a photographer who offers free adoption photo sessions in your area. Some will come to the airport to photograph your homecoming, so you'll need to set that up in advance.

- File a mail hold using the USPS website and place a hold on your newspaper.

- Inform credit card companies and your bank that you are going to China so they know any charges made are okay.

- Make arrangements to board the pets.

- If you have an alarm system, call them and let them know you will be gone.

- Arrange for someone to mow lawn and check on your house if it will be unoccupied.

- Let your neighbors know you will be gone, and buy a timer for lights in your home.

- Ask someone to make a trip to the grocery for you. Provide a grocery list for perishables to buy the day before you get home, so you don't have to run right out for bread, milk, and eggs.

- Things will be crazy when you return so plan ahead for meals. Make and freeze meals in advance, ask for restaurant gift cards when people ask what you need, and see if a friend or family member will organize meals for when you return.

- Make appointments with the international adoption clinic, pediatrician, and/or any specialists so they are all set up for when you return.

- If you are leaving other children, at home write up a power of attorney for the caregiver stating that they have permission to seek medical care. Be sure you leave the caregiver information so that they have the children's birthdates, any allergies, medical conditions, and insurance information. Include the location of your will and who to contact as trustee. Finally, you should leave a list of medications and dosages including OTC ones so that the caregiver can easily handle cold or fever symptoms.

- Notify your children's schools and pediatricians of your trip, and make sure you have filled out all forms needed to give your caregiver necessary permissions.

- If the caregiver for your children will also be taking them to activities or therapies, include the locations and phone numbers. If they are not familiar with the area, you might want to include a marked map or your GPS which includes the locations for the activities and appointments, but also places you drive to regularly or might need such as the grocery, pharmacy, and urgent care.

- Some parents like to make up "Countdown bags" for their children. This is a small bag or box for each day that you will be away. Ideas for contents include: candy, gum, stickers, small toys, or gift cards for a movie or ice cream.

- If someone is staying at your house with pets and/or children, leave a similar list of information which might be needed. You might want to include air conditioner/furnace repair, plumber, appliance repairman, vet. You could also include a list of household chores for taking care of pets or plants.

- Scan adoption documents onto a thumb drive to take along. You should also include your immunization records. Make copies of your credit cards and the international way to contact them if you have issues. Uploading these scans to a website such as Dropbox so that family members in the US can also have access to them if needed.

- Set up a VPN before you leave. This is needed in order to circumvent China internet restrictions. The most commonly used are Panda Pow, Strong VPN, and VPN Express.

Appendix 4

The Annotated China Packing List

You can poll 100 different adoptive parents on what you absolutely must not forget to pack for China and you would get 100 different answers. I remember that before I traveled I saw several experienced moms swear that you absolutely must take duct tape because you will always find something to use it on during the trip. I didn't pack it and didn't miss it. Some people pride themselves on packing "carry-on only", while others take the maximum allowable luggage and still wish they'd taken more. Allow me to give an illustration of how differently people pack.

Here are the results of a recent online poll--

- Items people most often wished they had packed more of: Clothing, snacks, and toys.

- Items people most often wished they had packed fewer of: Clothing, snacks, and toys!

So you see, you can stalk other people's packing lists all you want, but you will still end up being unhappy with what you packed if you aren't considering what you know about yourself when you travel. You know best whether you are a packing minimalist or if you will feel more secure if you take along many "just in case" items. You know which items you are most likely to need for comfort towards the end of a long trip. Instead of packing every single item suggested here, use it to create your own personalized list. I didn't pack half of these items and I was fine! Often I will list redundant items, so pick the one which you think you are most likely to use for several purposes rather than packing multiple items for a single use.

Baby Items if you are adopting a baby or toddler:

Bottles - You will want at least two in case your child is still taking a bottle. Your update information may or may not be accurate. Children are often bottle fed much longer in orphanages because it is faster and easier than solid food. Many people prefer the liner type to avoid having to wash the bottles in the hotel.

Nipples - Babies are often fed from a fast flow nipple, so you might want to pack toothpicks or small scissors to enlarge the opening.

Formula - You might want to buy the kind the orphanage uses, but you can begin mixing it with what you plan to use. For a toddler you might want transition formula for the vitamin fortification.

Bottlebrush and tongs for fishing the bottles out of boiling water, if you didn't choose the liner option bottles.

Sippy cup - If you child no longer takes a bottle the kind with a straw will still provide the soothing sucking to help calm them. If your child has an unrepaired cleft palate you need to pack a sippy cup which doesn't require suction.

Changing pad

Diaper rash cream

Non-latex gloves - Many children will come with a giardia, a parasitic intestinal disorder. Parents can catch giardia from changing dirty diapers. You might want to pack these for diaper changes. Be cautious of bathing children together for this reason.

Baby shampoo/wash/lotion

Portable snack container

Baby nail clippers

Baby toothbrush and toothpaste - Most children will never have had their teeth brushed so you might need to ease gently into brushing.

Baby sunscreen

Bibs

Carrier with a high weight limit - Ergo and Motherlode are frequently recommended

Clothing:

If you are traveling in the summer pack **cool and breathable clothing. Sun hat, sunglasses.**

If you are packing in the winter **pack layers**. If you are planning to wash laundry in the sink it will be easier to wash light under layers (**thermal underwear, leggings**) than to get heavy jeans and sweaters to dry. You can re-wear the heavy outer layers without washing.

Hat, gloves, hand warmers, and scarf.

For any season try to pack fewer items but ones which are mix and match.

Comfortable shoes - You will be doing a LOT of walking.

Pajamas, underwear

Swim wear, swim caps, swim ring, swim diapers, goggles - Even if you travel in the winter many hotels have indoor pools and swimming is a great bonding activity. Many hotels require swim caps be worn. They can be purchased inexpensively at Swimoutlet.com.

Comfort Items:

These are the items that people most often said they packed regardless of the space they took up because it made a difference to them. You should add whatever is most important to you to the list.

Favorite coffee cup

Instant coffee

Aeropress coffee maker or **French press** for making real coffee in the hotel room
(Sensing a coffee comfort theme here?)

Favorite snacks - Chocolate and peanut butter are most frequently mentioned

Slippers - For the hotel room

Something that provides a nice scent for hotel rooms - People suggest dryer sheets, Febreeze, and car deodorizers travel well.

Electronics:

Plug adaptors - The prongs on the cords of your US outlet products will not fit into the Chinese electrical outlets. The majority of hotels used by adoption agencies will have dual outlets because they cater to foreign business travels. Still, you can pick up an international travel plug adapter set inexpensively so you are covered just in case you need them.

Cell phones plus charger and cables

Laptop/tablet plus charger and cables

Camera

Small flashlight

Surge protector - You've got to plug all those chargers in somewhere.

Travel alarm clock - If you're old school and haven't switched to using your phone as an alarm clock.

Travel router - Hotels will provide wi-fi but it is often slow. A travel router will boost your signal so that you can watch videos or post pictures online. Models are available for under $25.

Food:

Oatmeal or cream of wheat packets

Granola bars

Trail mix

Dried fruit

Peanut butter crackers

Travel packs of peanut butter

Applesauce, pudding, or fruit cups

Tuna in the vacuum sealed pouch with some mayo packets

Yogurt meltaways

Cheerios

baby food squeeze packets

Note: you will find an entire aisle of ramen noodles when you go shopping in China, so no need to pack those. If you are unsure you will like Chinese flavors, bring only the flavor packets from the ones you like at home so you don't have noodles taking up space.

Laundry related:

Dish soap - Some people use this for both dishes and laundry

Laundry bar/Tide travel detergent packs - For washing laundry in the sink or bath tub

Portable clothesline/laundry hooks - For hanging clothes to dry. Wire hangers are also fairly light to pack if you don't want to make any special purchases.

Stain stick/Tide pen - If you pack lightly on the outfits, you don't want them to get stained.

Miscellania:

A real knife - For cutting food you eat in the room.

Tape - Duct tape, scotch tape, even painter's tape has been packed by people.

Binder clips/clothes pins - These serve multiple purposes. Besides office supplies and laundry they can hold the hotel curtains closed when you're desperate for sleep.

Sharpie

Gifts for officials and **Red gift bags**

Big diaper pins

Zip ties - I have no idea. I just wrote it down in case you know why.

A poster mailer tube - If you think you might buy calligraphy or artwork, having a tube will make it easier to pack in order to get it home undamaged.

Paper products:

Toilet paper - This is not provided in public restrooms. Some people carry around a full roll in a Ziploc while others use travel tissue packs.

Paper towels - These come in handy in the hotel room. Restaurants provide tissues rather than the napkins you are used to, so bringing a few paper towels for meals will make cleanup easier.

Antibacterial wipes - Depending on how germ-phobic you are, many people carry these around to wipe down restaurant tables, surfaces in the hotel, etc.

Toilet wipes - Same reason as toilet paper but some people prefer the wet variety.

Baby wipes - Use them to clean the baby, your hands, etc.

Insect repellant wipes - Even though you will be in large cities there are still bugs, particularly in semi-tropical Guangzhou. Many people forgo the malaria meds but pack these.

Feminine supplies - Travel can throw off your schedule. You'd rather be prepared than trying to figure out how to ask where they're located in a Chinese Wal-mart and decipher the boxes to figure out your options.

Diapers - Those who adopted in the 1990's did not find diapers generally available but you will not have that problem. However, Chinese diapers are less absorbent and leak-resistant than the American brands. You'll want to pack at least a small amount so that you have some on hand before you go shopping with your guide and for days when you are traveling.

Plastics:

Disposable plastic grocery bags - For dirty diapers, wet clothes, carrying purchases, supplementing the tiny trash can in your hotel room, etc.

Solo bowls/Gladware - It gets tricky trying to make ramen or eat take out in only the coffee mugs provided in the hotel room. These are disposable enough to toss at the end of your trip but will hold up to washing in the sink.

Plastic utensils - For eating in the room or taking along to restaurants. For those who are chopstick-challenged.

Ziploc bags in a variety of sizes - For packing, or other uses. Keep one or two along in an accessible location for when you are traveling in case of motion sickness. Don't get motion sick? I wasn't actually thinking of you. Most children being adopted haven't traveled by car before because they don't usually leave the orphanage. They can get very queasy on the trip.

Plastic shower curtain - Many people pack these along because they don't want their children to play on dirty hotel carpet. Other people liked to lay them on the floor when eating in the hotel room to prevent food from getting on the carpet.

Toiletries:

Hotels will provide a hair dryer but if you want a **curling or flat iron** pack that yourself.

Shampoo and conditioner - Some people like to have the comfort of their own products, but hotels will provide travel sized ones so others will forgo to save on space.

Soap - See above.

Washcloth or bath pouf/loofah - Hotels will provide towels but wash clothes are not commonly used in China. They are sometimes available in hotels which cater to western travelers.

Toothbrush, toothpaste , and dental floss

Deodorant

Razor and shaving cream

Make up

Hair styling products

Hand lotion

Lip balm

Nail clippers

Cotton swabs

Glasses cleaner or contact supplies

Your **back-up glasses** if you normally wear contacts

Small nail scissors - These come in handy for a variety of purposes.

Tweezers

Lady Anti-Monkey Butt Powder - This anti-chaffing product is a favorite among adoptive moms, particularly those traveling during the summer heat.

Toys:

Stacking cups- Rated #1 most popular with toddlers by parents

Bubbles

Balloons - The kind with the rubber band attached for bopping if you want to be extra fancy

Beach ball - Packs small and easier on the hotel breakables

Small cars or dolls

Small magnadoodle

Crayons

Bubble bath

Travel play dough

Travel Items:

Travel pillow

Compression socks

Ear plugs

Money belt / necklace style passport holder

Packing cubes or giant packing ziplock bags - Both are highly touted for helping to keep your suitcase organized and compress air to fit more items.

The Pharmaceutical Section:

Items for your traveling medicine cabinet usually take up more space than anything else on packing lists. As always, this is not intended as medical advice.

Hand sanitizer - This should really have gone in the paper products section with all the toilet paper and wipes. Soap is not provided in public restrooms so you will want to always have this available while you are out and about.

N95 or Vogmask if you choose to take face masks due to pollution

Any prescription medications you usually take

Something for diarrhea

Something for constipation

Motion sickness remedies

A sleep aid - melatonin is often used as a non-drug option

Vitamins

Cold remedies

Allergy medicines

Pain relievers

Saline spray

Antibiotics

Cough medicine

Lice remedy - frequently needed for children from orphanages

Prescription scabies cream - another orphanage related need

First aid supplies - Be sure to take band aids in case you guessed wrong on the comfortable shoes and end up with blisters.

Simethicon (gas) drops

Probiotics

Gatorade packets

Triple antibiotic ointment

Dental irrigating syringe - If your child has an unrepaired cleft palate, food getting stuck is a frequent concern. Some parents use this to try and dislodge the food with water.

Any specialty item needed for your child's special need

Appendix 5

Souvenirs to Buy in China

If you have any money left over from the adoption you're sure to want to spend it on keepsakes from your trip to China. Many families think ahead and buy gifts for their children for future birthday, holiday, or other special occasions. You may never have the chance to return to China so make the most of your opportunity! Here are some items which are popular choices with adoptive families.

- **Silk clothing for your child** - Remember to buy a range of sizes so you're prepared for Chinese New Year celebrations for the years ahead. These are much less expensive if purchased in Guangzhou than in the official silk factory, though the actual silk content is questionable.

- **Pearl jewelry** - Many families buy a pearl necklace for their daughter to wear on her wedding day or for a son to give to his bride. You can choose long strings of pearls which the store employee will mount on fastenings for you. One long string will make a necklace with matching bracelet and earrings.

- **Jade** - Jade family balls are available in a variety of sizes. Jade jewelry is also a great keepsake. Jade bangle bracelets are popular with women while a jade disc necklace is more appropriate for a man.

- **A carved stone name stamp** - This is known as a "chop" and an artisan will personalize it with your child's name. They are available in a variety of materials. Purchasing one in province can make it a particularly nice keepsake for your child.

- **Calligraphy** - You can find many calligraphy artists around the tourist attractions who will custom paint a scroll for you.

- **Cloisonné** - Vases are common here but in China you can find a variety of cloisonné times to choose from including ornaments for your Christmas tree.

- **Porcelain tea sets** - These come in a variety of sizes and small doll sized sets pack easily. Many can be purchased that fit into a case which is more likely to make it through the trip home intact.

- **A specialty from your child's province** - Some provinces are known for porcelain and others for embroidery. Do some research ahead of time or ask your guide so you can bring home a piece of your child's home with them. I was able to buy a beautiful hand painted glass bead from an artisan in my son's hometown.

- **Chopsticks** - These are available everywhere and come in many different materials.

- **An ornament to hang from your rearview mirror** - The red mandarin knots are most popular, but you can get everything from Chairman Mao to the Five Goat statue which is the city symbol of Guangzhou.

- **Toys** - Parents have been known to bring home an entire suitcase of Legos, swearing that you'll never find prices as cheap as those at the toy market. Puzzles made in the shape of China are another option, and if you can find them the little dolls wearing minority ethnic group costumes are quite beautiful.

- **Fans and kites** - Two more items which really say China and are available everywhere.

Suggested Reading

Websites:

http://www.rainbowkids.com/
https://www.lovewithoutboundaries.com/
https://creatingafamily.org/adoption/
http://empoweredtoconnect.org/
http://www.nohandsbutours.com/
http://adoption.com/
http://www.adoptionarticlesdirectory.com/ArticlesUser/

General Adoption Books:

Ballard, Robert L., editor. Pieces of Me: Who do I want to be?
Warren, NJ: EMK Press, 2009.

Cogen, Patty. Parenting Your Internationally Adopted Child.
Boston: The Harvard Common Press, 2008.

Eldridge, Sherrie. Twenty Things Adopted Kids Wish Their
Adoptive Parents Knew. Delta, 1999.

Gray, Deborah D. Attaching Through Love, Hugs, and Play.
Philadelphia: Jessica Kingsley Publishers, 2014.

Green, Melissa Fay. No Biking in the House Without a Helmet.
New York: Sarah Crichton Books, 2011.

Hopkins-Best, Mary. Toddler Adoption: The Weaver's Craft.
Philadelphia: Jessica Kingsley Publishers, 2012.

Keck, Gregory. Parenting the Hurt Child: Helping Adoptive Families Heal and Grow. Colorado Springs, CO: NavPress, 2009.

Purvis, Karyn B. The Connected Child. New York: McGraw-Hill Education, 2007.

Rowell, Katie. Love Me, Feed Me: The Adoptive Parent's Guide to Ending the Worry About Weight, Picky Eating, Power Struggles and More. Family Feeding Dynamics LLC, 2012.

Books on Chinese Culture:

Bowen, Jenny. Wish You Happy Forever. New York: HarperOne, 2014.

Chang, Jung. Wild Swans: Three daughters of China. New York: Touchstone, 1991.

Chang, Leslie T. Factory Girls: From village to city in a changing China. New York: Spiegel & Grau, 2009.

Fallows, Deborah. Dreaming in Chinese: Mandarin lessons in life, love, and language. New York: Walker & Co., 2010.

Hessler, Peter. Oracles Bones. New York: Harper Perennial, 2007.

Hessler, Peter. Country Driving. New York: Harper Perennial, 2011.

Xinran. Message from an Unknown Chinese Mother. New York: Scribner, 2010.

Acknowledgements

I would like to thank my husband, Matthew Meineke for his encouragement for me to take the leap from blog to book. I appreciate my children being such good sports every time I said "Not now, I'm writing!" I also would not have been able to write without the support of my mother, Alicia Roades, mother-in-law Linda Meineke, and my two good friends, Barbara Cobb and Audra Douglas. Thank you to Jessica Zeeb and Beth Smith of Holt, Meagan Smith of Lifeline, and especially Elizabeth Rose of WACAP, who answered countless questions about the China program. My thanks to Li Zhao for being my cultural advisor. The help of Mary "the Number Fairy" Miotke was essential in understanding the post-LOA process timeline. Finally, my gratitude to the following people for proofreading some or all of the rough draft: Julie Brown, Audra Douglas, Dana Duff, Jenny Herbert, Liberty Joy. Melissa Treece deserves special recognition for her thorough editing of my final draft.

About the Author

 A native of Kentucky, Kelly Mayfield now resides in Columbus, Ohio with her husband and six children, of whom the two youngest were adopted from China. While it is not a particularly relevant qualification for writing a book on adoption, Kelly holds a Master of Arts in Theology from St. Meinrad Seminary in St. Meinrad, Indiana. She blogs at http://www.mineinchina.wordpress.com

CPSIA information can be obtained
at www.ICGtesting.com
Printed in the USA
LVOW04s1012110916
504133LV00018B/408/P

9 781534 666443